COMMUNITY, LIBERALISM AND CHRISTIAN ETHICS

This book explores some current issues on the borderland between moral philosophy and Christian theology. Particular attention is paid to the issues at stake between liberals and communitarians and the dispute between realists, non-realists and quasi-realists. In the course of the discussion, the writings of Alasdair MacIntyre, George Lindbeck and Stanley Hauerwas are examined. While sympathetic to many of the typical features of post-liberalism, the argument is critical at selected points in seeking to defend realism and accommodate some aspects of liberalism. The position that emerges is more neo-Barthian than post-liberal. In maintaining the distinctiveness of Christian ethics and community, as determined by divine revelation, the book also seeks to acknowledge a measure of common moral ground held by those within and without the church.

DAVID FERGUSSON is Professor of Systematic Theology in the Department of Divinity with Religious Studies at the University of Aberdeen. He is a consultant editor and director of *Scottish Journal of Theology* and Chair on the Editorial Board of *Theology in Scotland*. His publications include *Bultmann* (Geoffrey Chapman, 1992), *Christ, Church and Society: Essays on John Baillie and Donald Baillie* (T. & T. Clark, 1993), and *The Cosmos and the Creator: an Introduction to the Theology of Creation* (SPCK, 1998).

NEW STUDIES IN CHRISTIAN ETHICS

General Editor: Robin Gill
Editorial Board: Stephen R. L. Clark, Anthony O. Dyson,
Stanley Hauerwas and Robin W. Lovin

Christian ethics has increasingly assumed a central place within academic theology. At the same time the growing power and ambiguity of modern science and the rising dissatisfaction within the social sciences about claims to value-neutrality have prompted renewed interest in ethics within the secular academic world. There is, therefore, a need for studies in Christian ethics which, as well as being concerned with the relevance of Christian ethics to the present day secular debate, are well informed about parallel discussions in recent philosophy, science or social science. New Studies in Christian Ethics aims to provide books that do this at the highest intellectual level and demonstrate that Christian ethics can make a distinctive contribution to this debate – either in moral substance or in terms of underlying moral justifications.

COMMUNITY, LIBERALISM AND CHRISTIAN ETHICS

DAVID FERGUSSON

CAMBRIDGE
UNIVERSITY PRESS

PUBLISHED BY THE PRESS SYNDICATE OF THE UNIVERSITY OF CAMBRIDGE
The Pitt Building, Trumpington Street, Cambridge CB2 1RP, United Kingdom

CAMBRIDGE UNIVERSITY PRESS
The Edinburgh Building, Cambridge CB2 2RU, United Kingdom
40 West 20th Street, New York, NY 10011–4211, USA
10 Stamford Road, Oakleigh, Melbourne 3166, Australia

First published 1998

Printed and bound in Great Britain by Biddles Ltd, Guildford and King's Lynn

Typeset in 11/12.5pt Baskerville   [CE]

A catalogue record for this book is available from the British Library

Library of Congress cataloguing in publication data

Fergusson, David.
Community, liberalism and Christian ethics / David Fergusson.
p.   cm. – (New Studies in Christian Ethics)
Includes bibliographical references and index.
ISBN 0 521 49678 0 (hardback)
1. Christian ethics. 2. Communitarianism. I. Title. II. Series.
BJ1275.F47   1998
241 – dc21   97–47493   CIP

ISBN 0 521 49678 0 hardback

Contents

General editor's preface

This book is the thirteenth in the series New Studies in Christian Ethics. It provides an expert analysis of some of the most central themes in the series. David Fergusson combines skills as both a theologian and a philosopher, and uses them here to give a Christian response to one of the most challenging debates of our age – the moral debate between communitarians and liberals.

Alasdair MacIntyre's *After Virtue* has succeeded beyond most other recent books in setting an agenda which has challenged many philosophers and theologians alike. Most of the other contributors to New Studies in Christian Ethics have made use of this seminal work. However, there has yet been no substantial philosophical discussion of it in the series or of the more specifically theological contributions of Stanley Hauerwas and George Lindbeck. David Fergusson's new book, *Community, Liberalism and Christian Ethics*, provides this. What he offers is an appreciative, but finally critical, account of this debate, which takes communitarianism seriously without abandoning all of the achievements of realism and liberalism. Unlike theologians such as Stanley Hauerwas and John Milbank, he offers an account of theology which is radical but not radically post-modern. In doing this, he sees himself more as a neo-Barthian than as a post-liberal.

What is at stake here? Within modern theology there is an increasing division between those who see themselves as a part of the liberal arts, engaging with secular disciplines and seeking to influence the wider political order from within, and those, in contrast, who argue that theology must abandon liberalism in any form, looking instead to the unique resources of the Christian community, and building up a radical theological critique of post-Enlightenment thought. Within secular social and political thought there is also an increasing division between libertarians, who emphasise the autonomy of the individual and the centrality of individual choice, and communitarians, on the other hand, who stress the need for community, tradition, and interdependency. David Fergusson seeks to offer a bridge between these polarised positions. For him, it is essential that Christian ethics *is* distinctively Christian, albeit focused less upon the church than upon God made known in Jesus Christ. He is suspicious of those who exaggerate the distinctiveness of actual Christian communities and believes, instead, that Christians must still engage centrally with secular society. Liberalism has made real gains both within society and within Christian communities which do need to be recognised more frankly than is apparent in the writings of MacIntyre or Hauerwas. For David Fergusson, an appreciation of their distinctive contribution can be combined with a positive account of some of the central features of liberalism.

All of this admirably fulfils the two key aims of New Studies in Christian Ethics – namely, to promote monographs in Christian ethics which engage centrally with the present secular moral debate at the highest possible intellectual level and, secondly, to encourage contributors to demonstrate that Christian ethics can make a distinctive contribution to this debate. This book is a very welcome contribution to the series.

ROBIN GILL

Preface

This book explores some boundary issues in theology and moral philosophy. Its particular focus is on the current series of disputes between communitarians and liberals, and realists and anti-realists. The central argument is of a Barthian character. There is a distinctive ethos governing Christian conduct. Human action must be seen in relation to the divine act and being which precede it and to which, at best, it bears the character of faithful witness and correspondence. The knowledge and service of God within the church, therefore, shape the moral perception, motivation, commitment, and seriousness of the Christian life. However, in relation to some recent ecclesial approaches to ethics, I seek to argue that the priority of God's action must be stressed over against the secondary reality of the church's *polis*. This in turn enables Christian theology to recognise, without compromising its central theme, how the will of God may be done beyond the walls of the church. I shall argue, in consequence of this, that theology has some stake in philosophical arguments for moral realism and that, within pluralist societies, the church can recognise common moral ground – thus making common cause with other forces, agencies, and movements – even in the absence of common moral theory.

I owe a debt of gratitude to many whose advice has assisted me in this project. I am grateful in particular to Robin Gill, the series editor, for his patience and encouragement in awaiting an overdue manuscript, and to Alex Wright whose support was important at an early stage. My Aberdeen colleague and friend, Iain Torrance has been an invaluable source of advice and reading suggestions. His expertise in the field of Christian ethics has been of much assistance, as has his readiness to share so many teaching and administrative tasks.

Earlier drafts of some sections were delivered at the Society for the Study of Theology and the Society for the Study of Christian Ethics, and I have benefited from comments made at these occasions. The completion of the project was made possible by a six-month period of research leave which was spent at the Center of Theological Inquiry, Princeton. I am grateful to Dr Wallace Alston, the Director of the Center, and to Bishop William Lazareth and my fellow members for their encouragement, support, and constructive criticism of my work on numerous occasions during our very happy stay in Princeton. I am also grateful to the Carnegie Trust for the Universities of Scotland for their financial support.

Since returning from Princeton, I have had the privilege of attending in Aberdeen the fourth in the annual Scottish Journal of Theology lecture series delivered by Stanley Hauerwas. Although I have not been able to assimilate this material in the present study, I wish to record my indebtedness to his writings and to the stimulus he has provided, even where we have parted company.

This book is dedicated to my parents for their interest and support over many years.

David A. S. Fergusson

CHAPTER ONE

Introduction

THE SOCIAL CONTEXT

This study explores some recent communitarian contributions to Christian ethics by way of comparison with current trends in moral philosophy. It is preoccupied with questions concerning Christian ethical distinctiveness and overlap with other theories, communities, and convictions. Christian communitarianism draws strength from the increasing dissociation of church and civil society in the western world. The emergence of pluralism and secularism in the late-twentieth century have led to the breakdown of any clear Christian consensus undergirding the standards, assumptions, and policies of multiracial and multi-religious societies. This social predicament has led to calls for greater Christian authenticity. We can no longer assume that Christian ethics simply endorses what everyone recognises to be good for human beings *qua* human beings. There is neither consensus as to what being truly human entails, nor universally available criteria for establishing this. The time has therefore come, it is argued, to bear witness to the specific virtues of the Christian life, through reference to its setting within the church under the guidance of Holy Scripture and the lordship of Jesus Christ. Christian moral formation is not to be seen as the pursuit of moral principles which are knowable by people in all times and places. It is not the promotion of an ethical viewpoint which can be set out apart from and independently of the particular assumptions which sustain the existence of the church. Christian witness in this social context bears the character not of seeking common ground with those who dwell *extra muros ecclesiae*, but of articulating a vision that is distinctive and sometimes counter to the prevailing culture. Parallels can be drawn here with the early church which contested and provided an alternative moral vision to that regnant in the Graeco-Roman world. This was achieved not through mapping out common moral ground, but through speaking decisively of a new way that had been disclosed and enacted in Jesus Christ and his followers. I shall be concerned largely to defend this position while holding simultaneously that greater recognition needs to be accorded to the presence of genuine moral insight and practice outside the church. While there is no common moral theory, there is none the less some common moral ground which needs to be identified. I shall argue that this requires a theological explanation which can be presented in terms that are broadly Barthian. For Barth, it is not the uniqueness of the church that is decisive, but the uniqueness of God's self-revelation in Jesus Christ. Accordingly, he maintains the possibility of witness to the Word of God outside the church, albeit witness the validity of which must be tested by reference to Scripture, the theological traditions of the church, and its impact for the life of the Christian community in the world.

Some writers often identified as 'communitarian' do not admit the label. While I shall explore the reasons for this, I shall argue also that the expression has some legitimate application in terms of the epistemological significance assigned to the church, claims for Christian distinctiveness, the criticism of liberal ideology, and the recognition that moral codes can only be understood *vis-à-vis* forms of social life and inherited traditions. Although it may be the church rather than any generic notion of community that is morally significant, one must understand this approach in light of its more general criticisms of liberal philosophy and society.

Theological variants of communitarianism have become significant for sociological and philosophical reasons, as well as theological ones. For this reason, philosophical parallels will be pursued at some length in this study. In an age of increasing cultural and religious diversity, the particular shape of a religious community is important for the way in which its members understand themselves and the world. In both the UK and the USA, there is not only a greater diversity within Christianity, but a burgeoning of options in ancient and new age religion.[1] This growing diversity is part of a wider social situation in which traditional patterns of communal life are breaking down. Much philosophical reflection has now been devoted to this phenomenon.

In the mid-nineteenth century, Alexis de Tocqueville drew attention to the way in which voluntary association in American civic life was vital to the working of a democratic society. This was particularly true in the absence of aristocratic forms of life which, in European societies, had contributed to civic cohesion through the definition of social roles. De Tocqueville, in work which showed remarkable prescience, argued that the voluntary associations formed by citizens contributed significantly to the creation of trust, a sense of collective responsibility, and a concept of the common good. In a polity which emphasises the equality of individuals, the common good can only be articulated through voluntary association. De Tocqueville sensed that this was part of the explanation for the economic success and vitality of American society.

> The first time I heard in the United States that a hundred thousand men had bound themselves publicly to abstain from spirituous liquors, it appeared to me more like a joke than a serious engagement, and I did not at once perceive why these temperate citizens could not content themselves with drinking water by their own firesides. I at last understood that these hundred thousand Americans, alarmed by the progress of drunkenness around them, had made up their minds to patronize temperance. They act in just the same way as a man of high rank who should dress very plainly in order to inspire the humbler orders with a contempt of luxury. It is probable that if these hundred thousand men had lived in France, each of them would singly have memorialized the government to watch the public houses all over the kingdom.[2]

Within this analysis there lurks a warning. If there is a decline within the network of voluntary associations which regulate society, the burden of individual expectations that are subsequently placed upon central government will prove too great.

According to various social commentators today, this negative prophecy is being fulfilled. In 1985, Robert Bellah and the four co-authors of *Habits of the Heart* (the title itself is an expression of de Tocqueville) explored sociologically the way in which the network of associations that make up civic life is being eroded in the lives of modern American citizens. By reflecting on religious and political affiliations, and the changing patterns of family life and leisure pursuits in the responses of their subjects, they reach the conclusion that the quality of human life is deteriorating with the slow collapse of commitments to common goods.

[I]f we owe the meaning of our lives to biblical and republican traditions of which we seldom consciously think, is there not the danger that the erosion of these traditions may eventually deprive us of that meaning altogether? Are we not caught between the upper millstone of a fragmented intellectual culture and the nether millstone of a fragmented popular culture? The erosion of meaning and coherence in our lives is not something Americans desire. Indeed, the profound yearning for the idealized small town that we found among most of the people we talked to is a yearning for just such meaning and coherence.[3]

These social trends together contribute to a situation in which civic assocational ties are diminished. Here, the individual selects his or her own goods as opposed to owning social goods which are defined by traditions, stories, and communities of memory. The increasing absence of a notion of the common weal which commands the loyalty of the members of a society is widely lamented. Although it is doubtful whether we can or would genuinely desire to return to the past, this none the less creates a situation in which institutions like the church, which offer to create a common identity and a morally coherent world of meaning, appear highly attractive. It is against this social background that we need to understand the appeal of communitarian themes in Christian ethics.

Recent work in philosophy provides a related intellectual context within which the recent ecclesiological emphasis in theology must also be understood. So-called communitarians such as MacIntyre, Taylor, and Sandel have raised searching questions of the adequacy of post-Enlightenment liberalism to provide an adequate account of the moral life and a basis for modern pluralist societies. Of these philosophers, it is MacIntyre whose work has received the closest attention in theology. His writings form the basis of chapter 5 and contribute significantly to the position advocated throughout the entire discussion. The central and consistent thesis of his work is that, despite three centuries of moral philosophy and one of sociology, there is no adequate account of liberal individualism. By contrast, the approach of Aristotle can, upon suitable revision (in MacIntyre's latest work this is a Thomist revision), restore intelligibility to the moral life.[4]

The closest theological analogue of MacIntyre's philosophy is found in the writings of Stanley Hauerwas. He does not wish to be too closely identified with broader intellectual trends, since his project is to speak of what it is that makes the church distinctive, rather than to outline a moral theory, a social analysis, a narrative hermeneutic, or a defence of a generic notion of community. None the less, his frequent borrowing from philosophy and social theory makes it possible to view his work and its reception in this wider context.

For Hauerwas, our current situation is one in which the idea of Christendom needs to be abandoned. Attempts at correlating the moral ethos of the church and civil society must lead inevitably to a loss of ecclesial identity and a failure of Christian witness. The church's task is to be representative of the kind of people God has made possible in Jesus Christ; a people committed to forgiveness, to the service of God, to loving one another, and to making peace. References to the ethical significance of the celebration of the Eucharist abound in Hauerwas' writings. Perhaps this is surprising in a Methodist theologian. Yet his theology of the Eucharist is a powerful sign of the dependence of the church upon Christ crucified and risen, its unity through his lordship, and its fundamental calling to be the same body of Christ before the world. How this works out we shall discuss in chapter 3. It is clear, however, that Christian existence takes its bearing from the church founded upon Jesus Christ. It is here that we are taught how to live and die as Christians. This ecclesiogical orientation of Hauerwas' ethics makes for a distinctive Christian witness in the world, and enables him to launch a full-scale attack on the nostrums of modern liberalism.

The attractions of this position should not be underrated by world-weary academics. The call for greater authenticity and distinctiveness reminds a younger generation that the Christian life is an adventure. Many of the prevailing assumptions and trends in our society are to be contested. We are challenged to live out new patterns of community in a world which shows a bias towards individualism and the reduction of religion to the private and recreational spheres of our existence.[5] Moreover, this way of thinking about moral practice seems to make better sense of how we come by our standards than earlier types of ethical theory. We learn to act morally, not so much by the intuition of general moral principles, but through particular examples and communal instruction in how to comport ourselves. The communitarian perspective can make better sense of the roles of parents and teachers. It reveals why stories and historical examples are so important to our moral upbringing. As I write in Princeton, it is Martin Luther King day, a day marked by school holidays, public lectures, and McDonalds' TV advertisements in honour of the civil rights leader. Here, the particular takes precedence over the general. The recital and memorising of great stories shapes the moral progress of our little ones.[6] This is how we learn to think, react, and live in ways that are morally significant.

None the less, in seeking to expound recent communitarian trends in Christian thought, one is conscious of a range of problems that can be readily identified in the literature. These are explored throughout this study, and have led to a modified version of communitarian themes.

One problem concerns the spectre of relativism. If Christian moral standards are defined by reference to the polity of the church and to its distinctive beliefs, practices, and narratives, does this imply that the truth of these standards is constituted merely by their faithfulness to one way of seeing the world? By implication, it might be held that other moral positions are true by virtue of their consistency with the frameworks of belief and patterns of community which support them. Truth in morals is thus constituted by reference to the beliefs and practices of whichever community and tradition one owes allegiance to. The possibility of a rational discrimination between rival communities is thus ruled out of court. There is no Archimedean position from which such comparison can take place. There is no transcommunitarian fact at stake into which one can reasonably inquire.

As far as I am aware, such an unashamedly relativist position is not avowed in any textbook on Christian ethics, even in a post-modernist age. The exponents of communitarian ethics typically argue that there is truth to be discovered and practised which is not exhausted by reference to the rules of discourse and behaviour governing the life of a community. The truth is what God wills for us and all people, although this may only be known through divine revelation in history and the patterns that this establishes in the traditions of Israel and the church. Truth is thus not relative to a particular framework, although knowledge thereof is available only to those who inhabit the framework. The position may be described as ontologically realist but epistemologically relative.

This still leaves the problem of how moral perception outwith the Christian community is to be assessed. I shall argue that it must be assessed positively though critically, and shall defend the arguments in recent philosophical literature for moral realism. I am deeply sceptical about strategies which enthusiastically deconstruct all other forms of moral consciousness, while making the strongest realist claims possible for moral perception within the church. Apart from the intrinsic implausibility of this position – can one subscribe to arguments which seek to undermine all forms of moral realism while claiming immunity for one's own particular form? – it is at odds with much of what Christian theology has historically tried to articulate in terms of natural law, common grace, and the orders of creation.

A further problem posed by the communitarian turn in Christian ethics concerns the way in which the church has often adopted the concepts and precepts of secular theories. The image of Christian discourse as a language game with its own grammar and forms of life has to be squared with the borrowing and appropriation of materials from other sources. This is a problem for Christians who are deeply conscious of inhabiting and being committed to more than one community. How should they comport themselves? Has the Christian community anything to learn from alternatives or should it pay exclusive heed to its own Scriptures and traditions? Stated thus starkly, this is a difficult if impossible position to defend in mainstream Christianity given the manner in which feminism, ecology, and an increased awareness of other faiths shape our understanding of the modern world and condition our reading of Scripture. A related issue concerns the criteria by which a community is determined. Where does one community begin and another end? What are the limits of a community? The concept of a community is not univocal and has probably not been subjected to sufficiently rigorous analysis.[7]

This second cluster of issues gives rise to a third which is perhaps the most fiercely contested. Many mainstream churches in western societies feel a strong sense of responsibility for their civil polities. This is reflected partly through a commitment to some of its institutions, e.g. parliamentary democracy, the forces of law and order, welfare provision, etc., but also through a desire to speak critically of the status quo and to call for change. This stake in the political and social order is conditioned by the way in which the church has historically shaped the societies in which it has existed. Yet, with the increasing dissociation noted above, problems arise as to the stake the church has in identifying and seeking to promote a social consensus. Is there a moral basis to the civil order which the church can support or supply? If so, in what language should that be couched, given that many of our contemporaries espouse another or no faith? The response that one makes to this problem will tend to be determined by the relative weight one attaches to the priorities of witnessing to what is distinctive on the basis of Scripture and tradition, or seeking common cause with other groups and agencies. Closely related to this dispute is a fundamental question about the theological propriety of the discourse of human rights. The language of rights is the only current candidate for a universal moral discourse. Should this be welcomed throughout the *oikumene*, or should it be viewed with suspicion as lacking any genuine basis and as frequently hijacked for a plethora of incompatible claims which are corrosive of community and informed moral choices? This question will be revisited in the closing stages of the discussion.

Beneath these contested issues there lies a controversy about the doctrine of the church. Recent communitarian approaches to Christian ethics suggest a revival of a radical Reformation ecclesiology.[8] The church is a distinctive community set apart from the world. It does not speak for society at large, but develops its own moral ecology. The idea of a Christian society has now been discredited, or so it is argued, and it is no coincidence that the traditional practice of infant baptism is increasingly being called into question within Protestant theology. Thus the co-ordination of church and civil society that one finds in Roman Catholic, Lutheran, and Calvinist ecclesiologies is regularly queried.

In order to assess this approach to Christian ethics, I shall look backwards and sideways: backwards, by assessing its recent theological ancestry; sideways, by comparing it with recent parallel trends in moral philosophy. In this way, communitarianism will be seen to be neither theologically nor culturally egregious. At the same time, however, these theological and philosophical evaluations will reveal some of the weaknesses of the approach and suggest ways in which it should be refined.

THE MORAL ECOLOGY OF THE EARLY CHURCHES

Any new development in theology will tend to seek support from historical examples in the Christian tradition and from Scripture itself. Recent communitarian approaches have coincided with a range of studies which draw attention to the importance of community in the moral world of the New

Testament and the early church. This is worth sketching at the outset since there are some vital resources here for communitarian approaches, as well as some pressing questions.

The New Testament, of course, does not contain any clearly worked out meta-ethical theory. It is none the worse for this. In part, this reflects its thorough integration of the languages of theology, doxology, exhortation, and witness. Ethics is not compartmentalised in the manner of a modern theological syllabus. The early Christians are urged to imitate the example of Christ, to follow his teachings, to keep the precepts of what became known as the Old Testament, to bring forth the fruits of the Holy Spirit in their living, to observe and even surpass standards already recognised in the ancient world.

The question has often been asked as to what new ethical norms the church introduced into the ancient world.

> What can this Gospel of Jesus be?
> What Life & Immortality
> What was it that he brought to Light
> That Plato & Cicero did not write?
> The Heathen Deities wrote them all,
> These Moral Virtues, great and small.[9]

To discover the moral significance of the early church for the ancient world, it is not sufficient merely to list its ethical precepts and exhortations. One will find strong similarities both with Judaism and pagan culture. Parallels can be drawn with many ethical precepts in the New Testament. Yet the particular social context and configuration of ecclesial forms, symbols, and beliefs provide a new framework for moral practice. The description of early Christian 'socioecology' has been undertaken in several recent studies by Wayne Meeks.[10] His project is to approach early Christian morality not by asking at the outset what the church taught about marriage, war, or slavery, but by delineating the new ecclesial setting within which ethical deliberation and guidance took place. In converting to the faith, Christians described their new life with the most radical of metaphors. They are chosen (1 Thess. 1:4) and called (1 Thess. 2:12) by God. They have turned from idols to God (1 Thess. 1:9). Their new life is a source of estrangement but also the means of their solidarity with others who share the same faith even though they be scattered throughout the world (1 Thess. 2:14). This dual sense of estrangement and solidarity is emphasised throughout early Christian literature. Christians are described by Paul as a new creation in Christ in which the old person has passed away and a new life begun (2 Cor. 5:17). Those who were once no people have now become a chosen race, a royal priesthood, a holy people, whose real home is in heaven (1 Pet. 2:9–10). One of the distinctive features of this new community of faith is that it has a strong moral cast by comparison with other religious cults. In this regard, it is more reminiscent of a philosophical school than a religious sect.[11]

The sense of being set apart, of entering a new life, and of being bound together with Christ and with one another is strengthened by the rituals of baptism and the Lord's Supper. In Romans 6, Paul uses an elaborate series of metaphors to describe the way in which baptism signifies dying and rising with Christ. The discontinuity between life before and life after baptism is stressed, as is the practical implication that Christians should walk in newness of life. Indeed, post-baptismal sin on this reading is highly anomalous. In the weekly Eucharistic meal, the memorial of the Last Supper in 1 Corinthians 11 is a reminder to Christians of the equality that arises from belonging to the body of Christ.[12] This subverts the traditional manner in which a meal reinforced social stratification. Here, guests were treated in different ways according to their social status. This practice is contested by Paul as deeply inappropriate within the church. The unity evoked and demanded by the Eucharist is given wider expression in the famous passage from the *Didache*, sometimes used in contemporary liturgies. 'As this broken bread was scattered upon the mountains, and then was gathered together and became one, so may your Church be gathered together from the ends of the earth into your kingdom.'[13]

In being called into this new community, Christians are faced with a range of practical problems about how they should dispose themselves with respect to others in the church and to those outside. Their ethical practice in these situations arises out of the nature of their calling to the church. The moral exhortation of the apostles is integrally related to what it means to be a particular kind of people. In this respect, being takes priority over doing. The kind of people Christians are called to be results in their behaving in particular ways. A similar relationship of imperative to communal identity can be found in Jewish communities throughout the Diaspora. The keeping of the law is the way in which Jews maintain their identity as the covenant people of God. 'The first point in each form of the variety of Jewish ethics, therefore, is to be Israel.'[14]

Following Lohfink, Richard Hays makes the point that Jesus did not have to found a church, because there already was one: Israel.[15] Prior to the church, the Hebrew notion of the covenant people already provided a model of community life. Jesus' calling of twelve disciples signals the restoration of Israel; Paul understands the Gentile communities to whom he ministers as 'Abraham's offspring, heirs according to the promise' (Gal. 3:29). They are the spiritual descendants of the Exodus people, all of whom drank from the one spiritual rock that was Christ (1 Cor. 10:4). The communal identity of the church, therefore, is determined by the nature of Israel as the chosen people of God under the law of God.

Although ethical practice has to be understood within the context of communal identity, it is also true that the practices of the community contribute to its character.[16] There is a mutual enrichment of character and habitual activity. The importance of showing hospitality to strangers is a prominent Jewish theme which appears in the New Testament and in the literature of the post-apostolic period. This practice helps to forge links with Christians from other parts of the world. It is a way of supporting the church's itinerant ministers. It also has the symbolic function of reminding Christians of their own identity as 'resident aliens' since they have in this world no abiding city (Heb. 13:14). Similarly, the gathering of funds for Christians in other parts of the empire is an important expression and reinforcement of belonging one to another, as is the regular support of the sick and widowed within each congregation. 'Would not the very act of dropping those hard-earned coins

into a jar every Sunday have an effect on the way the partici-
pating members of the church would henceforth think about
the morality of wealth and poverty?'[17]

The new communal identity determined the character of its
members and called for their highest loyalty, even when this
occasioned martyrdom. The sacrifice made by Jesus was itself,
in part, a model of martyrdom. Yet the polity of the church did
not require Christians to abandon all previous commitments,
social ties, and standards. In this respect, there is an ambivalence in Christian orientation within the wider world. The
manner in which Christian groups often had their focus around
a particular household reflected social patterns in the Graeco-
Roman world. The members of the household were engaged in
the life of society at large. This gave rise to the type of problem
manifested in 1 Corinthians 8–10 where some Christians
participated in dinner parties at which meat previously sacri-
ficed to idols was consumed.

The ethical injunctions of Paul and other New Testament
writers bear some formal similarities to the conventions of
Graeco-Roman moral exhortation. 1 Thessalonians opens by
dwelling on the friendly relations between writers and recipi-
ents. It reminds the readers what they already know. There is
an emphasis upon imitating the example of others. More
significantly, most of the virtues and vices listed can be found in
pagan literature. Meeks presents an aggregate of vices found in
eighteen different lists in the New Testament.[18] He concludes
that all can be widely found elsewhere, although there is a
particular emphasis upon sexual impropriety and idolatry in
the Christian lists. Much of Paul's parenesis in 1 Thessalonians
4 would be familiar to non-Christians. Sexual purity, marital
fidelity, brotherly love, leading a quiet life, and minding one's
own business are all commended. What is interesting in this
context is that Paul goes on to assert that others, on observing
such conduct, will respect and trust those who belong to the
church. Implicit in this claim, which was later to be developed
by the second-century apologists, is the idea that the heathen
can recognise the high moral standards set by the followers of
Christ.

In the early church, we can find moral standards and practices which are not dissimilar to those acknowledged elsewhere. Yet their context in a particular socio-ecology gives them a distinctive focus and significance within the Christian life. The rationale of the moral life and the way it is practised reflect the particularity of the Christian faith. Not only moral perception, but also the motivation, commitment, and seriousness of the moral life are reconfigured by one's ecclesial belonging. The moral world of the first Christians cannot be understood except with reference to Jewish morality, the example of Jesus, the relations within and across congregations, and the symbols and rituals practised within the body of Christ.

Prior to the fourth century, the early Christians bound themselves to a minority religion which was often misunderstood and sometimes violently persecuted. The church comprised small but active groups of Christians whose commitment to their congregations was intensified by a sense of their standing out from the majority.[19] The demands of following Christ together with the tensions experienced within the church produced some significant emphases. Divisions of race, class, wealth, and gender were more acutely felt within the *koinonia* of the Holy Spirit. This gave Christian ethics a stronger social dimension than one finds in the traditions of Plato and Aristotle.[20] In the writings of John Chrysostom in the late fourth century, there is a strong sense of a common humanity which imposes obligations upon slave-owners and the rich. It is impossible to enter the kingdom of God without the giving of alms. It is the heart of virtue. The best way to utilise wealth, he counselled the rich, was to disburse it to widows, orphans, the sick, and prisoners. Domestic slaves are to be treated with respect. They are neither to be beaten nor separated from their spouses. Friendship between master and slave, *contra* Aristotle, is to be desired.

Think not that what is done towards a servant, [Christ] will therefore forgive, because done to a servant. Heathen laws, indeed, as being the laws of men, recognise a difference between these kinds of offenses. But the law of the common Lord and Master of all, as doing good to all alike, and dispensing the same rights to all, knows no such difference.[21]

None the less, despite the high moral standards expected by Chrysostom of followers of Christ, there is a constant recognition that all are sinners and dependent upon the grace and forgiveness of God. This means that there can be no pride or unseemly claim to virtue on the part of the Christian. It also demands an attitude of humility and a readiness to forgive as God forgives. This stress is less apparent in the pagan moralists of antiquity.

The most theologically significant features of this new life are the way of Jesus and the authority of what became the Old Testament. These are underemphasised by Meeks.[22] This may have something to do with a sociological approach which tends inevitably to understate the significance of theological factors. Thus Childs, while not denying the validity of the approach, wishes to accord greater emphasis to the way in which the community is addressed by Paul in the name of God who is 'the source of Paul's comfort, authority, and the norm of Christian behaviour'.[23] We know that the early church preserved the sayings of Jesus and that Paul attaches a higher authority to them than his own ethical advice (1 Cor. 7:12). Writing almost a century later, Justin sees in the example and teaching of Christ, the incarnation of that wisdom whose seeds are present in the teaching of Socrates. The nature of the Christian life as a calling by God to believe and respond to the gospel of Jesus Christ as members of his body, the church, bestows upon that life a definite orientation. We have here the principal criterion for the nature of the life to which Christians are called. Their calling is to serve the God of Israel who has been most fully revealed in Jesus Christ. This is the source and criterion of their new life. The grace of God as the origin of the church explains why the early Christians were compelled to attach such ethical significance to humility, forgiveness, and love. The Christological criterion does not provide the church with ready-made ethical solutions for every occasion. The wrestling with particular issues that Paul engages in throughout 1 Corinthians testifies to this. None the less, the foundation of the church upon Jesus Christ provides an authority which cannot be forgotten. This is especially true of his teaching on the Sermon on the Mount which is impossibly exacting. It provides an intensification of Old Testament law which cannot be ignored. This is reflected in later Christian discussion of war, marriage, divorce and forgiveness.[24]

The attitude towards the world that all this evokes is strangely ambivalent. The church worshipped Christ crucified, a stumbling-block to Jews and foolishness to Greeks (1 Cor. 1:22ff.). It could not forget that its Lord had been crucified by the civil state. Christians were called to a new *polis*, the full reality of which would only appear at the end of the world. According to the Fourth Gospel, Christians are chosen out of the world and cease to be of the world (John 15:19). They are told to anticipate the hatred of the world just as Christ had known it (John 15:18). Yet the world remains the creation of God through the divine Word. It is the object of God's redeeming love and in it God's Word becomes incarnate.

The ambivalence of Christian attitudes to the world is already reflected in 1 Thessalonians. There, as we have seen, Christians are urged to live quietly and to mind their own business. Elsewhere, Paul claims that the secular authorities are ordained by God and deserve the recognition that is appropriate to them (Rom. 13:1ff.). He urges those within the church to live peaceably with all people (Rom. 12:18). On the basis of the analysis offered, we must assume that Christians continued to show commitment to the institutions and practices of the world out of which they had been called. This was a necessary condition for the presence of 'households' at the centre of Christian congregations. While many later followed a strict ascetic line by withdrawing from the civil world, this was not the rule for the majority. Peter Brown recounts the extraordinary witness of those who made an ascetic commitment, but notes that the silent majority must have been those who married, raised children, preserved households, and thus contributed to the survival of the church.[25] At the same time, apocalyptic strains in early Christian literature foretell the final destruction of earthly civilisations and polities. In this respect, the Christian attitude to the state is eschatologically critical. The church must live in the knowledge that the secular powers are only provisional and may even be corrupt.[26]

The ambivalence of these attitudes towards the world may be endemic to any theology of creation and redemption. In a world created and fallen, yet still loved by God, the church might expect to be confronted both by hospitality and hostility. It is significant that this ambivalence was removed most effectively in the theology of Marcion by denying outright the orthodox doctrine of creation through a disjunction of creation and redemption.

The ethical orientation of Christian writers in the early church reveals neither an exclusive differentiation from surrounding society nor an assimilation to conventional norms. One cannot ignore the ways in which Christian moral exhortation draws unashamedly upon pagan sources. Ambrose's treatise *On The Duties of the Clergy* explicitly borrows from Cicero's discourse by recommending, for example, the four cardinal virtues of temperance, prudence, courage, and justice. In the same context, Ambrose also repeats the point, found in earlier Christian writers, that the great philosophers were expounding wisdom that they had originally derived from Moses. Basil's *Address to Young Men on How They Might Derive Benefit from Greek Literature* commends the moral example set by Pericles, Euclid, Socrates, and others. These remain instructive when set within a Christian context.

Also of significance is the way in which patristic writers regularly appeal to natural law, often citing Romans 1–2. This was not presented in the systematic way that was later to characterise Thomism, but used in an *ad hoc* fashion to indicate the possibility of ethical recognition throughout the created order. This can be seen in the writings of Clement, Basil, Chrysostom, and Augustine.[27] Some commentators have even discerned a natural morality in the words of Jesus. 'If you then, who are evil, know how to give good gifts to your children, how much more will your Father who is in heaven give good things to those who ask him?' (Mtt. 7:11)[28]

The Hebrew notion of 'wisdom' provided an interpretive

principle for recognising moral order everywhere throughout
the cosmos. 'She reaches mightily from one end of the earth to
the other, and she orders all things well' (Wisdom 8:1). Apologists of the second century – Aristides, Athenagoras, and Justin,
for example – could expound the Stoic notion that the universe
was governed by an order which was discernible in some
measure by all rational persons. This order was identified by
Justin Martyr with the divine Logos through which all things
were created and which had become incarnate in Jesus Christ.
The appeal to a universal moral order had a dual function. It
enabled the apologists to recognise the moral perception of
pagan society at its best, thus demonstrating that the Christian
religion did not directly contradict what was already known in
part. But it also had the purpose of showing the distinctiveness
of Christian practice over against the customs of the host
society. Thus the apologists can point to the *polis* of the church
as morally exceeding the highest standards known in the
ancient world.[29]

The apologists might be perceived as adopting a craven
though understandable posture towards pagan morality. Yet
many of their themes are present in later writers and can be
detected in Augustine. Rowan Greer has argued that the
dominant model for configuring the relationship of church to
world is that of alien citizenship.[30] This is the paradox of
belonging provisionally to earthly polities, but simultaneously
and finally to a greater polity, the city of God. This strange
relationship of church to state is set out in the anonymous
Epistle to Diognetus around CE 130.

[I]nhabiting Greek as well as barbarian cities, according as the lot of
each of the natives in respect to clothing, food, and the rest of their
ordinary conduct, (Christians) display to us their wonderful and
confessedly striking method of life. They dwell in their own countries,
but simply as sojourners. As citizens, they share in all things with
others, and yet endure all things as if foreigners. Every foreign land is
to them as their native country, and every land of their birth as a land
of strangers. They marry as do all; they beget children, but they do
not destroy their offspring. They have a common table, but not a
common bed. They are in the flesh, but they do not live after the flesh.
They pass their days on earth, but they are citizens of heaven. They

obey the prescribed laws, and at the same time surpass the laws by their lives. They love all people, and are persecuted by all. They are unknown and condemned; they are put to death and restored to life.[31]

The writer goes on to compare the relationship of Christians to the world to that of the soul to the body. The soul dwells in the body but is not a part thereof. The soul is imprisoned in it and is persecuted by it, yet the soul loves and preserves the body it inhabits. Through bodily hardship, the soul prospers. Likewise, through persecution the church increases in number. It is stressed, furthermore, that the church is no earthly invention. It is brought into being through the action of God in sending the Son into the world to be its Saviour. It is by his healing of our corrupted nature that Christians are made citizens of heaven. The community of the church thus understands itself not as a human creation but as constituted by God. This theological *prius* becomes the criterion for the form and content of the church's polity.

The tension between commitment to the civil society and the church was sometimes broken in the inspiring example of the martyrs. This led to a disowning of any stake in worldly society, as for example in Tertullian's later writings. The tension could also be broken in less praiseworthy ways, especially after the conversion of Constantine. The order of the empire could too easily be identified with the order of the kingdom of God as, for example, in the tributes of Eusebius to Constantine. However, Augustine, in *The City of God*, returns to the model of alien citizenship. The earthly city cannot be identified with God's sacred order. It is a community of corrupt people in a fallen world. Its institutions must always remain imperfect. Yet it is capable of attaining a measure of peace and order through the restraint of evil forces. The people of God whose home is the heavenly city none the less have a stake in this earthly peace.[32]

Augustine also echoes Stoic themes about the eternal law of God reflected throughout the creation. This is apparent even within the earthly city, although our supreme end can only be known and enjoyed through divine grace.

God, then the most wise Creator and most just Ordainer of all
natures, who placed the human race upon earth as its greatest
ornament, imparted to humans some good things adapted to this life,
to wit, temporal peace, such as we can enjoy in this life from health
and safety and human fellowship, and all things needful for the
preservation and recovery of this peace, such as the objects which are
accommodated to our outward senses, light, night, the air, and waters
suitable for us, and everything the body requires to sustain, shelter,
heal, or beautify it.[33]

Peace is found, for Augustine, in the well-ordered obedience of
faith to God's eternal law. This involves the love of God, the
love of oneself, and the love of one's neighbour. This love
(*caritas*) is infused into our hearts by the Holy Spirit. The
understanding of the source of this love dominated Augustine's
ethical reflections and led to the subordination of the four
cardinal virtues of Stoicism to the theological virtue of love.[34]
We do this not through external imitation, but through 'putting
on Christ' by the grace of God, and thereby knowing the full
measure of divine love. The pursuit of order through the love of
God, self, and neighbour entails significant moral restrictions
upon the waging of war (this leads to the just war theory) and to
a ban on suicide (which the church has since held to). The
dominant image of the Christian life is that of pilgrimage to the
heavenly city.

   This pilgrimage has a communal dimension. It takes place
within the body of Christ. We are supported by the angels who
already dwell in that glorious city. Within our mother church
alone Christians receive training and instruction. It is the
discipline, exhortation, and fellowship of the church which are
necessary for our earthly journey. It is there that we learn how
to honour our children and love our partners in marriage. It is
there that we learn how to be good citizens and rulers, and how
to relate to people of other nations, cultures, and races.[35] The
heavenly city may be assisted by that measure of peace granted
the earthly city. The temporal stability of society and the
regulation of human life are useful to it in its state of pilgrimage.

This heavenly city, then, while it sojourns on earth, calls citizens out
of all nations, and gathers together a society of pilgrims of all

languages, not scrupling about diversities in the manners, laws, and institutions whereby earthly peace is secured and maintained, but recognising that, however various these are, they all tend to one and the same end of earthly peace.[36]

Where does this preliminary sketch leave us? One should beware of any attempt to see the early Christian communities as ethically or culturally monochrome. Diverse attitudes can be detected. A similar diversity can also be discerned in Jewish communities throughout the Diaspora.[37] None the less, it seems clear that the early Christians understood their lives to be shaped by their commitment to Christ and their belonging to the church. The Christian life was a following of Christ's commandments, which reflected also elements of the Torah. It was also a learning to live in fellowship with Christians from different backgrounds and of different social status. Towards the civil authority, it was a working out of attitudes which, without seeking confrontation, expressed a higher commitment to God. In all this we find an eclectic borrowing from pagan writers and a recognition of examples of goodness outwith the Christian community. None the less, both borrowing and recognition are positioned within a Christian framework. The moral life is part of the life of faith, of life within the church, and of one's earthly pilgrimage. In this respect, it is neither a following of the dictates of natural reason nor allegiance to a set of self-evident autonomous moral principles. For the New Testament and the early church, morality is determined by its position within the life of faith as the response that God's grace calls forth. While there is significant overlap with pagan ethical precepts, the new context for ethical behaviour provides a heightened awareness and intensifying of its significance. We can see how this aspect of early Christian life is retrieved by recent communitarian trends in theology.

CHAPTER TWO

Christian ethical distinctiveness

Recent ecclesial or communitarian trends in Christian ethics can draw support from a variety of ecumenical sources. These lie in close theological proximity to current debate. The contours of these sources will be briefly sketched in this chapter.

KARL BARTH

Some imperious claims for Christian ethical distinctiveness can be found in the writings of Karl Barth. Although he is generally studied for his contribution to dogmatic theology, ethics remained a fundamental preoccupation throughout Barth's life. The lectures given in Münster (1928/9) and Bonn (1930/1) now comprise a posthumously published volume of over 500 pages.[1] The second half of *Church Dogmatics* ii/2, the entirety of iii/4, and the material originally designed as iv/4 are all devoted to ethical themes. This is in addition to numerous other writings and portions of the *Church Dogmatics* which are of ethical import. All told, therefore, one can make the surprising claim that Barth is one of the most prolific Christian ethicists of the twentieth century.

For Barth, there is no sphere of human life which is not governed by the divine intention. The doctrine of election declares that God's purpose in the creation of the world is the establishment of the covenant of grace in Jesus Christ with all human beings. There is no province of human existence which is not determined by this purpose. God's election is not exclusively about divine action. It is a divine action which by its nature summons a human response. Its goal is covenant partnership. In this partnership, human beings acknowledge and obey the divine rule. The gospel thus determines human action, and in doing so it has the character of law. God wills to take us into the divine service. We are commissioned for a share in God's own work.[2]

The Word of God, according to Barth, is always laden with ethical import. Theology thus includes the problem of ethics.[3] In determining our action, God's activity is always primary and human activity secondary. One consequence of this is that human goodness must be described in terms of sanctification. As the Word of God addresses, redeems, and sanctifies human life, so genuine goodness becomes possible. It is for this reason that Barth deals with ethics in terms of the leading concept of the divine command. Moral imperatives are occasioned by the command of God which governs human existence. The divine command, however, is neither abstract nor general. It comes in a particular way to each one of us in the historical circumstances of our lives. It carries an indispensable reference to Jesus Christ and to Holy Scripture. All Christian living bears witness to Christ, in whom the eternal decree of God is revealed and enacted. God wills to be for us in Christ, and in doing so calls us to be the witnesses and servants of Christ.[4] What this entails is revealed in Scripture which itself is an indispensable witness to Christ in the dual form of promise and fulfilment. Ethical action thus has the character of attesting the righteousness of God.[5]

[P]recisely because perfect righteousness stands before them as God's work . . . they are with great strictness required and with great kindness freed and empowered to do what they can do in the sphere of the relative possibilities assigned to them, to do it very imperfectly yet heartily, quietly, and cheerfully. They are absolved from wasting time and energy sighing over the impassable limits of their sphere of action and thus missing the opportunities that present themselves in this sphere. They may and can and should rise up and accept responsibility to the utmost of their power for the doing of the little righteousness.[6]

It is clear from the outset that Barth's approach to ethics is dependent upon his understanding of the sovereignty of God, the determination of human beings for covenant partnership in Jesus Christ, and the uniqueness of Scripture as witness to the Word of God. His ethics gives the highest priority to the divine command, to the person and work of Christ, and to the church as the community which hears and testifies to the Word of God. Situated in this way, Christian ethics is distinguished in form and content from every other form of ethical belief.

The besetting question is whether distinctiveness is purchased at too high a price. Is this approach to ethics excessively abstract in ignoring both the ways we are customarily taught to be virtuous and the rules that are an integral feature of most ethical systems?[7] Is it merely a historical accident that Protestant ethics produced in the 1960s situationism, a theory which held that all ethical instruction could be reduced to the one value of love? One possible rejoinder is that Scripture clearly specifies a range of moral rules which are expressions of the divine command. Thus we do not merely intuit the will of God in the particular circumstances of our lives. We are given distinct expressions of God's will in the Decalogue and the Sermon on the Mount. Yet there are two related reasons why Barth must qualify this response. First, the divine commands in Scripture cannot be abstracted from the history in which they arise and assume significance. They must be set in the context of the story of Israel and the life of Jesus. As such, they summarise the lines along which human behaviour should proceed rather than providing absolute injunctions which provide a blueprint for all subsequent human activity. Barth is here tilting at forms of Christian legalism. The commandments not to kill and to love one's enemies summarise a concrete command given to Israel and the disciples within particular historical situations. It is possible, Barth claims, that different things may be required of us in different circumstances albeit in accordance with the general orientation of human behaviour which is revealed in these biblical commands.[8]

The second, related reason why Christian ethics cannot be reduced to a set of rules delineated in Scripture concerns Barth's 'actualism'. This refers to the way in which the Word of God always assumes the character of a dynamic event rather

than a static deposit controllable by the human subject.[9] The
capacity of the Bible to become the Word of God depends upon
the activity of the Holy Spirit in the present to appropriate its
words. In ethical terms, this implies that the will of God cannot
be encapsulated in a set of general moral rules.

God wills that (we) should be called and gathered to this people of His
choice to share in its office of witnessing . . . How strangely would the
Bible deviate from its proper theme and content if it presented
matters otherwise than it actually does in the shape of this, so to
speak, historical ethics, if it were to describe the will of God as the
establishment and proclamation of general precepts and rules which
can be filled out only on the basis of the reflection and decision of
man![10]

Barth treads a fine line between an ethical occasionalism on
the one side and a casuistic system on the other. He denies that
the command of God appears from nowhere in the instant of
each new ethical decision. His ethics is not a form of divine
command intuitionism. God's command belongs to a history in
which the Word of God has been disclosed. This is the history
narrated in the stories of Israel, Jesus, and the church. Our
human activity has the task of corresponding to the central
events in that history, namely the birth, life, death, and resurrection of Christ. It has a visible shape, therefore, and one that
calls for our obedience not merely in theonomous terms.[11] On
the other hand, he is deeply suspicious of casuistic systems
which provide rules and procedures for determining the will of
God on each and every occasion.[12] Furthermore, Barth repeatedly insists that the divine command liberates rather than
enslaves.[13] This is what distinguishes it from every other
command. It appears to us as our highest good, *pace* Kant, and
not merely as our highest duty. God's command comprehends
all that is right and friendly and wholesome.[14] It is the source of
our joy and delight. In this respect, obedience to the Word of
God fulfils our deepest human aspirations, even as these aspirations are thereby redefined.

Yet a further problem that arises for this account of ethics is
how it relates to ethical precepts and examples which are not
specifically Christian. We are taught how to behave by parents

and teachers who often make no reference to the command of
God. The ethical discussions that are conducted in modern
societies seldom refer to Scripture or the divine will. How is
Barth's ethical viewpoint to be positioned in relation to other
ways of speaking about human action? In his discussion of the
relationship of theology to philosophy, Barth is adamant that
theology cannot tolerate any ethical system which opposes the
view that 'all ethical truth is enclosed in the command of the
grace of God'.[15] In this respect, his divine command theory is
exclusive. Theological apologetics is proscribed in so far as it is
an attempt to justify theological claims on the basis of their
relation to foundational truths which are accessible both to
believer and unbeliever. No such common starting-point exists.
If it did it would compromise the nature of God's grace in Jesus
Christ. Here Barth's criticism of the doctrine of the *analogia entis*
has ethical force. The relation of nature to supernature in
Thomist theology presupposes that, by virtue of our created
nature, we can know of God and goodness. This facilitates a co-
ordination of moral philosophy and moral theology, of nature
and grace, and of reason and revelation. Barth argues that here
the sub-structure of nature inevitably becomes a foundation on
which the super-structure of revelation must be placed.[16] This
is to be rejected because of the way in which it decentres the
eternal decree of the covenant of grace. Revelation loses it
character as the event in which God wills to be gracious to us in
Jesus Christ. This event is itself the basis by which every other
claim to knowledge of God's will is relativised. There is in
Thomism a foundation which the Christian gospel cannot and
must not admit. While this characterisation of Aquinas' moral
teaching can be questioned, it is none the less clear that Barth's
divine command ethics is intolerant of any rival claims about
the source and content of genuine moral knowledge.

Throughout much of his ethical writings, Barth is concerned
with describing the context of the Christian life. Thus, Christian
ethics includes what is often characterised as 'the spiritual life' as
well as the problems of 'the moral life'. It is significant that his
treatment of special ethics in *Church Dogmatics* III/4 begins with
an exposition of the Lord's Day as the day of worship, confes-

sion, and prayer. In similar vein, *The Christian Life* offers an extended reflection on the opening petitions of the Lord's Prayer as a way of describing the moral world of the Christian. This is not the expression of a quaint piety. It shows rather the way in which ethical belief, deliberation, and action are shaped by the character of the Christian life as a glad and grateful response to what God has already done. This fundamental setting determines the moral universe of the Christian. As Webster remarks, 'For Christian ethics, the world is a different place, and part of a Christian theory of morality is a careful delineation of that difference.'[17] This aspect of Barth's ethics provides a place for concepts of 'virtue' and 'character' which appear to be lacking from his divine command theory. To do God's will involves learning how to live as a member of the church in the world. This means responding to God's grace and finding one's position in a covenant history that has been established in Christ. It involves the development of forms of activity such as confession, invocation, thanksgiving, and service.[18]

On the other hand, Barth insists that Christian ethics must not adopt an isolationist stance. There can be no diastasis between Christian and other forms of ethical reflection. This would lead to the unwelcome consequence of a theological ethics concerned only with the province of the Christian moral consciousness.[19] The secular moral consciousness would then need to be described in terms of an alternative theory. Yet the command of God is the source of all ethical truth, and it determines not only the church, but all who are elected for the covenant of grace in Christ. Theological ethics is therefore interested in philosophical representations of human thought, affection, and agency. Barth uses a variety of terms to describe an approach which resists a common foundation but denies a lack of all positive relation. Theological ethics can 'comprehend', 'absorb', and 'annex' claims that are made by philosophical ethics. The term 'annexation' (*Annexion*)[20] is used repeatedly throughout his ethical writings. While it is an aggressive metaphor, it none the less reveals Barth's conviction that ethical insights from outwith the church can be positively appropriated.

This is further reflected by some surprisingly positive endorsements of non-Christian ethical action, especially in Barth's later work. Non-Christians are not be rigidly separated from Christians. They can be thought of as those whose calling lies before them in the future.[21] Everyone must be considered as living in the context of the uniting of all things that has already taken place in Jesus Christ. Each human being must be approached and dealt with on the basis that he or she is one for whom Jesus Christ is Lord whether that fact is acknowledged or not.[22] While this does not eradicate the significant difference between Christian and non-Christian, it seems to point to the possibility of God's work in the lives of those outwith the church. This is underscored by Barth's discussion of secular parables of the Word of God. Here there is genuine witness to God *extra muros ecclesiae*, although its adequacy must be tested by reference to Scripture, the confessional traditions of the church, and the upbuilding of its common life.[23] This possibility is already recognised in the context of his earlier discussion of the divine command.

In all ages the will of God has been fulfilled outside the Church as well. Indeed, to the shame of the Church it has often been better fulfilled outside the Church than in it. This is not in virtue of a natural goodness of humankind. It is because Jesus, as the One who has risen from the dead and sits at the right hand of God, is in fact the Lord of the whole world, who has His servants even where His name is not yet or no longer known and praised.[24]

The possibility of genuine ethical perception and action, outwith the community where the command of God is attested, is thus affirmed by Barth. He speaks positively of a non-theological ethics which does not make absolute claims that controvert those of the Christian faith, but which, within its own limits, offers illuminating reflection upon the problems of human life. Here Barth refers to the work of novelists, such as de Balzac, Dickens, and Tolstoy, and to the philosophical moralists. 'Thanks to the wisdom and patience of God, and the inconsequence of humankind, it is quite possible in practice that Christian insights and deduction may actually exist where their Christian presuppositions are wholly concealed, or where a closer investigation would reveal all kinds of presuppositions that are only to a small extent Christian.'[25]

Yet this is not merely to be thought of as the result of an occasional action of the Holy Spirit or the reconciled status of all people in Christ. The possibility of ethical perception and action beyond the church is recognised not only under the second and third articles of faith, but also under the first. The doctrine of creation provides a context in which the sharing of convictions and insights can be recognised. By virtue of the basis on which the covenant of grace is enacted, all human beings find themselves in social spheres which are under the command of God. Creation is thus central to Barth's theological ethics, although its significance cannot be understood apart from its eschatological goal. The action of God in creating the world has 'in view the institution, preservation and execution of the covenant of grace, for partnership in which He has pre-destined and called' humankind.[26]

In his early ethical work, Barth deployed the Lutheran concept of the orders of creation. These are described as creaturely standards by which the will of God meets us in the kingdom of nature.[27] Despite the way in which Barth subsequently adverts to Scripture and Christ, there is some tension with his earlier dismissal of a theory of nature which discerns, in independence of revelation, a knowledge of the will of God. This largely accounts for his decision to drop the concept of orders of creation in his later work and to prevent the publication of the earlier lectures.[28]

Although the concept of 'orders of creation' does not appear explicitly in Luther's social ethics, he wrote of the *status economicus*, which included marriage and family life, and the *status politicus* as orders which governed all human life.[29] Through these orders, human beings are bound in a network of relationships which carry responsibilities and obligations. In nine-teenth-century German Lutheranism, the notion of the orders of creation (*Schöpfungsordnungen*) describes the ways in which human beings by virtue of their social nature are aware of roles and obligations apart from and prior to belief in Jesus Christ. In the orders of creation we have a consciousness of the divine command outwith the province of special revelation. This provides an ethical basis for civil society, and a set of accessible moral standards which can command the allegiance of Christian and non-Christian alike.[30]

Understood in this sense, the concept is rejected by Barth. It establishes a source and norm of ethical knowledge prior to what is given in the self-revelation of God in Jesus Christ. It fails to perceive that creation must be understood in the light of the covenant of grace. It makes law prior to the gospel of grace, rather than a form of the latter. This is a crucial theme in Barth's theology which, in contradistinction to Lutheranism, locates ethics within dogmatics. The grace of God is the source of the command of God. In determining us by grace, God also summons us to action. Both the gospel and the law are rooted in God's eternal decision to be gracious towards us in Jesus Christ. The law is the form of the gospel, and should not be understood as prior to it or knowable independently of it.[31]

In *Church Dogmatics* III/4, the concept of the orders of creation is rejected by Barth in his criticism of Brunner and Bonhoeffer. To argue that we have a knowledge of God's will within the orders of creation is to posit a revelation of God prior to God's Word in Jesus Christ. Barth poses some critical questions. Where does this knowledge come from? Does it not presuppose a static understanding of the orders which makes it too easy to identify God's will with the status quo?[32] Yet despite this rejection of the orders of creation, Barth recognises that something vital is here receiving improper expression. The Word of God does not come to us in a way that is inexplicable and irrelevant to our created nature. It comes in such a manner as to make sense of the social nature of human beings. It engages us in the sexual, economic, and political dimensions of our natural existence. While rejecting the language of the orders of creation, Barth continues to speak of the 'spheres' of activity in which the command of God addresses us.[33] What we are to do in these spheres is known only through God's Word, but its directing of our lives comprehends the fundamental features of social existence.

[I]f it is true that the divine command and human action cannot be understood apart from them, it is just as true that they themselves must not be understood apart from the divine command and human action, but only as the reality of the event in which these two meet. Thus the emergence of these spheres, relationships or orders does not make possible a return to casuistry. They are not universal ethical truths, but only the general form of the one and supremely particular truth of the ethical event which is inaccessible as such to the casuistical grasp.[34]

In his theological anthropology, Barth describes the social nature of human existence by the leading concept of co-humanity (*Mitmenschlichkeit*). The fundamental shape of human nature has not been destroyed by human sinfulness although it is everywhere defaced by it. It is disclosed by Jesus Christ who is not only the one for God but also the one for others.[35] The being of Jesus for others corresponds to his eternal relationship to God the Father. The eternal love within the Godhead is also the love which is offered by Jesus to all other human beings. Barth can thus speak of an '*analogia relationis*'.

This theology of the human person is determined by a description of revelation. But, since the account is of human nature within and without the Christian community, we should not be surprised if there are parallels with philosophical formulations. Barth makes specific mention of Confucius, Feuerbach, and Buber.[36] He argues that this partial correspondence is to be acknowledged and read as indirect though unnecessary confirmation of what is asserted from a theological perspective. Where ethics is concerned, we should not be surprised in light of this account of human nature to find some similarities between the content of moral beliefs inside and outside the church. The possibility of good moral practice beyond the circle of faith is thus a feature of Barth's doctrine of creation as well as of his doctrines of reconciliation and redemption.

In attempting to offer a brief characterisation of Barth's ethics, one is struck by the different nuances in his thought. His strong realism is apparent in the insistence that what is right is determined only by the command of God which is always beyond human control. This divine command is sovereign and cannot be set out in a system of rules. Yet it is not an occasional event which bears no reference to the history that God has established with Israel and in the sending of Christ. Its direction is given us by the witness of Scripture. There is no source or norm of moral knowledge in creation which can precede or be set alongside the Word of God. Yet creation is characterised by spheres or orders which set the context within which the command of God is heard and obeyed. What constitutes goodness is known only from the side of faith, within the Christian community, and by the action of the Holy Spirit. Yet the will of God can be done, and witnesses can be found far beyond the sector of the church. While asserting the distinctive bases of Christian moral perception and action, Barth is also anxious to affirm activity that takes place on other bases. One might summarise this as an attempt to recognise common ethical ground with those outside the faith, without requiring any common ethical theory. The existence of such common ground is itself explained in terms of a distinctive theory about the work of God as creator, reconciler, and redeemer.

The capacity of Barth's theological work to provide a distinctive basis for Christian political witness was nowhere more apparent than in the Barmen Declaration (1934) of which he was the principal author. This continues to exercise influence as a model for Christian proclamation and political action. The Barmen Declaration asserts the unique sovereignty of God's Word in Jesus Christ, and its unlimited scope in determining every area of life. 'Jesus Christ as he is attested for us in Holy Scripture, is the one Word of God which we have to hear and which we have to trust and obey in life and in death.' The influence of Barth's theology can be discerned in theological protests against apartheid[37] and in recent reactions to ecclesiastical connivance at the proliferation of nuclear armaments and American foreign policy. George Hunsinger thus calls for a confessing church which will protest on a doctrinal basis against the cultural captivity of much modern American Christianity. 'The Lordship of Jesus Christ over and beyond all relativities of human culture is, so far as the church is concerned, a matter of life and death, a binding truth and a decision of ultimate significance.'[38]

The symposium devoted to Hunsinger's essay contains eighteen responses and counter-responses. Together, these reveal the continuing influence of Barth and the main lines of reception to his ethical work. The need for a distinctive Christian ethical witness is affirmed. Yet it is recognised that this is problematic in democratic societies which attach a high premium to values of tolerance and pluralism. It is urged that faithfulness must take priority over considerations about effectiveness in our current social situation. Yet this must happen without isolation in an ecclesiastical enclave. The trappings of an easy consensus and a tacit collaboration need to be admitted, even while the possibility of making common cause with others outside the church is endorsed.

The Church does not confront the world in absolute antithesis and mutual exclusion (sectarianism), nor does it simply surrender itself to the world's agenda, as if it were merely a valuable resource for the accomplishment of secular ends (acculturation). The Church's solidarity with the world allows it to seek valid forms of contextualization while guarding against flaccid conformism. Yet its precedence over the world requires it to maintain its essential distinctiveness without retreating into rigid isolation.[39]

POST-LIBERALISM

An important trend in recent theology reinforces some of these Barthian claims for Christian ethical specificity through linking them to a more general account of religion. Post-liberalism is a label that has come to be applied to theological trends associated with the Yale theologians, Hans Frei and George Lindbeck.[40] Although it is not a monolithic movement, it gained clearer focus with the publication of Lindbeck's *The Nature of Doctrine* in 1984. Little more than 120 pages in length, this has probably been the most widely discussed theological text of recent years. Two related aims can be discerned in *The Nature of Doctrine*. First, there is the ecumenical goal of understanding doctrines as rules governing Christian speech, action, and belief. In this way one can resolve apparent contradictions between doctrines by understanding them as rules which are to be applied in discrete ways under specific circumstances. Apparently conflicting rules may be reconciled by a better understanding of their context of origin and proper application. Thus there may emerge an underlying compatibility between, say, the Eucharistic doctrine of transubstantiation and its Protestant rivals. These 'can be interpreted as embodying rules of sacramental thought and practice that may have been in unavoidable and perhaps irresolvable collision in certain historical contexts, but that can in other circumstances be harmonized by appropriate specification of their respective domains, uses, and priorities'.[41] To support this understanding of the function of doctrine, Lindbeck sets out a second aim of his study, the articulation of a cultural–linguistic theory of religion. This understands religious utterances in the context of the practical, linguistic, and textual shaping of religious communities. It is contrasted with two alternatives; a propositionalist account of religion and an experiential–expressivist account. The cultural–linguistic theory construes a religion as being like a language in several vital respects. A religion is neither primarily a range of beliefs nor a set of symbols expressive of basic attitudes or experiences. It is a conceptual scheme which makes possible patterns of experience and the holding of beliefs. It is a public phenomenon which is the necessary condition of individual feeling and cognition. It comprises a vocabulary and a grammar which are rooted in a form of life. Thus beliefs, values, and experiences are shaped by the communal life forms which are their necessary conditions.

Lindbeck's presentation of the cultural–linguistic theory draws explicitly upon the work of scholars in philosophy and the social sciences, including *inter alios* Wittgenstein, Kuhn, Berger, and Geertz. He considers the more original theme of his work to be the rule theory of doctrine, and expresses surprise at the debate occasioned by his presentation of the cultural–linguistic theory.[42] He claims modestly that this merely reproduces work that was carried out previously and is in wide circulation. Yet the attention that his cultural–linguistic theory has commanded can be explained in two ways. On the one hand, its lapidary and finely illustrated presentation has helped to clarify the main options in the study of religion today. As Hans Frei has reported, many on reading *The Nature of Doctrine* are struck with the realisation that it states what they had already believed for some time but could not articulate properly.[43] On the other hand, the defence of the cultural–linguistic theory by way of rejection of propositionalist and experiential–expressivist positions has attracted theological criticism from both the right and the left. This is not surprising given the way in which Lindbeck's defence of his approach maps out a post-liberal theology, particularly in the final chapter of *The Nature of Doctrine*. Although the cultural–linguistic theory of religion may, in principle, be theologically neutral,[44] it is clearly being deployed here to support a definite theological orientation. David Tracy has commented, not without some justification, that 'Lindbeck's substantive theological position is a methodologically sophisticated version of Barthian confessionalism. The hands may be the hands of Wittgenstein and Geertz but the voice is the voice of Karl Barth.'[45]

Lindbeck's post-liberal theology attempts, partly through the annexing of insights from philosophy and the social sciences, to articulate a distinctively Christian position. This is done through his understanding of the church and its position *vis-à-vis* contemporary culture. In a time of increasing dissociation between church and society Lindbeck argues that the Christian future will be a sectarian one. The primary task of the church is not to baptise whatever elements of secular culture seem most religiously promising. Its task is to make greater Christian authenticity possible by socialising its members into a new way of life. This way of life is structured by the canonical texts of the community and the ways in which they recite the stories of Israel and the church. These stories, as they are read and followed by the church, have the communal power to shape belief, experience, and action. Here Lindbeck's cultural–linguistic theory draws on resources from Frei's narrative interpretation of Scripture. The Bible offers an identity description of an agent, namely God. This description reaches its climax in the story of Jesus, the divine–human agent, crucified and risen. The task of the church is to live out its communal life and represent reality in light of God's character as depicted uniquely and unsubstitutably in the story of Jesus.[46] For the theologian, therefore, the task of Christian self-description takes priority over all attempts to correlate religious with other forms of belief.

Pagan converts to the catholic mainstream did not, for the most part, first understand the faith and then decide to become Christians; rather, the process was reversed: they first decided and then they understood. More precisely, they were first attracted by the Christian community and form of life. The reasons for attraction ranged from the noble to the ignoble and were as diverse as the individuals involved; but for whatever motives, they submitted themselves to prolonged catechetical instruction in which they practised new modes of behaviour and learned the stories of Israel and their fulfillment in Christ. Only after they had acquired proficiency in the alien Christian language and form of life were they deemed able intelligently and responsibly to profess the faith, to be baptized.[47]

Lindbeck's sectarianism is of a sociological rather than theological type. The sectarian church must learn to live in a manner differentiated from its host society. Yet it continues to live in continuity with the catholic or ecumenical church across space and time. It confesses the ancient faith in the unique and final lordship of Jesus over the whole world. To maintain its catholicity today, it seems, the church must become more sectarian in the sociological sense.

The differentiation of the cultural–linguistic theory from propositionalist and expressivist theories has prompted lines of criticism from both sides. These criticisms circle around the charges of pragmatism and isolationism. Troubled by the rule theory of doctrine and the Wittgensteinian proposal that meaning is deeply connected with social use, one set of critics claims that Lindbeck reduces theological truth to a function of correct performance in accordance with the communally authorised rules for speech and action. This criticism gains plausibility from Lindbeck's notion of intrasystematic truth which invokes the criterion of coherence with the total relevant context. 'Thus for a Christian, "God is Three and One", or "Christ is Lord" are true only as parts of a total pattern of speaking, thinking, feeling, and acting.'[48] He goes on to remark that the crusader's war cry 'Christus est Dominus' is false when used to authorise the slaughter of the infidel, even though the same words can be used in a different context to make a true utterance. Thus, truth seems to be reduced to a function of correct performance.[49]

On the other hand, Lindbeck works with a notion of truth not only as coherence, but also as correspondence. Coherence is a necessary but insufficient condition of ontological truth. Ontological truth is made possible by the categorial adequacy of the religion which obtains when forms of life shaped by Christian narratives 'correspond to God's being and will'.[50] Utterances can be ontologically true, therefore, when the conditions of categorial and intrasystematic truth are met. There is thus a clear realist intention within Lindbeck's appropriation of a cultural–linguistic theory, although the practical character of religious utterances entails that this is not to be construed as a simple isomorphism of proposition and reality. Within religion, truth is to be characterised in terms of a correspondence of a total way of life, which includes beliefs and propositions properly contextualised, with the divine being and action. Drawing upon the Thomist distinction between the *modus significandi* (mode of signifying) and the *res significata* (thing signified), Lindbeck suggests that, while the thing signified is beyond comprehension, the mode of signification may be fixed by the rules governing correct performance.

Seriously to commit oneself to thinking and acting as if God were good in relation to us (*quoad nos*) in the ways indicated by the stories involves asserting that he really is good in himself (*in se*) even though, as the canonical texts testify, the meaning of this latter claim is utterly beyond human comprehension.[51]

Whether this defence of theological realism is sufficiently robust to fulfil Lindbeck's intentions is questionable. Can one combine the unknowability of God, a pragmatic theory of religious meaning, and an ontological account of theological truth? At the very least, some account is required of how the mode of signification and the thing signified are related. This calls for a doctrine of revelation which defends the notion that, in some sense, God is, within God's own self, who God is for us in the stories of Israel and Jesus. At one point in his discussion, Lindbeck seems to concede this. The gospel stories, he remarks elsewhere, following Frei, 'unsubstitutably identify and characterize a particular person as the summation of Israel's history and as the unsurpassable and irreplaceable clue to who and what the God of Israel and the universe is'.[52] The narrative thus has a referential as well as a regulative function, the former acting as a warrant for the latter. In other words, the regulative functions of the religion are understood to derive ultimately from the being and action of God. That Lindbeck's theology has a clear realist hue is evident also from his strong commitment to the eschatological lordship of Jesus. His concern for the salvation of adherents of other religions in a way that does not compromise this commitment can only make sense in light of a strong Christian realism.[53] Lindbeck's intentions, therefore, are unashamedly cognitive and realist. The problem is that these seem to lie in deep tension with a thesis about the unknowability of God.

Some of the ambiguity in his position can be resolved by construing the concepts of instrasystematic and categorial truth as criteria of ontological truth rather than rival and incompatible accounts of the nature of truth. This is the reading of *The Nature of Doctrine* advocated by Bruce Marshall and subsequently endorsed by Lindbeck himself.[54] If correct performance and categorial adequacy are considered necessary conditions for utterances which are ontologically true, these may be construed in terms of justification rather than as what makes the utterance true. What makes the utterance true is the being and action of God, but for us to speak truly requires necessary conditions of behavioural coherence and the grasp of an adequate categorial scheme. This need not be perceived as an accommodation to a pragmatic theory of truth, provided we hold that truth values attach not to sentences as such but to particular token utterances. There is thus no sense in which the cry 'Christus est Dominus' can be true or false except as an occasioned utterance set in context. An appeal is made here to the Aristotelianism of

Aquinas. 'In Aquinas' intellectual setting, judgments, not sentences in abstraction from acts of affirmation, were propositions capable of being true or false.'[55]

This co-ordination of Lindbeck's different constructions of truth will allay some realist scruples. Yet Lindbeck's emphasis upon the significance of use for understanding meaning continues to cause realist anxieties with respect to his rule theory of doctrine. There resurfaces here the drift in a regulative and pragmatist direction. (Perhaps this is not surprising given the prominence of Wittgenstein, Kuhn, and Geertz in the articulation of the cultural–linguistic theory.) The rule theory of doctrine seems to be sustained in part by a conviction concerning the unknowability of God. According to Lindbeck, the Athanasian understanding of consubstantiality can be understood 'in terms of the rule that whatever is said of the Father is said of the Son, except that the Son is not the Father. Thus the theologian most responsible for the final triumph of Nicaea thought of it, not as a first-order proposition with ontological reference, but as a second-order rule of speech.'[56]

Lindbeck does not deny that these second-order rules of speech can also be used to make first-order propositional statements about the Godhead, but he claims that the priority belongs to the former function of doctrine. (It is hard to believe that Athanasius was not engaged at both levels.[57]) He is sceptical about the prospects of resolving this side of eternity first-order disputes such as that between eastern and western theologians about the nature of the immanent Trinity, but is more hopeful that agreement can be reached on the fundamental rules that are prescribed by Trinitarian language. He offers a comparison with scientific theories. Disputes between Aristotelian, Newtonian, and Einsteinian theories of space and time are scientifically assessed independently of the very different question of the way things really are.[58] Similarly, a doctrine is to be assessed in terms of its organisational function with reference to Scripture, tradition, worship, and the Christian life. This illustration seems to expose the central weakness in Lindbeck's position. A commitment to realism is somehow tempered by the assumption that 'the way things really are' is unknowable and irrelevant to the assessment of scientific theories and theological doctrines. We have here a collision between something like a realist theory of reference and an instrumentalist theory of meaning. This sits very uneasily with his earlier claims, drawn from Frei, for the gospel stories as the unsurpassable clue as to who and what God is.[59] It seems, therefore, that it is finally the stress on the unknowability of God which compromises Lindbeck's theological realism.

Differences within the so-called Yale school may be most crucial at this juncture. According to Thiemann, part of the logic of Christian discourse is that contextualised claims about the action of God for us carry implications about the identity of God. We cannot make sense of Christian faith, hope, and practice without the assumption that the God *pro nobis* is also God *extra nos*. Convictions about the prevenience of God's grace and the revelation of God to us are constitutive features of the church's canonical scriptures, sacramental practice, and eschatological hope. Unless we assume that there is some correspondence between God for us and God's self, the depth grammar of the Christian faith will be undermined. It is part of the meaning of the narrated promises of the gospel that it is not possible to think of God other than God as here depicted.

Faith is a response to the God who issues the promise and who alone establishes the possibility of the act of communication. Faith is a necessary though secondary element in God's act of promise. Thus we see again the same pattern of relation and priority. God's *extra nos* reality as the existent God who issues his promises to the reader through the text is recognized precisely as the *pro nobis* character of his reality is acknowledged.[60]

This relation of the *pro nobis* to the *extra nos* mirrors a characteristic feature of Frei's theology of the resurrection. The way in which the gospel portrays Jesus as risen entails that we must think of his presence here and now as enabled by his resurrection *extra nos*. The way in which the identity of Jesus is rendered requires that we think of his being raised from the dead as an event primarily for him and secondarily for us.

A very different line of critical inquiry has come from those who perceive the cultural–linguistic theory to be isolationist. It attaches too high a value to intratextual faithfulness and performance according to communal standards, as opposed to co-ordination with the best knowledge and insights available from other fields of inquiry. Thus, one reviewer could remark that Lindbeck had effectively shut the door on the criticism of religion. On the cultural–linguistic model, the 'community has generated rules to protect its intellectual self-understanding which have been made independent of reference to what lies outside the community'.[61] A more plausible version of the same point is advanced by David Tracy. He accuses Lindbeck of failing to perceive the ways in which exponents of the experiential–expressivist paradigm have been preoccupied with the ways in which experience is embedded in language, forms of life, and social practices. Their understanding of the relationship between language and experience is thus more sophisticated than Lindbeck gives them credit for. Yet Tracy perceives that Lindbeck's criticism runs even deeper than this and is, in principle, a protest against theologies of correlation. It is the repristination of a confessional over against a correlationist theology. For Tracy, however, there should be a mutually critical correlation of the meaning and truth of the tradition with the meaning and truth of the contemporary situation.[62]

Although Lindbeck eschews a correlationist approach, he can respond to the charge of isolationism (or fideism). The cultural–linguistic theory claims that religion in some important respects only is like a culture or a language.[63] This implies that in other respects religion functions in different ways. For example, the understanding that a religious community has of the world and its own canonical texts can change under the impact of external forces. Lindbeck is well aware of this mobility within Christian theology. He claims that the fundamental doctrinal rules governing the language of the faith and the constitutive narratives of the community do not change. None the less, within these parameters first-order truth claims change and vary 'from the application of the interpretive scheme to the shifting worlds that human beings inhabit'.[64]

Similarly, the notions of absorbing the world into the text and of *ad hoc* apologetics indicate ways in which a religion might evince its rationality and relevance in the modern world without capitulating either to foundationalist or correlationist strategies. To accuse Lindbeck of rendering religion immune from external criticism or encounter with other disciplines is well wide of the mark. As Marshall notes, his position may be imperialist, but it is certainly not sectarian in this sense.[65] Despite accusations of isolationism, Lindbeck, in the closing stages of *The Nature of Doctrine*, writes as a soft rationalist. A religion shows its reasonableness through its powers of assimilation. This is done by offering a plausible interpretation of 'the varied situations and realities' its members confront.[66] Apologetics can be conducted in an occasional manner provided it is not 'systematically prior and controlling in the fashion of post-Cartesian natural theology and of later liberalism'.[67]

Lindbeck's defence of a cultural–linguistic model of religion within Christian theology reflects a substantive position on the relationship between church and civil society. It is not in the interests of withdrawal from society that he advocates a church which differentiates itself sharply from its host culture. It is because he reckons that such a church will better witness within the world and will provide its members with the appropriate skills and practices for its reshaping. Although not overconfident that this is what the future holds, he judges that 'provided a religion stresses service rather than domination, it is likely to contribute more to the future of humanity if it preserves its own distinctiveness and integrity than if it yields to the homogenizing tendencies associated with liberal experiential–expressivism'.[68]

Despite its problematic account of theological truth, Lindbeck's post-liberalism provides a way of construing the Christian religion and the position of the church in such a way as to support the distinctiveness of Christian ethics. If experience and belief are conditioned by the particular rules and vocabulary of Christian speech set within discrete forms of life, then both moral obligation and perception will have a particular configuration. The rationale for moral action will make reference to the canonical stories and patterns of life prescribed by the language of the religion. Christian moral discourse will involve 'thick description' which derives from the theoretical and practical resources of ecclesial life.[69] This discourse, however, need not be radically incommensurate with other forms of moral language. The possibility of absorbing the world and engaging in *ad hoc* apologetics suggests that partial similarities and correspondences may be sought and found.

'VERITATIS SPLENDOR'

The 1993 papal encyclical addresses some fundamental questions in moral theology. In doing so, it sets out a framework for dealing with matters of moral perception which shows some striking similarities with recent Protestant attempts to defend the distinctiveness of Christian ethics.[70] It is significant that the encyclical opens with a sustained reflection upon the encounter of the rich young man with Christ. (Karl Barth likewise devotes careful attention to this passage in his ethics.[71]) Questions about what is good and what ought to be done are to be answered only by reference to Christ. Faith and discipleship provide the context for a Christian understanding of moral law in terms both of its content and of its goal. All goodness derives from God, and the purpose of life is to live for the praise of God's glory. The moral life is a response to the grace of God in both Old and New Testaments.[72] To follow the precepts of the second table of the Decalogue is integrally related to the love and obedience owed to God in the first table. This setting of the moral commandments in the context of one's life in Christ is apparent to some degree also in the ordering of material in the recent *Catechism of the Catholic Church*. The exposition of the natural law and the Decalogue is set within Part Three which deals with 'Life in Christ' and expounds first the human and the theological virtues.[73] As in Karl Barth, ethics is set within the context of Christian dogmatics.

Christ, the incarnate Son, is the perfect expression of God's wisdom. To follow him is 'the essential and primordial foundation of Christian morality'.[74] This is not a matter of merely heeding his ethical teachings. It means holding fast to his very person, being conformed to him, and becoming a member of his Body, the Church, by the grace of the Holy Spirit. In the church our lives are reconfigured to the service of Christ through baptism and the Eucharist. By being created anew in this way we find our true freedom. All this is summarised at the opening of chapter two.

> Our meditation on the dialogue between Jesus and the rich young man has enabled us to bring together the essential elements of revelation in the Old and New Testaments with regard to moral action. These are: the subordination of man and his activity to God, the One who 'alone is good'; the relationship between the moral good of human acts and eternal life; Christian discipleship, which opens up before man the perspective of perfect love; and finally the gift of the Holy Spirit, source and means of the moral life of the 'new creation' (cf. 2 Cor. 5:17).[75]

The exposition of the gospel encounter with the rich young man is of considerable methodological significance in the argument of the encyclical. It situates later teaching about human freedom, conscience, and natural law within some Scripturally shaped assumptions. Thus we are told that freedom is not an absolute but is dependent upon the truth. The freedom that is to be valued is that by which we discover, acknowledge, and follow what is true. Conscience does not itself determine the criteria for what is good and evil. It applies the universal knowledge of what is good to particular situations. Conscience is described, following Bonaventure, as 'the herald and messenger of God'.[76] The natural law is rooted in the eternal wisdom of God, and is its human expression. Although human beings can discern good and evil by the use of their reason, the encyclical stresses the need for reason to be guided by revelation and faith.[77] This is reinforced by the description of 'connaturality'. The forming of conscience requires not merely a knowledge of God's law. It requires a 'connaturality' of the human person and the true good. This is developed through the cardinal and the theological virtues, and is also assisted by the church and its magisterium.[78] The teaching office of the church thus enhances rather than overrides the individual conscience. The position that is mapped out is described as a 'participated theonomy'.[79] The source of goodness and law is in God. It is revealed in Scripture and taught by the church. But it corresponds with our created nature, reason, and conscience as these are ecclesially shaped.

The religious setting of the moral life is emphasised by the encyclical's stress on Christian witness. Faith itself is a truth to be lived out. It involves a commitment to God's commandments. In living faithfully we bear witness to the goodness of God. 'Christ's witness is the source, model and means for the witness of his disciples.'[80] The supreme work is that of charity and the supreme witness is that of martyrdom by which one imitates the sacrificial love of Christ. In this witness, however, Christians are not alone. One may see the moral sense of those shaped by 'the great religious and sapiential traditions of East and West' as reflecting the work of God's Spirit.

The encyclical has engendered controversy within the Roman Catholic Church mainly on account of internal disputes within its moral theology. The attacks on 'proportionalism' and the distinction between the fundamental option and particular choices are intended to safeguard the view that certain acts are, by virtue of their object, intrinsically evil. This has been perceived as an attempt to provide theoretical support for the dubious prohibition on artificial contraception. Many perceive this as the leading subtext of the encyclical.[81] Other scruples concern its use of Scripture,[82] the failure to recognise the evangelical message of justification by grace, the gratuitous use of non-inclusive language, its mariology, and its invocation of papal authority at the expense of other magisterial resources within the Roman Catholic Church.[83]

Leaving these criticisms aside, however, the encyclical still stands as a powerful late twentieth-century defence of theological ethics over against secular trends. It connects a decline or obscuring of the moral sense with the dechristianisation of a community. This comes about through the loss of awareness of Gospel morality and the eclipse of fundamental principles.[84] The dissociation of freedom from divine truth leads to an assertion of the autonomy of the individual. We find this reiterated even more strongly in *Evangelium Vitae* with its criticism of the autonomous self devoid of reference to common value and a truth binding upon all. In this moral context, 'everthing is negotiable, everything is open to bargaining, even the first of the fundamental rights, the right of life'.[85] Thus there is a risk of an alliance emerging between democracy and ethical relativism.[86] It is probably its robust response to this situation through restating Scriptural and theological themes which has elicited widespread support.

By going behind particular issues to focus on the instrumentality and plasticity of modern moral reason, the Pope has gone to the heart of a philosophical situation in which all Christians now find themselves. If there is a place for a Petrine office in the Church (a matter on which I keep an open mind), surely this encyclical is a creditable example of the kind of service it may render.[87]

The way in which the encyclical positions natural law theory in relation to positive theology and Scripture reflects a further trend in the recent reading of Thomas Aquinas. The disjunction between the natural law and a distinctively Christian life which once characterised Catholic moral teaching has now been called into question. For Aquinas, the natural law derives from the eternal law of God which is first in the order of being. Although some rudiments of the natural law are present in the minds of all rational creatures, this does not provide a free-standing basis for an adequate moral theory.[88] Our grasp of the natural law is clouded by sin and error. There are cultural variations in perceptions of it. Moreover, his account of natural law is presented in the *Summa Theologiae* in the context of more extensive treatments of the cardinal and theological virtues. To understand the natural law and its application to human affairs one must acquire a range of virtues, most notably prudence and charity. Prudence is necessary to determine a substantive theory of the good, while charity is the supreme organising principle of the moral life. Through the supreme virtue of charity, the individual participates in the mind and will of God. This enables him or her to understand the will of God in particular situations while also transforming his or her affections and actions. Thus, although Aquinas maintains that human creatures everywhere can know the most basic requirements of the natural law, for example the prohibition on killing the innocent, his moral theory presupposes a network of specific philosophical and theological commitments which makes it more contextual than has often been recognised. The cardinal virtue of prudence is truly and perfectly present only where grace directs the whole person to his or her final good.[89] No true or perfect virtue is possible without the greatest of the theological virtues, since our ultimate end is the enjoyment of God which is attained through the gift of charity.[90]

The arguments of *Veritatis Splendor*, together with recent readings of Thomas Aquinas, indicate a greater measure of contextualism in Roman Catholic moral theology.[91] Ethics is to be understood in terms of the good life which embraces religious concerns. The rich young ruler is directed to a life in which the One who alone is good can be found. The insights of the natural law are fragmented and rudimentary until illumined by the truths of revelation as these are known within a life of faith, hope, and charity. The dignity of the human being, while affirmed in different ways by the secular conscience, is threatened by the corrosive trends of a social life which loses sight of its theological and transcendent context. In the following chapter the most powerful attempt to develop an ecclesially specific ethics in recent theology will be explored at greater length.

CHAPTER THREE

Ecclesial ethics – Stanley Hauerwas

A turn towards ecclesial ethics[1] can be detected in the writings of John Yoder, James McClendon, and Stanley Hauerwas amongst others. This approach represents a significant trend in recent Christian ethics, and resonates with wider theological, philosophical, and sociological trends. In this exposition of ecclesial ethics, attention is devoted mainly to the writings of Hauerwas, principally because he is the most prolific and widely discussed in this context. His approach can be introduced by way of his criticism of liberalism and congruent patterns of thought in theological ethics.[2]

THE FAILURE OF LIBERALISM

The crisis of liberalism can be seen in the increasing fragmentation of western societies and the dissociation of citizens from moral traditions, institutions, and communities. The project of liberalism was one of establishing a moral basis for the democratic state and the market economy. This was done in a variety of ways, each of which shared the common feature of isolating the individual and his or her own interests. A common morality was sought which could underwrite liberal societies and which did not require specific appeal to religious beliefs, historical traditions, or contested metaphysical notions. According to Hauerwas, the impossibility of this project has been manifested in several ways.[3]

The individual of liberal theory does not exist. Our societies comprise very different types of individuals who reflect in their interests and goals specific beliefs and commitments which have been mediated by their inheritance of historical traditions and communities. The secular state, therefore, represents a compromise between a range of competing interests, rather than embodying a single moral theory to which all its citizens are committed. Interests are neither a fundamental nor transparent notion, but presuppose a prior description of a person's character, projects, and community. In order to create a corporate identity for liberal individualism, the nation state becomes necessary as a vehicle for articulating the interests of individuals, and this is often achieved only through violence. Social cohesiveness is typically acquired through a good war.[4]

The preoccupation of moral philosophy with 'quandary ethics' reflects the ethical assumptions of liberal society.[5] It is assumed in much moral debate that ethical dilemmas can be resolved either by clarifying the empirical facts or by ascertaining the correct application of some principle(s). In the case of the abortion debate, the central issues are often depicted as whether the foetus is a human person or whether the rights of the foetus take priority over the rights of the mother. Yet the way in which the abortion dispute seems incapable of resolution suggests that the differences between the ethical perspectives of the disputants run much deeper. '[T]his kind of analysis fails to see that the issue is not one of principle or fact, but one of perception determined by a history of interpretation.'[6] The context for one's moral judgment involves notions pertaining to the way we perceive children, human sexuality, the body, and human birth. These notions can only be displayed by reference to historical traditions which provide examples of how life is to be lived and understood. 'Deontological or utilitarian theories that try to free moral notions from their dependence on examples and the narratives that display them prove to be too monochromatic to account for the variety of our notions and the histories on which they are dependent.'[7] Moral principles, for Hauerwas, only make sense when set within the context of an understanding of what human life should be. In other words, an account of moral principles involves some account of the virtues or, which is the same thing, of moral character.

The crisis of theological ethics stems from attempts ever since

Kant to show that Christian theological insights overlap secular insights and can be accessed by those outwith the Christian community. In many respects, this was a worthy undertaking since it enabled Christians to advocate social improvements without requiring the acceptance of theological presuppositions to recognise their desirability. For example, the post-war churches in the UK could advocate the creation of the Welfare State without implying that the Beveridge Report be under-written by theological principles. There could be a constructive moral contribution from the church to a religiously pluralist society. However, the danger in this strategy is twofold. First, there is a tendency to accept tacitly the underlying structure of the society which is being reformed. The need for the church to challenge and confront its host society can thus be overlooked. Second, the attempt to present Christian moral insights to a secular audience often results in the theological dimension of ethics appearing either unnecessary or marginal. If the moral principles underwritten by Christian beliefs can be known and practised independently of these beliefs, then the latter start to look redundant.[8] This is confirmed by the way in which theological statements can usually be detached from the conclusions presented in many textbooks without those conclusions being unduly weakened. For Hauerwas, a proper Christian contribution to society begins with the recognition that Christian convictions make a difference and presuppose the particularity of the Christian community. This point is also argued by Yoder in *The Politics of Jesus*. In surveying recent approaches to Christian ethics, Yoder shows how often writers were able to sideline the commandments of Jesus and thus to present ethics in terms of principles or procedures which could be established on the basis of what was natural. These strategies, which reduced the teaching of Jesus merely to its eschatological or existential significance, thus prevented the emergence of a distinctively Christian approach to ethics centred on the polity of the church.[9]

Hauerwas also follows the recent assault on foundationalist epistemologies in his attack on liberalism. The project of estab-lishing foundations of knowledge on self-evident principles, incorrigible sense-data reports, or propositions commanding universal consent is now doomed, he claims. It was a misguided epistemological adventure of the Enlightenment which ignored the way in which many of our most deeply held assumptions are embedded within the particular traditions and forms of life we inhabit. Hauerwas is clearly hostile to foundationalism,[10] although his recent writings suggest that he does not wish to be positively identified as an anti-foundationalist.[11] None the less, his writings share the now familiar attack on liberalism and its doctrine of the unencumbered self.

VIRTUE, COMMUNITY, AND NARRATIVE

Hauerwas shows a fundamental preference for the language of virtue over against the language of moral principles. His justification for this is similar to arguments advanced for Aristotelianism by Alasdair MacIntyre. An agent's being takes priority because moral actions only make sense within the context of who we are, what sort of people we are seeking to become, and the moral traditions and communities from which we take our bearings. This, of course, presupposes a standard account of the proper ends of human nature, and for this we must have recourse to a moral tradition which, through story, precept, example, and training, enables us to live well. Hauerwas' first monograph was devoted to the concept of character, and argued that moral discourse could only make sense when set against some account of the development of an agent's character. Thus moral principles, divine commands, and ethical decisions all require to be placed within the context of an account of the formation of moral character. The self must be understood as an agent whose character explains action without that action being construed mechanistically or deterministically.[12]

The significance of character in determining an agent's moral choices requires that we have some account of what virtues ought to be acquired and practised. These are our habitual dispositions to act in ways that are morally praiseworthy. Moral character is shaped by the development of the virtues. This, in turn, points to the ethical significance of the

communities to which we belong. Contrary to standard typolo-
gies, this account of virtue does not necessarily imply a preference for teleological theories of ethics over against
deontological theories. It is possible within an account of the
virtuous life to make sense of a range of deontological principles. For example, the creation of a community in which the
virtuous life is possible may require respect for some fundamental rules. In this way the virtuous life would require respect
for duties binding upon all members of the community. 'The
recognition and performance of duty is made possible because
we are virtuous, and a person of virtue is dutiful because not to
be so is to be less than virtuous.'[13]

The nature of the virtues is such that they can only be
learned, practised, and developed in human communities. To
be truthful, humble, and just presupposes a particular way of
relating to others, which can only be acquired within a social
form of life. Without the requisite community moral character
cannot be developed. There is thus a shift in emphasis from
Hauerwas' more individualistic treatment of character in *Character and the Christian Life* with its stress on sanctification, to a
stronger ecclesial emphasis in *The Community of Character*.[14] The
concept of virtue is integrally related to the social concept of a
practice. The notion of performing well or virtuously in choral
singing, family life, building bridges, or writing poetry only
makes sense with reference to a social practice and the tradition
in which these activities have been developed.

Given the epistemological significance of community, the
moral vacuum in liberal societies is a political rather than a
theoretical problem for Hauerwas.[15] The distinctiveness of
Christian convictions is dependent upon the existence of a
discrete community in which these convictions are represented
and fostered. Christian ethics thus requires a church which is
independent of the secular state and the prevailing culture. 'It is
my suspicion that if theologians are going to contribute to
reflection on the moral life in our particular situation, they will
do so exactly to the extent they can capture the significance of
the church for determining the nature and content of Christian
ethical reflection.'[16]

The tradition of Christian virtues must be borne by a community in which historical examples are remembered and interpreted in the light of new circumstances and problems. The emphasis on tradition and authority need not, in this respect, be reactionary. The tradition must be learned and extended under new conditions, but this can only take place in relation to the past and to the examples which constitute the tradition. Hauerwas' ecclesial epistemology may be seen as an attempt to overcome the textbook distinction between Christian doctrine and ethics. 'A christology which is not a social ethic is deficient.'[17] Christian confession is ethically situated in the form of life which Jesus makes possible. In this respect, Jesus and the community which knows him are indispensable for Christian ethics. Hauerwas appeals here to Lindbeck's cultural–linguistic model of religion. Learning Christian faith is not so much understanding a set of propositional truths as learning like a child to speak the language of its community. This involves participation in the social forms of life of that community.

This sets up an important ethical criterion for the truthfulness of Christian convictions. The polity of the church, and hence of the Christian tradition, is to be judged by the character of the people it produces. In the same way as the fruitfulness of scientific theories in terms of their explanatory and predictive power is a mark of truthfulness, so the ability of the Christian community to generate moral character is a mark of the truthfulness of Christian beliefs.[18] This is a surprising move for a Protestant theologian to make. The dominant image of the church is not that of a community *simul iustus et peccator* but of a pilgrim people sanctified by God as a sacramental sign before the world. 'I am not a good Lutheran, and I want to argue that the metaphor of the journey is and surely should be the primary one for articulating the shape of Christian existence and living.'[19]

The claim that Christian beliefs are acquired and tested only by the forms of life in which they are embedded, risks being construed as a non-cognitivist or regulative account of faith. Christian belief might thus be reduced to a commitment to a specific form of life. In the manner of a prescriptivist theory of ethics, Christian confession is to be analysed in terms of adherence to and recommendation of a particular way of life. Yet, it is clear that this is not Hauerwas' intention. Although he relates belief and practice very closely, he is careful at times to distinguish these.[20] We might say that, for Hauerwas, ethical fruitfulness is a criterion of the truth of Christian claims but does not actually constitute their truthfulness. This is constituted by the way things are with respect to God, Israel, and Jesus independently of Christian confession. In this respect, Hauerwas' theological ethics displays a strong realist commitment. None the less, it has to be said that Hauerwas does not have a great deal to say about the truth of Christian convictions over and beyond their ethical fruitfulness, and some of his statements seem almost to imply a regulative theory of theological truth.[21] Doubtless, this relates to his fear that Christian confession can all too easily be divorced from the practices within which it alone becomes intelligible. As a Methodist, he inveighs against trends in Protestantism which proclaim a gospel of justification by faith divorced from the social forms that the gospel creates and within which alone it can be received and proclaimed.[22]

Hauerwas' ontological realism and epistemological relativism are apparent in his exchange with Julian Hartt, who charges him with failing to distinguish adequately between aesthetic truthfulness and theological truth. The former is appropriate to the stories of fiction and construes 'true' in the sense of 'authentic' or 'true to life'.[23] Yet the Christian faith traditionally claims that the gospel narratives are 'true' in some further sense. They are 'true' in virtue of their characterisation of God (what Hartt calls 'truth in the ontological mode'), and it is this truth which enables and sustains the Christian community. Hauerwas' response is simply that the truth is such that it can only be apprehended in a truthful manner.[24]

The category of 'narrative' or 'story' plays a central role in Hauerwas' ethics.[25] Narrative is described as 'the connected description of action and of suffering which moves to a point'.[26] It is the cumulative description of how character is formed both by what one does and what happens to one. In this respect, a narrative can provide insight into how life should (or should not) be lived, and is thus an indispensable vehicle for moral appreciation. The presentation of moral principles independently of an account of the way in which these can be embodied and held together in a human story leads to distortion. The primacy of being over doing is reflected in the need to assess particular actions in the context of a narrative in which character unfolds. In the case of the abortion controversy, an adequate assessment of the issues requires the moral agent to consider the place that abortion has within a particular narrative.[27] Its relation to other notions which require narrative display is crucial to any rational decision in the face of a moral dilemma. The relatedness of moral decisions to narratives does not imply relativism, for it is possible to judge one story as better than another. Criteria such as 'unity', 'wholeness', 'consistency', 'integrity' can be invoked, although these criteria themselves can only be grasped through being trained to appreciate 'a good story'. Thus the category of story is epistemologically fundamental, and the moral criterion for assessing each story is the character it forms.

Moral principles and decisions are informed by the unity of virtues to be realised in a human life. The unity of virtues can only be articulated in terms of narrative patterns combining action and suffering. To be virtuous is, in one sense, therefore, to allow one's life to be determined by a narrative in which virtue is displayed. The value of such determination can be assessed in terms of its moral effectiveness. 'By their fruits you shall know them.' Hauerwas sets out four positive effects that a narrative might have upon a human life: power to release us from destructive alternatives; ways of seeing through current distortions; room to keep us from having to resort to violence; a sense of the tragic, i.e. an awareness of the moral conflict that besets even our best endeavours in a finite and imperfect world.[28]

In the same way as a scientific narrative can demonstrate its truthfulness by the pragmatic criteria of explaining not only the data, but also the success of previous theories which it now surpasses, so a narrative of moral character can convince us by its ability to shape more effectively the lives of its participants.

This does not lead to a pragmatic construction of truth. While employing pragmatic criteria for determining truthfulness, it does not reduce the concept of truth to pragmatic efficacy. In this respect, Hauerwas' realism, as we have already seen, retains a distinction between the criteria for truthfulness and the constitution of truthfulness. This will become apparent as we assess his reading of the specific narratives of Israel and Jesus.

Hauerwas' focus upon narrative has the aim of signifying the importance of the Christian community for the shaping of virtuous lives. Without the narrative resources of the community, the conditions of virtue will be absent from contemporary society. The church is a community whose life is shaped by the specific content of the narratives of Scripture. Here, considerations more specific to Christian theology become apparent. The narrative of Scripture is not simply a configuration of human stories constituting a social ethic. The narrative of Israel and Jesus is the story of God's self-revelation in history. It is, in a crucial sense, God's story before it is ours, although because it is the story of God with us it can and must become our story also. The nature of God and the type of community that God's action makes possible cannot be disengaged from the particularity of Jesus and the kingdom he proclaimed. The gospel narrative is indispensable, for it describes the form in which Jesus becomes paradigmatic for the Christian community. The relationship of particular to universal is crucial at this juncture. The story of Jesus is not to be read as a particular instance of some universal truth. His significance is not merely illustrative. If this were so then Christian ethics could be set out independently of Jesus and his story without any material loss. For Hauerwas and the school of thought he represents,[29] this reverses the proper relation of particular and universal in Christian theology. Jesus is of universal significance because of the constitutive power of his particular story. This implies a belief in the eschatological ordering of everything in the light of that one story. It is on the basis of the person and work of Jesus that God relates to us and is significant for us. For the Christian community, there must be continual reference to the gospels' narrative rendition of Jesus as the one in whom every human life finds its meaning and purpose.

The story of Jesus is dominated by the message of the kingdom proclaiming God's gracious rule over all creation and history. As the story unfolds, however, Jesus' proclamation of the kingdom becomes the church's proclamation of Jesus crucified and risen. Jesus thus represents the kingdom in person – the *autobasileia*, to use Origen's expression[30] – and the only way to know the kingdom is to know Jesus. Knowledge of Jesus takes the form of discipleship. Only by knowing the way in which his life, death, and resurrection make the polity of the church possible can one know him. The disciples can know Jesus in their common life by taking up the cross and following him. Thus the confession of Jesus Christ, the witness to God's kingdom, the life of the church, and social ethics all stand together.

The way in which the coming of Jesus is also the coming of a new social order in history is argued more extensively by Yoder. He resists any attempt to construe the work of Christ independently of the polity of justice and peace that he advocates and instantiates in his earthly life. It is his ethico-theological commitment which results historically in his crucifixion. If we construe the cause of his death only as the necessity of getting immolated to satisfy the metaphysics of the atonement, we break the link between the ethics of Jesus and those demanded of the church.[31] Similarly, the doctrine of justification is not given expression except in terms of the new social reality that God's declaration of our righteousness in Christ brings about. According to Ephesians 2, it is by the blood of Christ that our estrangement from God and from one another is overcome. The work of Christ creates one new humanity in which former divisions are overcome.[32]

For both Yoder and Hauerwas, the quality of peace-making is, above all, the characteristic of the Christian community in the world. This is a constant theme across their writings. The life of Jesus enacts the power of non-violent resistance. He eschews both the sectarian (Essene) option and the militarist (Zealot) option. The cost of non-violent resistance is crucifixion. The resurrection is the sign of God's vindication of Jesus' way, which enables us to live at peace with one another. The need for violence arises through fear or the desire for control and power. These are negated by the gospel narrative which brings a kingdom in which human differences are overcome and in which the future rests secure in God's love. This is what provides Christians with the means to be peace-makers and to be witnesses against the power of violence in the world. '[L]ove is the nonviolent apprehension of the other as other. But to see the other as other is frightening, because to the extent others are other they challenge my way of being. Only when my self – my character – has been formed by God's love, do I know I have no reason to fear the other.'[33]

As the central virtue of the church, peacemaking is directed towards the world. It challenges the false peace and uneasy compromises which are based on power rather than honesty.[34] It challenges the apparent necessity of violence in the face of provocation and threat. In a subtle argument which relies upon Yoder, Hauerwas claims that the Christian narrative creates possibilities which contest the assumption that violence is some-times the only way. Defending my welfare and my property cannot be paramount for anyone who acknowledges the Chris-tian story. The overall effect of non-violent action is difficult to calculate even when the short-term effects appear tragic; yet the providential pattern found in the story of Jesus and his followers provides grounds for confidence that are not found elsewhere.

Christians have held that the death of a Christian believer, as a result of his behaving in a Christian way at the hands of the agents of evil, can become through no merit of his or her own a special witness and a monument of the power of God. The death of that Christian disciple makes a greater contribution to the cause of God and to the welfare of the world than his staying alive at the cost of killing would have done. For ever after it is looked on with respect. Why not accept suffering? Jesus did.[35]

CHRISTIAN HOMOGENEITY

In a range of writings, Hauerwas has argued imaginatively for the normative ethical significance of the Christian narrative and the forms of life it makes possible. In this respect, his own writings on applied ethics confirm the claim he makes for the distinctive contribution of the church to the world. Although these are not the focus of the present study, they merit reference since Hauerwas' contribution cannot be assessed except in the light of its specific ethical outcomes.

According to Hauerwas, the standard debates between pro- and anti-abortionists are too formalised and abstract in their concentration upon the rights of the mother, the rights of the foetus, and the question of whether and when the foetus becomes a person. By engaging in debate on these terms, the Christian ethicist has surrendered too much. Abortion must be seen within the context of the community's understanding of the significance of life and the meaning of procreation.[36] It is only in terms of the community's commitment to children as a sign of our trust and confidence in life that the scandal of abortion can be fully appreciated. This is not to say that abortion must always and everywhere be wrong – the tragic dimension of life may occasionally necessitate it – but the establishment of abortion on demand in any society is funda- mentally at odds with the political complexion of the church.

The church believes explicitly in the providential care of the God who is both creator and redeemer. Its task is to witness to this providential rule as a historic community of faith. In its life, therefore, it looks back to the inheritance of faith and pledges its hope for the future by creating and nurturing new life in its midst. For children are our anchors in history, our pledge and witness that the Lord we serve is the Lord, not only of our community, but of all history. The family is, therefore, symbolically central for the meaning of the existence of the Christian people.[37]

It is within this narrative and communal setting that Christian convictions about the sanctity of life become intelligible. Hauerwas talks not about the inherent value of life, but about life as 'the locus of God's creating and redeeming purpose'.[38] As a precious gift of the sovereign God, life is not ours to deny or to destroy. In this respect, there must always be a presumption against abortion as the destruction of new life. The first task of Christian witness is not to shape public policy by seeking common moral ground with all opposed to abortion. The first task is to make clear why we believe in children and why we desire to create and nurture new life in the community of faith. This witness to the character of the church is the most important contribution that Christians can make to public controversy.

Parallel considerations are advanced in support of marriage as a specifically Christian institution. Rejecting romantic and personalist approaches to marriage, Hauerwas appeals to the uniqueness of the church's witness to the kingdom of God. Here, both the single and married states can be justified; the single because the church grows through witness and conversion; the married because children are a sign of our hope for the future, a hope grounded in faith in God. Both marriage and the family appear in a distinctively theological perspective by virtue of their witness to God's faithfulness to us and our response to God. 'Our commitment to exclusive relations witnesses to God's pledge to his people, Israel and the church, that through his exclusive commitment to them, all people will be brought into his Kingdom.'[39]

The campaign for nuclear disarmament is supported by Hauerwas, but not on the secular basis that nuclear warfare threatens the future of life on our planet. This ground for peacemaking is rejected as 'idolatrous'.[40] Disarmament receives a theological justification from the thought that peacemaking is a central aspect of Christian obedience, for we have been shown that this is the way God deals with the world. Opposition to nuclear warfare is built simply on the notion of obedience. Strategies of survival are inappropriate, since it is not our responsibility to ensure that history turns out all right. This has already been settled by God.[41]

In his essays on the subject of disability, Hauerwas offers a series of theological insights about the nature of Christian community. These challenge the way we tend to construe human status in terms of economic or physical power, or capacity for independence. Those who are disabled can remind us of our dependence upon one another and God; they can bring resources and gifts which build up the Christian community; they challenge our assumptions about normality. While eschewing 'a rights based' approach to those who are disabled, Hauerwas tries to bring particular Christian convictions to bear upon the debate in a way that is ethically constructive. In the church we seek to live without fear or resentment of one another. It is within this social context that we can erase many of the prejudices and stereotypes that frequently characterise our attitudes to the disabled. 'If we can be this kind of community, then we may find that we do not even need the label "retarded", and that we can explore more creative ways at once to help those different from us without that help becoming a form of discrimination.'[42]

Hauerwas' writings create an excitement which is attributable not merely to an elegant style, a provocative manner, arresting illustrations, his generosity, and wit. He succeeds in describing accurately aspects of our contemporary theological and philosophical environment. He provides a framework for thinking about Christian ethics which is lacking in much reflection upon ethical and political dilemmas, and he presents a persuasive argument for the distinctiveness of Christian considerations. This yields some dividends when he comes to reflect upon nuclear war, abortion, marriage, and the treatment of the sick and disabled.

His criticism of the defects of liberalism, though not original, is largely persuasive. In particular, its doctrine of the self and its inability to provide a coherent notion of the common good lead towards moral fragmentation and rootlessness. In drawing upon MacIntyre's *After Virtue*, he can point to the difficulties surrounding the so-called 'Enlightenment project' of justifying morality on the basis of claims the validity of which are recognisable by every rational agent, *qua* rational agent. The problems attending moral theories from Kant to emotivism illustrate this. By contrast, the emphasis upon community and tradition enables Hauerwas to argue that the church is indispensable for the moral training of Christians and for the knowledge of the people we are called to be in Christ. What is required for virtuous living is neither a philosophical argument nor an ethical theory. These have their places, but must always be parasitic upon the practice of communities and the inheritance of traditions. Christian ethics is thus no longer a list of ethical precepts, but is an adventure in following Christ and finding the skills by which to interpret our lives and our world in terms of his story. The knowledge of God and the practice of Christian discipleship are thus ecclesial activities. 'The church is the colony that gives us resident aliens the interpretive skills whereby we know honestly how to name what is happening and what to do about it.'[43]

Hauerwas speaks to those who are conscious of the increasing dissociation of church and culture in the late twentieth century. The old strategy of seeking to articulate a moral consensus for those within and without the church is breaking down.[44] Christian theology and ethics become distorted by attempting to stand on common ground with those outside the colony. 'Jesus was not crucified for saying or doing what made sense to everyone. People are crucified for following a way that runs counter to the prevailing direction of the culture.'[45] This stress upon the distinctiveness of the Christian community and its narrative purports to provide a stronger basis upon which ministry can be conducted. In a context of social fragmentation and moral disarray, greater Christian authenticity becomes possible. Having faded from the social landscape, Christian faith emerges as something radically different and compelling. Hauerwas and Willimon appear content to plead guilty to the charge that this makes a theological virtue of a sociological necessity.[46]

Hauerwas argues that the church's *raison d'être* is found neither in its transformation of society nor in its conversion of individuals, but rather in its witness to Jesus. Here he appeals to a typology of Yoder. Distinguishing the confessing church from the activist and the conversionist church, Hauerwas asserts that 'the confessing church finds its main political task to lie, not in the personal transformation of individual hearts or the modification of society, but rather in the congregation's determination to worship Christ in all things'.[47] The confessing church will be concerned with individual transformation and social improvement, but only in the context of its primary aim of confessing Christ in every area of life. There are unmistakable echoes of the Barmen Declaration here, and a strong sense of a be-leaguered Christian community making a distinctive and provo-cative witness before a hostile world. We should not underestimate the extent to which Hauerwas is calling for a distinctive church. His hints as to what we should actually do in our current situation are sometimes oblique and uncertain, but he suggests, for example, that the church should not admit to the Lord's Supper those who make a living from building weapons,[48] that Christians should publicly declare their income in the fellowship of the church,[49] that separate Christian schools are what we need,[50] and that vegetarianism may be an appropriate witness to the eschatological vision of creation.[51] It is, perhaps, the fact that Hauerwas' position cannot easily be labelled as 'right-wing' or 'left-wing' which gives his work a prophetic quality.

His theology also seeks to give central place to the virtues of hope and patience in a way that facilitates ministry in our current situation. The hope of the Christian community is an eschatological one. The future is secured only by the grace of God, and it is guaranteed and announced in the resurrection of Jesus Christ from the dead. This liberates the church from a sense of having to be successful in numerical terms or in its general influence. It yields an eschatological hope which enables witness, discipleship, and service in a world that is often strange and alien. It also enables the community to live and to worship patiently, since the justification of Christian disciple-ship is defined Christologically and eschatologically, rather than in secular terms. For the church, this implies that faithfulness rather than success is paramount. The measure of the minister's effectiveness is not in terms of numbers or of secular influence. It is the community which in its worship and fellowship witnesses to the gospel. 'The church is the visible, political enactment of our language of God by a people who can name their sin and accept God's forgiveness and are thereby enabled to speak the truth in love. Our Sunday worship has a way of reminding us, in the most explicit and ecclesial of ways, of the source of our power, the peculiar nature of our solutions to what ails the world.'[52]

THE SECTARIAN CHARGE

There are a number of criticisms which Hauerwas ecclesial ethics have provoked. These can readily be identified in the literature. One typical challenge comes from James Gustafson, who accuses Hauerwas of succumbing to 'the sectarian temptation'.

Sectarianism ensures a clear identity which frees persons from ambiguity and uncertainty, but it isolates Christianity from taking seriously the wider world of science and culture and limits the participation of Christians in the ambiguities of moral and social life in the patterns of interdependence in the world . . . At the meeting of the British Society for the Study of Christian Ethics in September last, I found enthusiasm for his work from theologians from the Church of Scotland, the Church of England, and the Roman Catholic Church. I asked that some thought be given to possible incongruities between the ecclesiology that is necessary for the sectarian ethics and the ecclesiologies of these churches . . . A few days later at the conference on Reinhold Niebuhr at King's College, London, I received an answer from a Scottish theologian. The sectarian ethic of discipleship is attractive because it made clear a historic confessional basis on which Christian morality could be distinguished from the culture, and how Christians could stand prophetically as Christians on matters of nuclear armaments and the like.[53]

This anonymous Scottish sectarian was Duncan Forrester. Whether or not this is an accurate account of the exchange that took place, sectarianism is certainly one of the charges most frequently levelled against Hauerwas.[54] For Gustafson, sectarian theology is an attempt to maintain the language and culture of a minority tribe without reference to knowledge that is available from other areas of experience and inquiry. It sacrifices relevance and coherence for some notion of historical faithfulness. In doing so, it fails to take into account the theological notion that the whole world and, therefore, all experience and knowledge are within God's creation. It ignores the sociological fact that members of the Christian community also belong to other communities and cannot be hermetically sealed up inside the church.

The term 'sectarian' is a contested and pejorative label, and

it is not always clear what is meant. If, however, it suggests that
Hauerwas and other advocates of ecclesial ethics beat a retreat
from the realities of the world into an ecclesial enclave then it is
manifestly unfair.[55] Their ecclesiology is world-affirming and
their writings wrestle with the major moral conundrums of the
day. By being the church, Christians have the task of disclosing
to the world its true identity. This may sound imperialist to
some, but it is not sectarian. Hauerwas' claim is that, by living
genuinely as a distinctive Christian community, the church may
have more impact in its surrounding society than by advocating
consensus solutions to the problems we face.[56]

McClendon points to the way in which H. R. Niebuhr's
typology of churches casts the 'sectarian' mode in an unfair
light. In *Christ and Culture*, Niebuhr presents a range of thinkers
from the author of the first Johannine Epistle through Tertullian
to Tolstoy as advocating a withdrawal from the world. Their
concern is primarily with the purity of the church, and reveals
an indifference to the surrounding culture. Niebuhr castigates
this type of ecclesiology for the way in which it is ensnared in
contradiction – we are all infected to some degree by our
surrounding culture – and by its divorce of creation and
redemption. 'At the edges of the radical movement the Man-
ichean heresy is always developing.'[57] Yet his typology ignores
the possibility that the development of a distinctive church may
be for the sake not of withdrawal but of witness and mission.
The purpose of a counter-cultural distinctiveness, it may be
argued, is not isolationism, but a proper contribution to the
wider social world. It is to be faithful as the disciples of Christ in
the world where the mission of the church is to be conducted. It
is world-affirming but from a distinctive perspective. Thus
McClendon writes of the so-called sectarians. '[E]ngagement
with the world was not optional or accidental, but lay at the
heart of obedient discipleship.'[58]

The charge of sectarianism is either false or misleading. It
would be better to drop this particular criticism and to examine
more carefully the underlying concerns that it represents. The
sectarian charge has arisen because of the way in which recent
ecclesial ethics requires a revitalisation of radical reformation

ecclesiology. This is demonstrated by Arne Rasmusson in his recent study.[59] Rasmusson argues that Hauerwas' theology requires a doctrine of the church which is analogous to that developed within the radical Reformation. His criticism of liberalism requires a relationship of church to state which is more antithetical than that found in the magisterial Reformers. The repeated denunciation of the heresy of 'Constantinianism' calls for an end to the legitimation of a particular secular order by the church. The ecclesiology that this requires is summarised by McClendon in terms of five characteristics. These are 'the awareness of the *biblical* story as our story, but also of *mission* as responsibility for costly witness, of *liberty* as the freedom to obey God without state help or hindrance, of *discipleship* as life transformed into obedience to Jesus' lordship, and of *community* as daily sharing in the vision'.[60] The church is here described apart from the world, but to characterise this as withdrawal is misleading. The description of mission in the second characteristic is strongly world-affirming in presupposing the church's responsibility for political witness and practice.

It might be countered, however, that this church advocated by Hauerwas nowhere exists. It is a fantasy community, the conception of which fails to reflect the ways in which the members of the church are also positioned within civil society. It does not correspond to any visible communion within the *oikumene*. Hauerwas' own status as a Methodist who describes himself as a high-church Mennonite under no particular ecclesiastical discipline reflects this dissonance between the church described in his theology and the church as we actually find it.[61] On one level, this criticism may be side-stepped by arguing that his proposal is prescriptive rather than descriptive. It is a call for the church to be the community that it ought to be rather than a description of any empirical reality. This imperative is made possible by the work of Christ which is already real and in our midst.[62] At the same time, Hauerwas and Willimon have struggled to show that the church they describe is present in the stories of many Christian congregations and lives. It is these which provide the most eloquent testimony and inspiration. 'Good communities are known by their saints. By naming these ordinary but theologically and morally impressive people, we discover resources that we did not know we had.'[63] A similar locating of the Christian story in the biographies of the saints can be detected in McClendon's writings. By reciting with care and insight the stories of Sarah and Jonathan Edwards, Dietrich Bonhoeffer, and Dorothy Day, he displays the way in which the pattern of discipleship can be learned from lived examples. Through recounting how individuals have exemplified the character of Christ under changing circumstances, the church can enlarge its moral perception and reinvigorate its moral will.[64]

The claim that this ecclesiology contains a critical standard by which to challenge the empirical church is necessary if Hauerwas is to meet feminist criticisms that his theology legitimises a patriarchal institution. This challenge is one instance of the typical criticism that communitarian ethics is characteristically oppressive and authoritarian. Thus Gloria Albrecht in a recent article review assserts, 'That Hauerwas can lavish praise upon the practices of an exclusively male, hierarchically authoritarian tradition, as a good example of Christian community, reveals important deficiencies in his epistemology and in his proposed ecclesiology.'[65] Albrecht's thesis is that the hermeneutics of suspicion needs to be applied not only to secular liberal culture, but also to the Bible and the institutional church.[66] Without this critical edge, ecclesial ethics will fail to liberate the oppressed from historical forms of servitude. If this charge is to be met, some distinction will be required between the church as it is and the church as it is called by God to be.[67] This, in turn, requires some criterion of theological truth over and against the particular claims of ecclesiastical tradition. In what follows, I shall try to argue that the principal weakness in Hauerwas' theology is its overdetermination of the distinctiveness of the church. This is reflected both in an attentuated reading of the person and work of Christ, and in a reluctance to describe the possibility of ethical perception and action outwith the Christian community.

THE NATURE OF THEOLOGICAL TRUTH

The link between truth and performance is a crucial feature of Hauerwas' theology. He insists upon the close relationship between Christology and ecclesiology to the extent that the truth about Jesus can only be perceived from within a life of discipleship in the community of the church. At times, this becomes an attack on Protestant individualism.[68] He even commends the insistence of Vatican II that tradition and Scripture together form one sacred deposit of the Word of God. The Bible should be withheld from Christians until they have developed better habits of discipleship to facilitate its correct understanding. This resonates with the emphasis throughout his writings that being positioned within the Christian community is the indispensable condition for confessing Christ.

As was argued earlier, Hauerwas does not attempt to reduce the truthfulness of Christian convictions to correct performance. The latter is more akin to an epistemological condition of the former. None the less, the way in which he seeks to integrate his description of the person and work of Christ with its ecclesial resultant raises a number of difficulties. These can be traced to his overdetermination of the doctrine of the church. In outlining the significance of Christ for the Christian life, Hauerwas frequently implies that Jesus is to be understood as the exemplar and initiator of a new social order, the kingdom of God.[69] The traditional language of the incarnation and atonement is muted by contrast with his insistence upon the importance of the life of Jesus as this is narrated in the Synoptic Gospels. This clearly arises out of a concern with the way in which the exposition of dogma can too easily prescind from the way in which Jesus' mission is loaded with ethical import.[70] Yet the outcome of this concern is that Jesus is generally characterised as the prototype of Christian existence, the founder of the church, and the one in whom God reveals how we are to live. The Christological language tends to be that of revelation rather than redemption. The latter seems confined to a quality of life realised only in the church.[71]

Despite the desire to integrate ethics and dogmatics, there is some imprecision in Hauerwas' exposition of dogmatic themes. In particular, it is not clear in what sense the work of Christ can be described as completed in his resurrection and ascension, or in what sense Christ is active in the church by the power of the Spirit. If his work is principally the establishment of a community, then its continuing significance must be defined in terms of an act of recollection by which that community is reminded of its constitution. Christ's continuing presence and activity to his disciples are thus a function of memory inspired by the sacramental re-enactment of a story. If, however, one construes the work of Christ as 'a once for all' achievement which is accomplished *extra nos*, as is suggested by the New Testament proclamation of his exaltation, then its relationship to the life of the post-Easter community is altered. Christ continues to be present and active in the life of the church and the world, but this presence and activity are dependent upon what is already accomplished in his life, death, and resurrection. The church is not the extension of the incarnation, but exists to bear witness and to live faithfully in light of this unrepeatable and unsubstitutable event.[72]

Symptomatic of a failure to distinguish adequately the life of the church under the third article from the work of Christ in the second, is a somewhat reductionist treatment of the doctrine of justification in Hauerwas. He is rightly uneasy about individualist and quietist readings of justification as the article on which the church stands. He aims to locate these notions in the context of a new social order that Christ has created. ' "Sanctification" is but a way of reminding us of the journey we must undertake it we are to make the story of Jesus our story. "Justification" is but a reminder of the character of the story – namely, what God has done for us by providing us with a path to follow.'[73] Yet this is hardly sufficient as a description of the church's dependence upon the person and work of Christ, and the New Testament description of the Christian life as 'in Christ'. Hauerwas points to the significance of the Eucharist in our coming to understand the story of Jesus. Yet the Eucharistic prayer is traditionally one of praise and thanksgiving which declares what God has already done in creation and redemp-

tion. Here, there is a commemoration of what God has brought
about in the birth, life, death, resurrection, and ascension of
Christ. Missing from Hauerwas' account in this context are
sufficient mention of Christ's overcoming of sin, evil, and death;
of our union with him by the bond of the Spirit; of the character
of the community as the Body of Christ; of the eschatological
expectation that his lordship will finally be exercised over all
creation. To make mention of this is not to seek to impugn his
orthodoxy nor to challenge the claim that the context of the
celebration of the sacrament is the life of discipleship. It is
rather to raise a query about the nature of the relationship
between Christ and the believer upon which the life of discipleship is established.[74] The agency of the church derives from the
activity of Jesus and continues through the Holy Spirit to be
dependent upon it. This relationship is more nearly described
by Barthian language of correspondence than by Hauerwas'
more linear notion of continuing what has been begun.[75] It is
perhaps symptomatic of his approach to Christology that the
books of the New Testament from which he most frequently
cites are the Synoptic Gospels. In his analysis of Hauerwas'
exegesis, Richard Hays points out that there are only occasional
references to Romans and 1 Corinthians, and almost no
mention of the Johannine writings and Hebrews.[76] His use of
Ephesians significantly appears to deal with the *Haustafeln*
rather than its rich Christology which understands the nature of
the church and the cosmos in relation to the ascended Christ.[77]

These concerns registered above may reflect some difficulties
inherent in Lindbeck's post-liberalism which has exercised an
influence upon Hauerwas. The criticism has frequently been
made that the cultural–linguistic model of religion reduces
theological truth to performance according to the form of life
created by the narratives of Scripture. Once the rules governing
correct use are mastered, a participant in the religion is enabled
to speak and behave truthfully. While capturing the self-involving nature of religious language – and thus the ethical dimension of Christian confession – this account seems to jeopardise
the realist claim that truth is not of our own making. It is
constituted by the way things are independently of and prior to

correct performance. To articulate this within one's theology, a distinction is required between the linguistic practices of the community, the words of Scripture, and that to which these ultimately refer. Transposed into theological categories, this entails that something like Barth's threefold stratification of the Word of God is necessary both for distinguishing and describing the patterns of dependence between the witness of the church, the words of Scripture, and Jesus Christ, the Word of God revealed.[78] The confession of the church depends upon the normative witness to Scripture. Yet Scripture itself only bears witness through the activity of the Spirit to its central theme and object, Jesus Christ. The church's story is truthful because of its dependence upon God's story. This story can neither be added to nor subtracted from by the church. We can hold to this account of theological truth without denying either that our knowledge of God is dependent upon the Bible and the Christian community, or that the witness of the Christian life is an indispensable sign of its truthfulness.

At stake in this attempt to rework Hauerwas is the nature of ecclesial dependence upon the person and work of Christ. This is central to Hauerwas' description of the virtue of patience and hopefulness as central to the Christian life. These virtues are made possible by the confidence that arises from knowing that the future of the world is finally secured not by our own ethical performance, but by the work of Christ which has already been accomplished once for all.[79] To be sustained, however, these virtues of the Christian life must be grounded upon a conviction about what God has promised rather than on prognostications concerning the church's efficacy.[80] Where a distinction is maintained between the church, the Bible and the Word of God revealed, the danger of a captivity of either Scripture within the church, or the Word of God by any one reading of Scripture recedes. Hauerwas' recent polemics against Protestant individualism lead him close to a position whereby the Bible can be domesticated by the institutional church. This grates violently with the way in which his own theology assails the church by frequent appeal to Scripture. In his writings, the Bible is time and again unleashed upon the church as much as upon the world. It is not clear what the theological rationale for this can be if the Bible can be read and understood only under the conditions of ecclesial life. Yet with a clearer stratification of church, Scripture, and revelation this problem can be eased. The revision I am pleading for shares some similarities with Reinhold Hütter's argument that ecclesial ethics needs a stronger pneumatology if it is to avoid the twin dangers of a 'quietistic inwardness' or a 'utopian activism'.[81] In particular, a surrogate 'works righteousness' is to be avoided by the recognition that the work required of us is by the power of the Spirit according to our determination by Christ. 'For we are what he has made us, created in Jesus Christ for good works, which God prepared beforehand to be our way of life' (Eph. 2:10).

In some respects, this reading of Hauerwas is curiously redolent of Barth's criticism of Bultmann. For Bultmann, there could be no expression of the significance of Christ which prescinded from the self-involving nature of faith. Christ could only be confessed in the language of non-objective existential utterance. The Hauerwasian analogue of this is that there can be no confession of Christ which prescinds from the ethical commitments of the Christian community. Yet, just as in Bultmann there is a slide from Christology into anthropology, so in Hauerwas there is a slide from Christology into ecclesiology. Barth's criticism of Bultmann was that the true nature of faith can only be expressed by speaking first of the priority of the person and work of Christ *extra nos*. The gospel story of Jesus is not an elliptical way of talking about the faith of the Christian. This might be transposed into a criticism of Hauerwas. The true nature of discipleship cannot be grasped simply in terms of a moral emulation of Jesus. The Jesus narrated in the gospels is not merely the prototype of Christian existence. Discipleship involves a recognition of the priority of Jesus, and our dependence upon his life and work *extra nos*.[82]

CHURCH AND WORLD

The excessive concentration upon the distinctiveness of the church in Hauerwas also generates difficulties in construing the

relationship of church to world. In one respect, this can be
interpreted as a hermeneutical problem. The Christian moral
conscience which interprets the Bible in the church is ineluctably infected by secular assumptions. For example, what Christians say today about the role of women in church and society,
the political significance of our equality in Christ, and the status
of homosexual relations reveals a debt to post-Enlightenment
secular culture that is sometimes unacknowledged by
Hauerwas. His dissociation of church and world may be over-
simplified. He arguably overdramatises the crisis of liberalism
and the counter-cultural force of the Christian polity. Symptomatic of this is his exaggeration of the differences between
Christian and secular marriage and parenting. This places him
at odds with both the Catholic and Protestant traditions which
have seen these institutions as wider in scope than the church,
and have detected good practice in non-Christians as well as
Christians. His remark that 'from the world's perspective the
birth of a child represents but another drain on our material
and psychological resources'[83] is, to say the least, hyperbolic.
His argument against abortion shows how a Christian perspective sets the issues in a new light, yet, if he is not to criticise
methods of contraception *pari passu*, he still needs to engage in
well-worn debates about when a human life begins, the moral
status of the embryo, and criteria for personhood. His pacifism
provides a perspective from which we can perceive the way in
which violence is endemic to our way of life, but to describe an
argument against nuclear weapons based on concern for the
future of life on this planet as 'idolatrous' is to depict secular
arguments in the worst possible light. While not only unfair on
much that is sane and decent outwith the church, this characterisation of an alternative position renders allies as foes and
hinders the process of making common cause. He appears also
to disjoin to an unnecessary degree the liberal discourse of
'innate human dignity' with the Christian recognition of the
claim of God upon each human person.

The problem with slavery is not that it violates the 'inherent dignity of
our humanity', but that as a people we have found that we cannot

worship together at the table of the Lord if one claims an ownership over others that only God has the right to claim.[84]

The 'secular' insight into the dignity of the human being differs from the Christian claim that human beings are created in the image of God, redeemed by Christ, and sanctified by the Holy Spirit. Yet the latter claim is capable of recognising that there is some wisdom in the former. In the light of Christian convictions about the status of the world as created, it should not be surprising if there are secular affirmations of the dignity of the human person. Instead of casting such assertions aside, the theologian needs to rehabilitate them within a Christian frame of reference. We shall touch on this issue later with reference to the contested discourse of human rights.

This further criticism relates to the earlier appeal to Barth. A theology which distinguishes more clearly between the Word of God *extra nos*, and the church's testimony to it, has the resource to account for the possibility of secular witness. The sovereignty of Word over church is compatible with the view that God may enable the church to hear the Word through the effects of forces, agencies, and examples *extra muros ecclesiae*.[85] This possibility, which is realised especially in Barth's later theology, is harder to assimilate in Hauerwas' ecclesial ethics. For Barth, the existence of secular parables of the Word of God is entirely compatible with claims for the distinctiveness of Christ. There is only one Word, but there can be witnesses to him outwith the church. Any putative witness must be tested by reference to Scripture, tradition, and the life of the church, but the conviction that God is the creator and redeemer of the world gives grounds for the confidence that such witnesses will be encountered.[86] The church enacts and witnesses to the eschatological kingdom before a fallen and hostile world, yet, since God has not abandoned the world, we may expect signs of that same kingdom in strange and surprising places. The community, as Barth says, is not Atlas bearing the burden of the whole world on its shoulders. Even within the world which opposes it, God can raise up witnesses to that cause. 'This is the message which the community has to learn through these true words of a very different origin and character. In this respect, too, it would be foolish and ungrateful if it closed its ears to them.'[87]

This critical accommodation of secular insights provides a means of contributing to the moral consensus which alone can sustain a pluralist culture. However fragile and problematic this consensus, it requires buttressing at selected points. Jeffrey Stout has pointed out that the moral disagreements in liberal societies tend to take place on the basis of a moral consensus on other issues.[88] There is a range of moral principles which are platitudinous, and, precisely because of that fact, do not receive the attention of philosophers and theologians. It is wrong to torture the innocent for pleasure; it is wrong to abuse sexually little children; disagreements between the major religions should not be settled violently; slavery is evil. Anyone who queried these platitudes would be regarded as a dangerous moral deviant rather than someone whose opinion is to be respected within the pluralism of the body politic. It may thus be possible to find common ground with those outwith the church even in the absence of any common theory which can be assented to by all parties. Stout's example of the moral culture of the nursery illustrates the ways in which our children are induced into a common morality irrespective of the religious tradition they inherit. The nursery is where infants are taught the value of friendship, courtesy towards strangers, fair play, truthfulness, benevolence, and ways of resolving disagreement without recourse to violence.

Michael Walzer has argued that different thick moralities typically display accounts of thin moralities.[89] These are minimal standards and practices which should be demanded of all people and societies. They are a function of thicker and culturally determined moral understandings, but the convergence of these on minimal common ground provides some basis for the maintenance of pluralist societies. It ought to be possible to provide a theological description of this phenomenon in terms of a (thick) understanding of our created and redeemed nature, without returning to earlier constructions of natural law and the orders of creation. Most Christian people in liberal societies do not belong only to the community of the church. They belong to other communities through their work, leisure, and political and cultural interests, and there they make common cause in a variety of ways with others who do not share their religious convictions. Some theological description of how this is possible and how they should comport themselves is owed them. Hauerwas himself wishes to acknowledge that the kingdom is not coextensive with the church.[90] What is required, therefore, is a reading of the church's constitutive narratives which displays the implications of this.

As we have seen, the ecclesial ethics of Hauerwas carries with it a relentless assault on the institutions of liberalism. He points to liberalism's failure to cope with moral disagreement, and to provide the resources of tradition, community, and practice necessary for moral formation. The moral vacuum within the liberal state is masked by the empty rhetoric of human rights and an idolatrous attitude towards the nation state, often sustained by war. The assumption that the church has a stake in this polity is disastrous for authentic Christian witness which needs to challenge rather than to endorse the state. Hauerwas' writings are thus replete with attacks on constitutional democracy in America.[91]

It is one thing to recognise the shortcomings and defects of liberalism, however, and another to appear to enter into wholesale condemnation. It is worth recalling in this context that the Enlightenment project did not simply spring from a misconceived epistemological programme, but had its historical context in the religious wars of the seventeenth century. Liberalism was thus borne of a desire to establish a civil order which could unite competing religious factions on moral grounds which everyone could assent to independently of particular traditions. While it is correct to point out that appeals for freedom of speech and religious toleration did not extend to some groups, for example Roman Catholics, the current need to incorporate more rather than less diversity within civil society actually strengthens these arguments for a pluralist polity.[92]

Stephen Toulmin has argued that greater attention must be paid to the historical context within which seventeenth-century thinkers operated. The first half of that century was a time of strife, social instability, and economic deprivation. Following the end of the Thirty Years' War in 1648, the nation states sought a greater measure of international peace and social stability. It is against this background that Descartes' search at the beginning of the century for an ideal method which transcended historical divisions must be understood. Similarly, Leibniz' interest in developing a universal language for international communication and the rational resolution of intellectual problems must be seen in the context of the years following 1648. Leibniz was a political activist and assiduous European correspondent, and it is a mistake to divorce his metaphysical concerns from these practical interests.

The three dreams of the Rationalists thus turn out to be aspects of a larger dream. The dreams of a rational method, a unified science, and an exact language, unite into a single project. All of them are designed to 'purify' the operations of human reason, by decontextualising them: i.e., by divorcing them from the details of particular historical and cultural situations.[93]

Eighteenth-century attempts to justify morality on bases which can be assented to by all rational persons irrespective of culture, language, or religion must be viewed against the concerns of early modernity. Although these attempts may be judged unsuccessful if one accepts MacIntyre's reading of the history of modern moral philosophy, the practical problem of the ethical bases on which a pluralist society is to be ordered becomes more rather than less pressing. If ethical perception is dependent upon particular communities, practices, and narratives, what is it that gives moral cohesion to a society comprising many overlapping sub-cultures?

One possible rejoinder to this problem is to argue that no common morality can be articulated and that to search for one is merely to compound the confusion. It would be better for Christian ethics to concentrate on making its distinctive contribution, on the assumption that this is more likely to be socially fruitful. This recalls Lindbeck's claim that a religion is more likely to be fruitful in preserving its own distinct identity than in seeking a shared one.[94] The weakness of this is that it neglects the possibility of some measure of translation between the moral language of the Christian community and other forms of ethical speech. The Christian whose working life is spent servicing institutions other than the church is left without the skills to translate the language of Christian virtue into those forms of discourse used in the workplace. Without some effort at translation, it is difficult to see how a constructive ethical criticism can take place. Similarly, the only plausible candidate for a universal moral discourse is that of human rights. This is fraught with problems, but to eschew it altogether is to leave one without the moral vocabulary for making common cause with agencies and forces whose goals are not wholly antithetical to those of the church. Christian theology has traditionally responded to these issues in terms of its doctrine of creation whereby human nature, even in its fallen condition, shows some awareness of those social goods required by human beings. The challenge that is thus posed for ecclesial ethics is whether it is capable of accommodating and reinterpreting older claims about natural law, the orders of creation, and natural rights.[95] Robert Jenson hints at similar criticism in one of the most perceptive remarks on Hauerwas' theology.

All address by the church to the world must indeed be 'violent' – as all mutual address by factions within the world undoubtedly must be – unless the church and the world are always antecedently involved in one conversation. That is, unless there is God and unless he is in converse with the world by ways others than by way of the church. We may not want, as I do not want, to construe this converse by the categories of 'natural' and 'law'. But Hauerwas has arrived at a position where he must acknowledge and construe it somehow, or end with a silenced church.[96]

All this implies a more ambivalent reading of the relationship between church and civil society than is suggested in Hauerwas. But, if the argument of an earlier chapter is valid, it is one for which we find Scriptural warrant. The early Christians were taught that their highest loyalty was to Christ and therefore to the church rather than the state or any other institution. This required a new orientation of their lives and often brought conflict, tension, and even martyrdom. Yet the virtues of the

Christian life, despite the way in which they were now resituated, sometimes displayed overlap with those advocated in the Graeco-Roman world. Christian writers could defend their practice by arguing that it reflected and often surpassed the highest standards acknowledged elsewhere. The state could be the enemy, but it could also exercise a legitimate authority and where possible Christians were urged to live peaceably with others. Thus a path was marked out between withdrawal and assimilation by those whose citizenship was ultimately in the church but who were called to serve God in other places and communities.

CHAPTER FOUR

Moral realism in recent philosophy

Claims for the particularity of Christian ethics have traditionally been tempered by the belief that some moral truths can be
grasped by every rational person irrespective of tradition,
culture, or upbringing. On account of this knowledge each of us
is worthy of praise or blame for our actions, and moral appeals
can be made by the church to those outside. This commonality
of moral belief has received a range of theological explanations
through the categories of natural law, the orders of creation,
and common grace. Similar assumptions about the universality
of moral knowledge informed the Nuremberg trials. Despite the
absence of any positive law, prosecution of war crimes took
place on the basis of there being natural moral truths which had
been seriously violated.

Christian ethics has historically been committed to two
closely connected theses about moral realism. First, there are
moral truths which are not of our own making and which have
been disclosed at least in part to us. Second, some of these moral
truths can, in limited ways, be recognised by those outside the
Christian faith. Theological ethics thus has a stake in defending
a realist construction of what has sometimes been called 'the
ordinary moral consciousness'. This, however, can be contested.
It is possible that there are moral truths which are known only to
those who have been illumined by faith and brought to a clearer
understanding of the theological source and mandate for ethical
action. On this basis, one might affirm moral realism on
theological grounds, while offering a non-realist account of the
moral beliefs and behaviour of those outside the circle of faith.
One might construe non-Christian ethics in terms of the

authoritarian imposition of codes of behaviour by social forces with vested interests. Alternatively, one might see 'the ordinary moral consciousness' merely as a confused amalgam of fragments of ethical traditions which have disintegrated in modern societies. Although I shall reject this position, it is one which will receive further consideration in the next chapter.

In what follows, attention will be devoted to recent philosophical discussion of moral realism. This is generally cast in global terms, in so far as its consideration of moral belief is not relative to any one religion, culture, or tradition. Although this debate has received little attention in theological discussion, it concerns arguments for moral realism in which Christian theology has a stake.

REALISM VS. ANTI-REALISM

Perhaps no metaphysical dispute is as fundamental as that between realists and anti-realists. At a time when far-reaching disputes about realism have dominated wider philosophical discussion it is not surprising that moral philosophy has internalised this debate.

Michael Dummett has argued that the realist is generally committed to the notion of a determinate reality which exists independently of our experience and language.[1] The world so conceived is mind-independent, and the truth value of our statements is determined by the way the world is. For the realist, therefore, meaning tends to be conceived in terms of truth conditions. We know the meaning of a statement when we know what it would be for that statement to be true. Since the world is mind-independent, it is possible that truth conditions may be unavailable to us. As such they are verification-transcendent. Many classes of statement fall in this category; those about inaccessible reaches of space and time, unrestricted generalisations, subjunctive conditionals, and the mental life of other persons.[2]

Dummett's attack upon realism concerns these verification-transcendent truth conditions. He argues that since our statements cannot possess such meaning the realist conception of the world is a delusion. A theory of meaning must also be a theory of understanding. It must capture what is involved in the understanding of a language so that an account of the meaning of an expression will explain what it is to use and understand that expression. Language-users are capable of constructing and understanding an infinitely large number of sentences through a knowledge of sentence components and an ability to combine them in appropriate ways. The task of a theory of meaning is to offer a theoretical account of this practical ability. The test of its adequacy will be whether it succeeds in showing in what that practical knowledge consists.

A theory of meaning must show that the language-user has the implicit knowledge that it ascribes to him or her. It must specify 'what counts as a manifestation of that knowledge',[3] and here, Dummett argues, the truth conditions theory of the realist breaks down. In our learning of assertoric language, we are exposed only to states of affairs that we are capable of recognising. States of affairs that we could not have been in a position to recognise could have played no part in our linguistic training. Hence, it is unclear how verification-transcendent truth conditions could have entered into our understanding of assertoric language. The realist assumes an understanding of language which we could in no way have acquired. Both the process by which we come to grasp, and the subsequent use we make of, statements of the disputed class suggest that we could not have derived from these any notion of what it is for a statement to be true independently of what we recognise as warranting its assertion.[4]

A mind-independent determinate reality which transcends our criteria of verification has no part to play in our understanding of how language works. Common-sense realism thus presents a beguiling view of reality. Meaning must now be elucidated by verification conditions and 'truth' must be construed as 'warranted assertibility'. The dramatic metaphysical consequences of this argument are brought out in passages like the following:

If we think mathematical results are in some sense imposed on us from without, we could have instead the picture of a mathematical reality not already in existence but as it were coming into being as we probe. Our investigations bring into existence what was not there before, but what they bring into existence is not of our own making. Whether this picture is right or wrong for mathematics it is available for other regions of reality as an alternative to the realist conception of the world.[5]

It is not necessary to discuss the merits of Dummett's arguments for a global anti-realism.[6] Our purpose here is to consider why some moral philosophers have opted for a non-realist interpretation of moral statements. But, before examining some of these proposals, it is worth noting the presence of similar (and perhaps better known) disputes within the philosophy of science.

A realist view of science typically holds that the entities to which scientific laws refer exist independently of our inquiries, while their behaviour is accurately described by these same laws. This realism asserts that true scientific laws can explain why observable phenomena are the way they seem and why the progress of science reflects an ever-increasing success in uncovering the structure of reality. Science is understood as a progressive enterprise in which we seek to characterise the most fundamental constituents of the universe, and thus to explain the way the world appears to us.[7] Yet realism in the philosophy of science has met with a number of serious objections which point towards the possibility of an alternative conception.

An instrumentalist philosophy of science denies the existence of unobserved entities postulated by scientists. These entities and the laws which characterise their behaviour are to be seen as heuristic constructs which enable us to make better predictions about what will happen in the empirical world. The goal of science is conceived in terms of maximising our ability to predict what will happen in the observable world. The attraction of an instrumentalist view of science lies in its apparent ontological simplicity and its links with a verificationist theory of meaning. Thus the early A. J. Ayer proclaimed all empirical hypotheses as no more than 'rules for the anticipation of future experience'.[8]

One major difficulty encountered by instrumentalism concerns the need to distinguish between observational statements and theoretical statements. The latter, it is claimed, are merely instrumental devices enabling us to organise and predict the former. As a rigid logical distinction, it is difficult to elucidate satisfactorily. An entity may at one time be postulated by a scientist but will later be detected under experimental conditions or through the use of a more sophisticated measuring instrument. Are we to say that what began life as an instrumental construct has now become an entity which actually exists? Are we to say that whereas once electrons were heuristic devices facilitating prediction they can now be said to exist and to feature in our ontology of observable entities.[9] The difficulty seems to be that the instrumentalist is construing a difference in degree as a difference in logical kind. Although what is observable can often be distinguished from what is postulated, this is not a hard-and-fast distinction. What is observable will often be relative to the state of scientific theory and the sophistication of measuring instruments at a given time.

More recent arguments against realism in the philosophy of science have utilised Thomas Kuhn's well-known thesis on the incommensurability of paradigms. Kuhn points out that the history of science is not an evenly paced progression towards ultimate truth. It is punctuated by sudden changes from one frame of reference to another. These paradigm shifts in the history of science, it is argued, lead to theories being generated within different frames of reference which render them incommensurable. There are no transparadigm standards such as 'meaning' or 'reference' which can measure shifts against one another. As a consequence, the notion of 'truth' seems to be relative to a given paradigm.

In a sense that I am unable to explicate further, the proponents of competing paradigms practice their trades in different worlds. One contains constrained bodies that fall slowly, the other pendulums that repeat their motion again and again. In one, solutions are compounds, in the other mixtures. One is embedded in a flat, the other in a curved matrix of space. Practising in different worlds, the two groups of scientists see different things when they look from the same point in the same direction.[10]

Although Kuhn's intention is mainly polemical, the upshot of his incommensurability thesis is a form of relativism which threatens the realist. If all our statements are relative to a given paradigm, then it cannot make sense to speak of terms referring to objects in a mind-independent realm. The nature of an object and the concept of reference only make sense within a particular paradigm. A paradigm itself cannot be thought of as measuring up to some *an sich* reality. We lack the conceptual tools even to make sense of such a notion. As a culturally determined matrix, each paradigm is likely to be superseded. Since there can be no trans-paradigmatic categories of assessment, there can be no question of which paradigm is closest to the truth. What we are left with is a world-view not dissimilar to Kant's transcendental idealism in which the noumenal world can only be described in terms of concepts which are of our own devising.[11]

Alongside Kuhn's incommensurability thesis, an inductive argument from the history of science is sometimes advanced to discredit the realist's position. In the same way as earlier theories in the history of science were replaced by later ones with different laws and terms, so, it is argued, our contemporary theories will be replaced by better ones in the future. If this is the case, then we cannot be confident that our present science succeeds either in referring to or in making true statements about the way the world is. This meta-induction undermines the realist conception of the world and the progress of science. The argument is eloquently stated by Richard Rorty.

We would like to write the history of the triumphs of rational inquiry in terms of gradual progress. But if we have a picture of knowledge as either in touch with the world or not – of language as either hooking or failing to hook onto the world – then it is hard to see how centuries of failure to name the real world could culminate in a sudden success in doing so. Secondly if we have to say that our ancestors quite literally did not know what they were talking about, why should we assume we are any better off?[12]

The realist response to this meta-induction is to claim that successive scientific theories are not simply true or false, but possess increasing verisimilitude. Realism must be seen as critical, not naive. Scientific progress must be viewed in terms of a gradual convergence upon the truth through a refining of old theories and the creation of new and more powerful ones. The strongest argument for verisimilitude, convergence, and critical realism is that by presupposing these we are led to greater success. This is to be explained by the truth of these hypotheses. This is the argument of Hilary Putnam in *Meaning and the Moral Sciences*[13] and is one of the most powerful that the realist has at his or her disposal. It can be extended to include the success of human behaviour and belief in general. The fact that our everyday actions are based upon a whole range of beliefs and are generally successful in outcome can be explained by the realist in a way not open to the non-realist. 'Realism is indeed confirmed day by day in innumerable ways.'[14]

Realist and anti-realist arguments in the philosophy of science are replayed, *mutatis mutandis*, in moral philosophy. The realist argues, typically, that the phenomena of moral judgment, discovery, disagreement, and convergence are to be explained by the world's manifesting moral characteristics. For the anti-realist, the phenomena of moral diversity and change are best explained in terms of a projectivist account of moral realities.

INTUITIONISM AND EMOTIVISM

In the early twentieth century, intuitionist accounts of morality prevailed amongst many British philosophers, before being eclipsed by emotivist theories. The issues at stake between intuitionists and emotivists adumbrate the more sophisticated debates that have taken place in the late twentieth century between realists, anti-realists, and quasi-realists.

Intuitionism sought to defend the assumption of the ordinary moral consciousness that moral beliefs are about the way the world is. That we are morally obliged to perform certain actions is a fact of which we are aware day and daily. This is as obvious to us as simple arithmetic truths. In addition to this, the intuitionists argued that moral truths were not reducible to, or necessarily entailed by, natural facts. There is always a logical gap between the description of a natural fact and the assertion of a moral truth. That I have a moral duty to help my child is not entailed by any description about his needs or my desires. My having a duty is a state of affairs *sui generis*, and is not entailed by any non-moral set of conditions. The upshot of this is the intuitionist view that moral truths are non-natural and are known by some special faculty held by all human beings.

According to H. A. Prichard, much moral philosophy has attempted mistakenly to answer the question 'Why ought I to be moral?' This is a mistake, because the procedure fails to notice that moral obligation is *sui generis* and cannot be reduced to anything more fundamental, for example the agent's interests.

[I]f, as is almost universally the case, by Moral Philosophy is meant the knowledge which would satisfy this demand, there is no such knowledge, and all attempts to attain it are doomed to failure because they rest on a mistake, the mistake of supposing the possibility of proving what can only be apprehended directly by act of moral thinking. Nevertheless the demand, though illegitimate, is inevitable until we have carried the process of reflection far enough to realize the self-evidence of our obligations, i.e. the immediacy of our apprehension of them.[15]

As an attempt to offer a theory which encapsulates much of the ordinary moral consciousness, intuitionism is bold and admirable. Yet the difficulties it generates are formidable. Three are relevant in this context.

First, it has trouble explaining morality as a practical project. If through intuition I discern various moral truths, it is not clear why these perceptions should motivate me to act in a particular way. On the standard model of explaining action, beliefs need to be accompanied by relevant desires. Yet no mention is made of desire in intuitionism, and it is not clear how the having of moral intuitions should move me to act accordingly. This gap between belief and action is not easily closed on intuitionist premises.[16]

Second, the faculty which makes moral perception possible is opaque. Given the non-naturalism of intuitionism, it seems that this must be some peculiar moral faculty possessed by human beings. It enables us to perceive moral truths as self-evident, in much the same way as we perceive mathematical truths. Yet, the more we inquire about this faculty, the more obscure it becomes, and the intuitionist account of how we arrive at our moral judgments becomes increasingly detached from the type of explanation that we would give in defence of the ordinary moral consciousness. We would appeal to upbringing, social context, the roles and commitments into which one entered to explain why we hold our moral beliefs. Yet, in order to preserve the non-naturalist thesis, the intuitionist has to posit a distinct moral faculty which is independent of these natural phenomena. It is hard to see exactly what this is and how it coheres with what we know about social conditioning.

Third, the disjunction between natural and moral facts leads to a certain banality in intuitionism. Its exponents tended to talk about the most general of moral concepts – goodness, rightness, and duty – and these were illustrated by commonplace moral examples, for example the importance of generally telling the truth. Yet intuitionism, almost by definition, has very little to say about disputes concerning contested moral concepts such as justice. If people have conflicting moral beliefs, how can these be resolved on an intuitionist basis which appeals to what is self-evident in defence of the ordinary moral consciousness?[17] All the problems permeating intuitionism seem to involve its abstraction from the particular needs, commitments, and projects of human beings which provide morality with its content and function.[18]

Emotivism was, in many respects, the fashionable successor to intuitionism in the analytic tradition. It appears better placed to explain both moral diversity and its integral connection with human practice. To achieve these it robustly eschews moral realism. Thus A. J. Ayer, writing in 1936, rejects the realism of the intuitionists by offering an altogether different account of morality.

The presence of an ethical symbol in a proposition adds nothing to its factual content. Thus if I say to someone, 'You acted wrongly in stealing that money', I am not stating anything more than if I had simply said, 'You stole that money.' In adding that this action is wrong I am not making any further statement about it. I am simply evincing my moral disapproval of it. It is as if I had said, 'You stole that money', in a peculiar tone of horror, or written it with the addition of some special exclamation marks. The tone, or the exclamation marks, adds nothing to the literal meaning of the sentence. It merely serves to show that the expression of it is attended by certain feelings in the speaker.[19]

Emotivism thus outlined can explain why moral belief involves a commitment to action. The expression of a moral opinion is, by definition, an account of the practical goals to which one is attached and is a recommendation that others commit themselves likewise. Unfortunately, its apparent success in explaining the practical nature of moral judgment is purchased at a high price. It no longer becomes possible to make sense of moral disagreement, for when the non-moral facts have been established disagreement can amount to no more than a difference in personal preference upon which one can make no rational judgment.

A more detailed defence of emotivism is offered by C. L. Stevenson. There are, he argues, roughly two different purposes for which language can be used; either to record, clarify, and communicate beliefs, or to express and influence the moods and actions of ourselves and other people.[20] It is with respect to the latter purpose that moral discourse is to be understood. The emotive meaning of moral terms has arisen through the history of their usage, and as a result they can produce significant affective responses. 'The word "good" has a laudatory emotive meaning that fits it for the dynamic use of suggesting favorable interest.'[21] When we attempt to get someone to change her mind, we do so by affecting her feelings in such a way as to alter her sympathy and temperament. In moral disagreement there can be nothing else taking place. The appeal to moral truth is met with incomprehension by Stevenson.

I can only answer that I do not understand. What is this truth to be about? For I recollect no Platonic Idea, nor do I know what to try to recollect. I find no indefinable property nor do I know what to look for. And the 'self-evident' deliverances of reason, which so many philosophers have mentioned, seem on examination to be deliverances of their respective reasons only and not of mine.[22]

Despite these protestations, there does appear to be something lacking on this account. In moral disagreement, we are not merely attempting to sway someone's feelings. We are attempting to change moral perception, to promote a different way of perceiving the situation. And this is done not by manipulation, but by reference to inter-personal evaluative standards. Raphael gives the example of two football supporters disagreeing over whose is the better team.[23] Their argument is not an attempt to bring about a transfer of allegiances so much as a discussion about the comparative standards of either side. Whether we are talking about football, cars, wine, or music there are always criteria governing the correct use of evaluative terms. In moral disagreement, we appeal analogously to objective standards of evaluation. The emotivist might attempt to argue that our assent to these standards is nothing more than the result of feeling, but here the theory starts to reduce to absurdity. What feelings are we talking about? Feelings can often vary or be entirely absent in particular cases of moral disagreement without the meaning of our utterances undergoing any significant change. Emotivism is thoroughly reductive. Instead of explaining the meaning of moral discourse, which Ayer and Stevenson purport to be doing, the theory now seems to abolish the discourse altogether. '[I]f and insofar as emotivism is true, moral language is seriously misleading and, if and insofar as emotivism is justifiably believed, presumably the use of traditional and inherited moral language ought to be abandoned.'[24] Emotivism undermines the apparently realist tenor of our ordinary moral discourse in a way that threatens to destroy morality as a social phenomenon. As this is neither desirable nor likely to happen, it is worth examining more recent and plausible attempts to wrestle with the issues surrounding ethical realism.

REALISM AND MORAL VISION[25]

Recent realist strategy in moral philosophy has appealed to analogies between moral and sensory perception. It has been argued that, just as our sensory apparatus can disclose certain features of the independent world, so our moral perception affords insight into the moral character of the world. The moral realist claims to do justice to various common-sense assumptions about morality. In making a moral judgment, we are generally inclined to the view that we are expressing an opinion about the way things are rather than the way we or others wish them to be. In acting in accordance with such a judgment, we often believe ourselves to be authorised by the facts of the matter rather than by any individual preference. (In this respect, almost all of us have some appreciation of Kant's distinction between hypothetical and categorical imperatives.) The realist is also impressed by the phenomenon of moral disagreement in which disputants appear to be making claims about what is or is not the case, in the hope that opponents can be defeated and even converted to a different way of seeing things. The ability of human beings to reach a moral consensus will carry more weight with the realist than the prospect of irreconcilable moral claims. '[I]t is remarkable and heartening to what extent, without losing hold of the sensitivities from which we begin, we can learn to find worth in what seems at first too alien to appreciate.'[26] In this context, the importance of moral training is often emphasised. In the same way as we have to be trained to appreciate the value of a work of music, art, or literature, so we have to be trained to perceive the appropriate moral features of the world. Thus morality is not solely concerned with the will. Moral perception has an indispensable role in right action.[27]

The non-realist while not insensitive to the above features of our moral discourse discerns too many problems in the realist hypothesis. It is not clear what sort of things moral properties or values are supposed to be, over and above the natural features of the world. Moreover, historical accounts of moral diversity and change will tend to be interpreted not in terms of convergence, but as confirmation of the hypothesis that values are largely invented by societies for a variety of human ends. And, finally, the anti-realist will note the crucial disanalogy with sensory perception. Moral beliefs are intimately connected with motives and generally possess action-guiding force. This characteristic of moral discourse (emphasised at the expense of others by emotivism and prescriptivism) can be better dealt

with in an account which stresses not perception of moral
properties, but the intrinsic connection between the institution
of morality and human interests. Once this connection is noted,
it is argued that the analogy with sensory perception becomes
redundant in any adequate description of the ordinary moral
consciousness.

John McDowell's ethical writings reflect the influence of Iris
Murdoch in their stress on the significance of moral perception
in stark contrast to non-cognitivist theories.[28] According to
McDowell, the question of what one ought to do should be
approached by first considering what it is to be a virtuous
person. Taking the virtue of kindness as an example, he argues
that a 'kind person has a reliable sensitivity to a certain sort of
requirement which situations impose on behaviour'.[29] This
sensitivity is likened to a perceptual capacity. He points out that
the knowledge of what kindness requires in certain situations is
conditioned by other conceptions relating to the fair treatment
of persons. In this respect, no one virtue can be fully possessed
independently of the other virtues. Here we have a revival of
the twin Socratic themes that virtue is knowledge and virtue is
one.

McDowell goes on to argue that moral action is not codifi-
able. It is not possible to specify what actions are prescribed of a
moral agent merely by citing a set of moral rules together with
procedures for their application. Moral sensitivity is too rich
and innovative to conform to this pattern. This generates a
further argument for the thesis of moral realism. If the conception of how to live virtuously cannot be spelt out by reference to
a hierarchical ordering of concerns (as in utilitarianism), some
other explanation of what is involved must be found. The realist
has recourse to the notion of moral perception as explaining
what otherwise remains inscrutable. 'A conception of how to
live shows itself, when more than one concern might issue in
action, in one's seeing, or being able to be brought to see, one
fact rather than another as salient.'[30]

One particular problem that this perceptual model of moral
realism faces is that of explaining how beliefs lead to moral
action. How, it might be asked, can a mere perception motivate

an agent? Does one not require to postulate a desire or an interest in morality which provides the agent with a reason to act in accordance with his or her moral perception? Once we have appealed to such a desire or interest in morality this will tend to provide the rationale for virtuous living and render the explanatory thesis of moral realism redundant. There will be nothing left for the realist to explain which has not already been elucidated by reference to the point of morality. The explanation of moral action will thus undermine the perceptual model of moral judgment. McDowell's response to this problem of moral psychology is to argue that the perceptual state of the virtuous person is itself practical and action-guiding. If we perceive one fact about a situation to be morally crucial (for example the possibility of assisting a friend in trouble) then that perception places us in a psychological state in which we have an overriding reason to act.[31] This, it may be countered, fails to explain why the agent should be committed to virtue in the first place. But McDowell's rejoinder is to argue that this type of strategy presupposes some external vantage-point which is essentially above moral concerns and which can pronounce on their rationality. This is an illusion, since the rationality of a practice can only be discerned from within the practice itself. One requires the necessary moral training and appreciation in order to perceive moral truths which are action-guiding. Just as one may have defective powers of sensory or scientific perception, so one may suffer from inadequate powers of moral perception. To presuppose some Archimedean point outwith the practice of virtue from which its rationality can be inspected is to embrace an erroneous 'scientistic conception of reality'.[32] When one has acquired the requisite powers of moral perception no further explanation is required as to why virtuous action follows.[33]

Moral vision requires the exercise of discipline and humility. In this respect, it cannot be attained except within the practice of a committed ethical life style.

If we resist non-cognitivism, we can equate the conceptual equipment which forms the framework of anything recognizable as a moral outlook with a capacity to be impressed by certain aspects of reality.

But ethical reality is immensely difficult to see clearly. If we are aware of how, for instance, selfish fantasy distorts our vision, we shall not be inclined to be confident that we have got things right.[34]

McDowell's perceptual analogy is developed in further essays which draw an analogy between moral awareness and our awareness of secondary qualities. The false 'scientistic conception of reality' identified above tends to assume that the only truly objective description of the world is one which makes no reference to the particular perceptions of sentient beings. Thus, an objective description of the world is one which would make no reference to colours or tastes since these secondary properties are the result of the impact of other primary properties upon our sensory surfaces. McDowell contests this hidden assumption by insisting that our perception of an object as red itself discloses something about the world, viz. that this object is such as to appear red to a sentient being under normal circumstances.[35] In this respect the analogy with secondary qualities can be used constructively to support the realist hypothesis.

Shifting to a secondary-quality analogy renders irrelevant any worry about how something that is brutely there could nevertheless stand in an internal relation to some exercise of human sensibility. Values are not brutely there – not there independently of our sensibility – any more that colours are: though, as with colours, this does not stop us supposing that they are there independently of any particular apparent experience of them.[36]

The significance of this argument is that it contributes towards demystifying the realist position. If Blackburn accuses the realist of positing 'a mysterious ability to spot the immutable fitnesses of things', McDowell can protest that this caricatures the position.[37] Unlike the intuitionists of the early twentieth century, he can explain why and how moral properties are perceived by some people but not by others. Perceptual capacities require to be developed for proper moral awareness. In this respect, those who have been trained in moral practice will be capable of a commensurate level of moral knowledge.

McDowell's realism has also been charged with the criticism

that it posits a realm of moral truths which bears no relation to human needs and nature. These are typically the stuff of ethical claims, yet their connection with the world of values is unclear. In his recent response to this difficulty, McDowell has taken pains to distance himself from a 'rampant Platonism' which sets out moral reasons in such a way as to leave untouched the description of the natural world. Our apprehension of ethical truth is not based upon inferences from the facts of nature, but is an apprehension which engages with the contingencies of our existence. Moral perception is described as a second nature which 'could not float free of potentialities that belong to a normal human organism'.[38] Thus while there is no inference from a non-moral description of the natural world to moral claims, none the less ethical perception is of that same world albeit in moral categories which are *sui generis*. This is a view which he attributes to Aristotle. It is also close to the Aristotelian thesis of MacIntyre in which the virtues are viewed as internal rather than external aspects of the good life. This will be examined in the following chapter. The realism of McDowell, however, can be further assessed by comparing it with its principal rivals in recent analytic philosophy.

J. L. Mackie's rebuttal of moral realism has strong affinities with Hume's ethical theory. For Hume, morality is essentially a device for offsetting the worst effects of a lack of external goods in the context of limited human benevolence. It is a social institution for regulating human affairs for the well-being of society and for enhancing the quality of personal life therein. The social and artificial virtues are those which contribute to the regulation of society (for example justice and truthfulness), while the natural virtues (for example temperance and cheerfulness) are those which tend to promote the well-being of their possessor and/or associates.

For Mackie, following Hume, morality is something that we invent for human purposes rather than something we discover within the fabric of the universe. None the less, he concedes that the ordinary moral consciousness is infected with the assumption of objectivity. 'Ethics, we are inclined to believe, is more a matter of knowledge and less a matter of decision than any non-cognitive analysis allows.'[39] In denying this moral assumption, Mackie expounds an error theory which explains both why it is untenable yet why we have come to hold it. The former task is discharged by appeal to two arguments; the argument from relativity and the argument from queerness. Together these undermine moral realism.

The widespread phenomenon of moral diversity is appealed to by Mackie in support of his contention that the values we adhere to cannot be the result of our perception of an objective moral reality. The facts of moral disagreement and diversity across space and time are best explained, he argues, not by varying perceptions of the same reality but by the different forms of social life in which moral values are embedded.[40] The argument from queerness addresses the unique nature of moral values and perception, and states that the obscurity of these entities and the faculty which perceives them must call into question the claim for objectivity. In important respects, Mackie rehearses the principal argument against intuitionism and claims that any commitment to moral objectivity is inevitably ensnared by the standard objections to the intuitionist. In particular, the problem of the relationship between the moral and natural qualities of actions, situations, character, etc. is particularly puzzling. The fact that an action possessing certain natural characteristics also possesses moral characteristics is not a matter of logical necessity. The moral characteristics must in some way 'supervene' upon the natural features, yet how or why this is so is hard to explain without reference to human desires, needs, and purposes. And as soon as these are intro-duced the objectivist model threatens to become redundant on Mackie's analysis.[41]

In this context, we can allude to a similar anti-realist strategy advocated by Gilbert Harman. He illustrates the difference between moral and scientific explanation by reference to two examples. In one case, a physicist seeing a vapour trail in a cloud chamber thinks, 'There goes a proton.' In another case, a spectator witnessing a group of children setting a cat on fire judges their action to be wrong. The crucial differences between these cases undermine moral realism. In the scientific instance, the physicist's judgments explain what is happening by describing the situation. In the moral instance, the spectator neither explains nor describes what is happening because this has already been done in purely natural terms, i.e. the children are burning the cat. The moral judgment merely explains something about the spectator and her moral sensibility. The explanatory chain between principle and observation is significantly different. In the one case, the principle explains why something happened, in the other it contributes nothing to the explanation of why it happened.[42]

Having exposed some overriding difficulties with the realist account of moral perception, Mackie can then explain the illusion of objectivity. Here he appeals to Hume's observation of the mind's 'propensity to spread itself on external objects'. The social dimension of morality makes it necessary that moral judgments be shared by all members of a given community, and the need to invest such judgments with authority results in their being read into the structure of the world itself. This pattern of objectification facilitates the point of morality by promoting a common acknowledgement of moral precepts, and it provides the non-realist philosopher with an explanation of the various moral phenomena which otherwise count in favour of ethical realism.

The strength of Mackie's position resides in its metaphysical simplicity and its ability to explain the necessity and purpose of morality within human societies. There is no need to populate the universe with obscure entities called values which supervene in mysterious fashion upon natural states. The nature of morality is to be explained by reference to the need for social regulation as a condition for individual prosperity. Without the order imposed by moral rules it would be impossible to live a life that would be desirable or worthwhile. An exponent of this position might appeal to the understandable lawlessness of emerging underclasses who no longer have a personal interest in the maintenance of our social institutions. Where human beings cease to have a stake in the regulation of society, they cease to have a reason for acting morally, except within the limited circle of their immediate acquaintances.

Perhaps the truest teachers of moral philosophy are the outlaws and thieves who, as Locke says, keep faith and rules of justice with one another, but practise these as rules of convenience without which they cannot hold together, with no pretence of receiving them as innate laws of nature.[43]

At the same time, the simplicity of Mackie's thesis entails an attenuated view of morality. The phenomena of moral disagreement, seriousness, conversion, and commitment are hard to accommodate on this account. The prospect of moral argument and revision appears to indicate that there is some fact of the matter about which disputants are concerned which is not reducible to mere disagreement about social efficacy.[44] Mackie's account explains morality in terms of its functional significance, yet this appears to preclude any account of the good life to which virtue is internally related. We shall see what this entails when examining the revival of the ethics of virtue, but in the present context it seems clear that Mackie's robust eschewal of moral realism in favour of a Humean account allows only for the notion that moral dispositions can be justified by reference to the non-moral goals that they promote. Yet many answers that have been given to the question 'how should I live?' make reference to moral ends which cannot easily be cashed out in non-moral terms. On Mackie's account, virtues are to be justified by reference to their social or personal utility. Any innate tendency towards such dispositions is to be explained in evolutionary (i.e. non-moral) terms.

A further development within recent analytical philosophy has been the emergence of a position which subtly lays claim to the strengths of the realist position without commitment to its metaphysical difficulties. This view is articulated by Simon Blackburn and there are hints of it also in some arguments of Bernard Williams. According to Blackburn, the realist view encounters insuperable difficulties which necessitate the formulation of an alternative account. He mentions three in particular which are reminiscent of Mackie's earlier argument.[45] First, the metaphysical fecundity of realism leads to the postulation of a realm of mind-independent values and an obscure faculty by which we become aware of this. By contrast, an account which explains morality by reference to human needs, desires, etc. which are projected on to the external world has a simplicity and explanatory power lacking in realist rivals. Second, the problem of how moral properties adhere to natural circumstances, i.e. supervenience, is difficult for the realist to resolve in the absence of any conceptual patterns of entailment. By contrast, an explanation is available to the projectionist in terms of human ends. 'From the anti-realist point of view things are a little easier. When we announce the A-commitments we are projecting, we are neither reacting to a given distribution of A-properties, nor speculating about one. So the supervenience can be explained in terms of the constraints upon proper projection.'[46] Third, the integral connection between moral evaluation and action is better explained on an anti-realist basis, since evaluative attitudes are more akin to commitments than beliefs. The explanation of moral motivation is already available by virtue of the anti-realist explanation, whereas the realist is typically beset with the problem of how a form of perception can explain moral behaviour.

In light of these criticisms, we can see how Blackburn's position shares many of the features of Mackie's anti-realism. The difference lies in their conflicting estimates of projectionism. For Mackie, the projecting of moral evaluations onto the external world is an error which is engendered by psychological, social, and even biological phenomena. In this respect, he shares Hume's scepticism about the objectivity of moral values and his desire to expose this illusion which grips our second-order moral discourse. Blackburn's position is more sophisticated in arguing that our projection of moral realities is an important feature of moral sensibility and reflection and one which it is vital to maintain. In this respect, his position is quasi-realist, although it is informed by some of the fundamental tenets of anti-realism. Quasi-realism argues that the features of our moral discourse which are so precious to the realist must be retained. The need for discussion, consensus, and improvement of sensibilities are all central to the function of morality, and can only be met by the adoption of realist forms of discourse. They cannot thus be abandoned as erroneous, as Mackie's error theory seems to imply.

Quasi-realism is the enterprise of explaining why our discourse has the shape it does, in particular by way of treating evaluative predicates like others, if projectivism is true. It thus seeks to explain, and justify, the realistic-seeming nature of our talk of evaluations – the way we think we can be wrong about them, that there is a truth to be found, and so on . . . [Q]uasi-realism at least removes the most important range of objections to projectivism – namely, that it cannot account for the phenomena of ordinary moral thinking.[47]

The quasi-realist thus seeks to take on board many of the features of moral phenomenology which the realist appeals to – moral disagreement, conversion, the training of our sensibilities – but without the unnecessary metaphysical encumbrance of realism. At the level of first-order moral discourse the quasi-realist leaves everything intact, whereas at the second-order level of explaining that discourse realism is eschewed. Quasi-realism thus attempts to harness the explanatory power of realism to the metaphysical simplicity of projectivism. Blackburn can appeal here to an analogy within the philosophy of mathematics. One might opt for a constructivist view of numbers and arithmetic formulae, but this would not lead one to doubt at the first-order level that $7 + 5$ was 'really' 12. The formula would be assented to with unshakeable conviction irrespective of whether one preferred a non-realist theory of numbers.[48]

Can the quasi-realist have his cake and eat it too? Blackburn has complained about the obscurity surrounding the realist's faculty for perceiving moral truths. But a similar obscurity may be held to surround the process of projection which leads to Hume's staining and gilding of the world with the colours of the mind.[49] How does this happen? When does it happen? Must it happen? If we revert to Mackie's explanation which has psychological, social, and biological ingredients, then we appear to be in the grip of a reductionism which undermines quasi-realism. We become victims of an illusion induced by forces external to us.

It is not clear that moral discourse could survive a quasi-realist construction. The function of a quasi-realist rendition of moral discourse is to promote discussion, sensibility, and agreement. Yet, without some moral distinction between how things seem to us and how they are, it is not clear how this will work. Stout writes about the significance in moral judgment of the logical space between what a competent judge holds and what actually obtains. Without this distinction, the nature of moral agreement and the criteria of competence are radically altered. Thus the judgement 'slavery is evil' does not reduce to a series of statements about what ideals observers would agree on. The truth of the statement, independent of anyone's judgment, explains why there is agreement and what competence in judgment entails.[50]

Is it possible to hold at one level that values are human inventions while acting and believing otherwise at another level? Analogies with quasi-realist theories of religion may give some credence to this notion, yet it must remain doubtful whether one can continue to experience and to believe in the authority of moral demands while convinced that at the deepest level of explanation they only have the force with which we have invested them. Blackburn considers the case of those who cannot live with the notion that values have a subjective source, and accuses them of being in the grip of defective sensibilities.

It might be that there are people who cannot 'put up with' the idea that values have a subjective source; who cannot put up with the idea that the meaning of their life and their activities is ultimately something they confer, and that even critical reflection on how best to confer them conducts itself in the light of other sentiments which must be taken simply as given. But this will be because such people have a defect elsewhere in their sensibilities – one which has taught them that things do not matter unless they matter to God, or throughout infinity, or to a world conceived apart from any particular set of concerns or desires, or whatever. One should not adjust one's metaphysics to such defects.[51]

The pejorative labelling of such realist scruples as 'defects' comes close to begging the question. It is precisely the search for some such notion which seems necessary in order to do justice to our realist discourse. If no such notion is tenable, then the sense of authority which pervades 'the ordinary moral consciousness' may indeed require to be abandoned as erroneous and in need of revision. In this respect, the position of quasi-realism may be thoroughly unstable. Charles Taylor has argued that quasi-realism is impaled on the horns of a dilemma. It tries to show the compatibility of ordinary moral experience and non-realism. Yet this experience itself is resistant to any non-realist construction. Either one must abandon the deliverances of moral experience or else reconsider the case for moral realism. Yet our use of thick moral terms is essential to the way we understand, explain, and judge ourselves and others. It is what we have to deal with, and will not vanish whatever our prejudices. 'Your general metaphysical picture of "values" and their place in "reality" ought to be based on what you find real in this way.'[52]

If the moral realist can make good sense of some fundamental features of our moral practice, there are also significant difficulties surrounding moral diversity and the queerness of values. Although the anti-realist can offer a simpler account and one which makes better sense of the integral connection between action and moral orientation, there are none the less difficulties here with explaining crucial features of moral thought and discourse. Much of this discussion, however, is narrowly focused and pays little attention to the historical and societal context in which moral judgments are made. The language of morals is not homogeneous but reflects in numerous ways the changing cultural matrices in which it is formed. Attention needs to be given to moral diversity and to the ways in which ethical judgments, rather than reflecting timeless principles, generally display the marks of their social history.[53]

MORAL PRAGMATISM

Unlike Mackie whose ethical irrealism is contrasted with scientific realism, Richard Rorty seeks to defuse at a global level all disputes between realists and non-realists. The concept of 'truth' cannot be cashed out in terms of correspondence or fittingness with the way the world is. The function of language is more like a tool enabling us to cope with the world rather than a medium through which the structure of the world can be grasped.

> The pragmatist . . . drops the notion of truth as correspondence with reality altogether, and says that modern science does not enable us to cope because it corresponds, it just plain enables us to cope. His argument for the view is that several hundred years of effort have failed to make interesting sense of the notion of 'correspondence' (either of thoughts to things or of words to things). The pragmatist takes the moral of this discouraging history to be that 'true sentences work because they correspond to the way things are' is no more illuminating than 'it is right because it fulfils the Moral Law'. Both remarks, in the pragmatist's eyes are empty metaphysical compliments – harmless as rhetorical pats on the back to the successful inquirer or agent, but troublesome if taken seriously and 'clarified' philosophically.[54]

Pragmatism is distinguished by three characteristics.[55] First, there is the adoption of an anti-essentialism towards key philosophical concepts such as 'truth', 'knowledge', and 'morality'. These concepts cannot be elucidated isomorphically. They should not be seen as providing us with images of the constitutive features of the world. Instead they should be understood practically in terms of what they enable us to do, what practices they make possible, and to what they commit us. A second characteristic of pragmatism is its dissolving of the traditional differences between science, morality, and art. It is impossible to drive a firm wedge between facts and values, between the objective truths of science and our subjective evaluations. All our judgments and commitments can only be assessed in terms of pragmatic criteria involving notions of coping, convenience, and control. Third, the constraints of inquiry are not realist – the nature of objects, the mind, or God – since we cannot make sense of these notions in realist terms. Rorty describes the constraints on inquiry as 'conversational'. What is true is what can survive criticism and objection. Since this cannot be anticipated, there can never be any assurance that truth is fixed or an inquiry closed. This conversational criterion has significant ethical consequences for Rorty. The notion of openness to truth is a central conviction of a liberal society. It suggests a community which is marked by tolerance and a plurality of opinions. Open-mindedness is to be sought merely for its own sake and not as a vehicle to ultimate truth. 'Truth' is to be defined as the resultant consensus from whatever open disagreements take place.[56]

There thus emerges within a pragmatic construal of moral truth some social norms which we ought to recognise. In this respect, Rorty avoids subjectivism and relativism. He advocates a form of pluralism which is conditioned by certain agreed norms, for example respect for other human beings, the prohibition of cruelty, the resolution of disputes by non-violent means, freedom of expression, etc. We have to learn to value these norms and the radical diversity within liberal societies without seeking an ultimate justification in terms of an essential human nature, objective moral realities, or the being and purposes of God. This is the position of the liberal ironist and the communities to which he or she belongs. The attempt to marry private ideals with social regulations is misplaced. The individual must be given the space within which to express and develop his or her interests. The only social norms that are justified are those which provide each and every individual with this opportunity. Rorty has even described the ideal world order as an 'intricately-textured collage of private narcissism and public pragmatism'.[57]

One problem that Rorty immediately faces is that of doing justice to the moral dissident. If moral truth is to be defined pragmatically in terms of what the community finds useful or convenient, how can we make sense of those who confront society with a moral alternative? Rorty's solution is to argue that the moral dissident is one who confronts society with the ideal of liberalism over against the shortcomings of the status quo. It is essential to a liberal society that it provide its poets and revolutionaries with the space in which to challenge conventional wisdom and practice.

In his recent Oxford Amnesty lecture, Rorty argues persuasively that the human rights phenomenon is now a brute fact of liberal societies and should be accepted as such. It is neither possible nor necessary to seek justifications of a Kantian sort for our belief in the inalienability of human rights. Such attempts make little philosophical sense and are of no practical use. We should not agonise over the unanswerable question that pre-occupied Plato: why should I be moral? Instead we should seek to stimulate the sympathies and sentiments which enable us to recognise other human beings as like us in important respects.

A better sort of answer is the sort of long, sad, sentimental story which begins 'Because this is what it is like to be in her situation – to be far from home, among strangers', or 'Because her mother would grieve for her.' Such stories, repeated and varied over the centuries, have induced us, the rich, safe, powerful, people, to tolerate, and even to cherish, powerless people – people whose appearance or habits or beliefs at first seemed an insult to our own moral identity, our sense of the limits of permissible human variation.[58]

Rorty's writings have something of a therapeutic quality. They force us to face the unpleasant fact that philosophy has been unable to resolve many of the traditional disputes that it engendered. The only alternative on offer is a pragmatism which offers operational substitutes for our key semantic concepts. Yet, when presented with this radical alternative, Rorty assures us that we can avoid nihilism. As good liberals we can hold on to the values for which our communities stand even in the absence of metaphysical justification. Learning how to do this is the vocation of the liberal ironist, and assistance can be found in the art and literature of our societies. Is this a tenable view?

Many of the difficulties which Rorty's position has encountered are of a general philosophical nature. Whether the concept of truth resists reduction to pragmatic criteria is a moot point. It may well be that the realist's conception of truth is one which the pragmatist cannot avoid even in formulating a different set of criteria.[59] A similar problem of self-referential coherence attends Rorty's reading of the history of philosophy. If this is presented as a true and objective account of what has happened, it is hard to see how Rorty is not commending his position in a manner that it judges impossible. This is the burden of Alasdair MacIntyre's complaint.

But at once the question arises of whether he has written a history that is in fact true; and to investigate that question, so I should want to argue, is to discover that the practice of writing true history requires implicit or explicit references to standards of objectivity and rationality of just the kind that the initial genealogical history was designed to discredit. Indeed when Rorty invites us to assent to the version of the history of philosophy which he has presented . . . he is surely not merely trying to elicit our agreement in the light of present *socially accepted* standards of work within philosophy and history. For he is – as philosophers characteristically are – himself engaged in advancing a philosophical theory about the nature of such standards. And this theory he presumably takes to be true, in the same sense as that in which realists understand that predicate. If not, then I am unclear just what he is claiming.[60]

A further difficulty in Rorty's pragmatism is that it leaves unexplained what seems to cry out for explanation. He acknowledges our feeling that there is a fundamental difference between the discourse of astrology and the discourse of particle physics, but in the end the only possible discrimination that can be entertained is of a pragmatic sort. We can only prefer physics if it is more useful; it can only be vindicated in terms of its providing us with a better tool than astrology. Why it is more useful cannot be explained. Yet here the realist can legitimately retort that there is an explanation in terms of the way the world is independently of our perceiving it.[61] To describe our predicament in terms of being trapped inside our conceptual scheme with no access to the independent world is to misrepresent our true position. It is in terms of our language that we attempt to describe the way the world is, the progress of physics being explained by our increasing success in doing so. The desire for understanding and the sense of discovery which characterise the work of practising scientists are not explained here. Thus Polkinghorne remarks, 'I have never known anyone working in fundamental physics who was not motivated by the desire to comprehend better the way the world is.'[62] Similarly, although there is no pure language of morals which infallibly represents ethical truths independently of historical context, this does not undermine the realist's case. As Stout argues, the fact that we can only talk about ethics in terms of a particular, culturally bound vocabulary, does not imply that we are not talking about something beyond our own culturally conditioned preferences.[63]

Bernard Williams has offered a plausible criticism of Rorty's treatment of the language of science. On the pragmatist account offered by Rorty, various features of natural science are left unexplained. It becomes difficult to make sense of the postulation of theoretical entities (for example electrons) at one stage in the history of science being confirmed *inter alia* by the observation of such entities (for example through an electron micrograph) at a later date.[64] Moreover, science itself has sought to explain, through evolutionary biology and neurological science, why its own enterprise is possible. We are beings who have evolved in such a way as to succeed in describing and understanding our environment. The self-explanatory power of science cannot be made sense of on pragmatic criteria. The most that we can say is that we find these accounts useful for self-understanding. Yet science is driven by the search for explanation, the quest for an adequate and not merely a useful account of reality. 'The sense that one is not locked in a world of books, that one is confronting "the world", that the work is made hard or easy by what is actually there – these are part of the driving force, the essential consciousness of science.'[65]

This leads Williams to a curious *reductio ad absurdum* of Rorty's proposal. For the enterprise of science, the most useful assumption is that it can explain with increasing power the way the world is. The pragmatist, however, in advocating the abandonment of such assumptions, threatens their usefulness, and this is self-referentially incoherent. The most pragmatic policy for the progress of science would therefore be the abandonment of pragmatism.

If Rorty's global pragmatism breaks down, this will inevitably have repercussions for his moral philosophy. While the pursuit of truth remains valid for science, it must at least be an open question whether it is valid also in ethics. Rorty's insistence upon the absence of absolutes, and also upon human rights as an unassailable fact for our culture, is questionable. The features of our moral discourse which constrain realism and which are present in much of Rorty's own moralising cannot be made sense of on pragmatist grounds. The banishment of moral realism is accompanied by a sense of the loss of moral discovery and authority. In this context, a criticism of Guignon and Hiley is worth registering. Noting that Freudian neuroses of oppression have been widely replaced by more recent neuroses of disorientation, lack of purpose, and lack of sustaining values, they ask whether Rorty's vision of free personal expression can do anything other than aggravate the current disorders of the self.[66]

Rorty's defence of moral pragmatism and the criticisms it has encountered direct us to wider issues surrounding the concept of the self, human communities, and the social ends of moral conduct. The most significant attempt in recent philosophy to recognise the significance of these without abandoning moral realism will be considered in the next chapter.

CHAPTER FIVE

Virtue, tradition, and God – Alasdair MacIntyre

THE ARISTOTELIAN CONSTANT

Since the publication of *After Virtue* (1981), Alasdair MacIntyre's writings have become a seminal philosophical influence in recent theology. While this work appeared to initiate a new phase in MacIntyre's career – one that has led him back to Christianity, though this time in a Thomist form – many of its characteristic themes are adumbrated in earlier works, *pace* Gellner.[1] Three of these deserve attention. His insistence that a study of ethical concepts must be set within a socio-historical purview of their context dominates his *Short History of Ethics* and sets it apart for its blend of sociology and philosophy.[2] This paves the way for his later apocalyptic pronouncements about the inevitable failure of 'the Enlightenment project' and his relentless assault upon modern liberalism, both of which, he claims, ignore the integral connection between standards of conduct and socially embodied practices based on agreement about those goods which are to be sought. This perception of the relationship between moral theory and practice may initially have arisen out of MacIntyre's study of Marx. In an early work on Marxism, written when he was 23, MacIntyre provides an exposition of Marx's view that philosophy must be evaluated in historical context if its true significance is to be shown. His remarks on Marx anticipate the striking claims of *After Virtue*. '[I]t is in Marx's own thought that philosophy has for the first time become conscious of its historical basis in seeking to transform that basis and has therefore passed beyond the limitations of earlier philosophy.'[3]

MacIntyre's admiration for Aristotle is also reflected in his earlier writings. There he claims that Aristotle correctly perceived, partly in reaction to Plato, that human action is to be evaluated in terms of its contribution to the proper ends of human conduct. The concept of the 'good' thus takes epistemological precedence over what is 'right', the virtues are central to ethics as those habitual dispositions which both facilitate and in part constitute human goodness, while ethics and politics are deeply intertwined insofar as the good life requires a particular social ordering of the *polis*. This invariant commitment to Aristotelianism entails that MacIntyre's ethical realism is of a more naturalist and historical cast than that encountered in the previous chapter. Moral truth cannot be isolated from claims about the purposes of human life nor from the social contexts in which these purposes are articulated and pursued.[4]

The argument of *After Virtue* expands and extends those earlier positions.[5] It might in part be seen as a research project which confirms the thesis of Elizabeth Anscombe in her 1958 article, 'Modern Moral Philosophy'.[6] The concepts of modern ethical theory from Kant's deontology onwards cannot be understood except in terms of the social and metaphysical context in which they emerged. Consequently, the Enlightenment project of justifying them, once detached from their proper context, leads only to the vacuous claims of emotivist and prescriptivist theory. The moral discourse of modern western societies is a survival of fragments from older traditions. Located outside these traditions, the discourse has ceased to make sense, as the spectacularly unsuccessful series of attempts to justify morality since the eighteenth century has shown. Without a strong theory of human nature to sustain them, the philosophical status of moral judgments will baffle us. Philosophical analysis of our current predicament must therefore be conjoined with a historical perspective.[7]

MacIntyre's criticism of contemporary forms of moral discourse resonates with other independent analyses. Basil Mitchell raises a similar query about the ability of liberalism to provide an adequate moral basis for social life. A society has no alternative but to make some moral decisions which presuppose ideals of human excellence. For example, legislation governing marriage and parenting must reflect substantive conceptions about how human beings should live and behave. These cannot be based entirely on thin concepts of equality, freedom, and tolerance. 'Ideals are not, as a rule, arbitrarily chosen but depend upon deeply held and broadly ramified convictions about human nature and the human predicament.'[8] Mitchell goes on to illustrate how traditional convictions about the sanctity of human life started to become puzzling when divorced from the theological framework which had sustained them. A symptom of this puzzlement was the emergence of intuitionism which affirmed various duties as incumbent upon us without any explanation of why we come to have them or how they are connected.[9] In this respect, his criticism of liberalism shares some strikingly similar features with MacIntyre's *After Virtue*.

MacIntyre's pessimistic analysis of modern moral theory is counterbalanced by a study of ethics in classical Greece, where the teleology of Aristotle is presented as possessing a coherence lacking in Enlightenment projects.[10] In Aristotelian ethics, the good life is largely elucidated in terms of citizenship in the city-state. Ethics is thus perceived as irreducibly social and political. The virtues are those habitual dispositions which will enable the citizen to achieve well-being, and in themselves they constitute a condition of such well-being. In this respect Aristotle's account of the virtues differs significantly from Hume's. The exercise of virtue is itself part of the good life and not merely something which accidentally affords pleasure. This formal feature of Aristotelian theory is shared by the New Testament and enables the later synthesis of Aquinas. Although there are important differences between the New Testament and Aristotle in their taxonomy of virtues – Aristotle, he claims, would not have admired Jesus – there are significant formal similarities. A virtue is that quality of character which enables us to live as we ought. Furthermore, its relationship to our final end is internal. It is not merely as a means to an end that we are called upon to develop the virtues of prudence and charity.[11]

Although the modern reader of Aristotle is struck by the relative neglect of rules in his ethics, none the less the virtuous life involves obedience to the laws of the city-state when these are properly enacted. These laws make possible the social framework and relationships without which the good life cannot be attained. To show contempt for civic law is to undermine the shared project of citizenship, and is necessarily at odds with the pursuit of the good. For the virtuous person, certain types of action are absolutely forbidden. Aristotle's position is teleological therefore, without being consequentialist. This account of the virtues as integral to the pursuit of goodness informs Aristotle's account of practical reasoning. The major premise of a practical syllogism that certain goods are to be pursued by an agent under certain circumstances can only be grasped by judgments about the goals of human life, judgments which themselves require the exercise of virtue.

In expounding and restating these elements of Aristotelian moral philosophy, MacIntyre also cites various weaknesses. It may be useful to delineate these for they are crucial to the sequel to *After Virtue* and, in particular, to the turn to Thomism in MacIntyre's own philosophy. The tension in Aristotle between the good as a social end and the good as metaphysical contemplation is never entirely resolved, although the presence of a theology in Aristotle is later used to claim Aristotle for Thomism over against the neo-Aristotelianism of Nussbaum and others.[12] The problem of how to reinstate Aristotelian teleology without Aristotelian metaphysical biology is noted. MacIntyre rejects as inadequate the suggestion that biological needs might in themselves provide a conception of the good life. While such needs place constraints upon human conduct, this approach ignores the extent to which culture shapes and generates rival conceptions of human well-being. Similarly, the provincialism of Aristotle's notion of well-being in the Athenian *polis* raises difficulties for the formulation of his ethical theory in larger and more pluralist forms of political organization which seek to accommodate different conceptions of human flourishing.

The setting of the Aristotelian taxonomy of virtues in context gives rise to three concepts that are crucial to the later development of MacIntyre's own thinking. These are the related concepts of a practice, a narrative, and a moral tradition.

A practice is a form of socially established co-operative activity through which certain goods are achieved through excellence. Those goods which are achieved are internal to the activity in the sense described above.[13] Football, chess, farming, and painting are all practices in this sense. Virtues are integrally related to practices in that they are those acquired qualities which enable us to achieve those goods which are constitutive of practices. To understand and master a practice one has to submit to the socially acknowledged authorities in the field. The idea of inventing standards of one's own without reference to those that are socially established is meaningless.

Every particular account of the virtues is also linked to some notion of how a life as a whole can possess a meaning and a shape. The goods which are sought in different practices must be ordered and harmonised, and this requires a conception of how life can possess a shape in which commitments are made and priorities set. This gives rise to the broader and more comprehensive notion of a history in which we are situated. As agents, the activities we undertake can only be explained by reference to the history of institutions. These histories require narrative display. One cannot understand the excellence that is appropriate to any of one's social roles except by reference to examples which explain and educate.

It is through hearing stories about wicked stepmothers, lost children, good but misguided kings, wolves that suckle twin boys, youngest sons who receive no inheritance but must make their own way in the world and eldest (*sic*) sons who waste their inheritance on riotous living and go into exile to live with the swine, that children learn or mislearn both what a child and what a parent is, what the cast of characters may be in the drama into which they have been born and what the ways of the world are. Deprive children of stories and you leave them unscripted, anxious stutterers in their actions as in their words.[14]

The narrative of a person's life history must inevitably intersect with someone else's narrative. This results from the social dimension of the practices in which we engage and the roles we occupy. Our histories are bound up with the histories of the institutions to which we belong and in which we participate, institutions such as the family, the university, the farm, the hospital, and the church. A tradition arises in part through a provisional consensus about how the goods sought in a wide variety of practices and institutions are to be ordered, and how they are to serve some overall *telos* of human life. Within a tradition, however, there is inevitably conflict, tension, and ongoing debate about the nature and ordering of such goods. In this respect, a living tradition must evolve and adapt. Conflict and criticism are two of its necessary features.[15]

This presentation of what constitutes a living tradition, however, contrasts sharply with MacIntyre's analysis of contemporary moral discourse in the closing stages of *After Virtue*. Except in those marginalized communities which retain strong links with the past, modern liberal societies can only draw upon the disconnected fragments of older traditions whose virtues they have ceased to practise. Modern politics no longer involves genuine moral debate, but rather the suppression of conflict through the use of rhetoric which masks the ethical rootlessness of our societies. The only flicker of light is the prospect of some neo-Benedict who can construct 'new forms of community within which the moral life could be sustained so that both morality and civility might survive the coming ages of barbarism and darkness'.[16]

THE TURN TO THOMISM

The sequels *Whose Justice? Which Rationality?* and *Three Rival Versions of Moral Enquiry* see MacIntyre's thought taking a remarkable theological turn. The wistful hope of a neo-Benedict has been replaced by a commitment to the tradition of Thomism, as the best alternative to a discredited liberalism and a Nietzschean nihilism. In *Whose Justice? Which Rationality?* the concept of a tradition of inquiry is developed and illustrated with reference to classical Greece, twelfth-century Europe, and Enlightenment Scotland. The focus of MacIntyre's inquiry is now upon the discontinuities in the history of moral inquiry and the need to provide an explanation for these.[17]

Modern disputes about the nature of justice are impervious to rational resolution, because the typical discourse of such disputes conceals the extent to which these rival conceptions are embodied in competing traditions of inquiry. Inquiry is situated within a tradition in the history of which standards of rational justification have emerged and been developed. The understanding of this context is a necessary condition for grasping its related moral standards. According to MacIntyre, rather than setting up incommensurable rival conceptions, this description of moral inquiry as tradition-situated enables us better to appreciate the nature of contemporary moral disagreement and to render it amenable to resolution.

He makes several further points in elucidation of this thesis.[18] Exponents of these traditions of inquiry need not have thought of themselves as expounding one of several traditions. It is only in circumstances of radical crisis and self-examination that an adherent of a tradition considers his or her most fundamental principles. Justification within traditions often proceeds by reference to first principles which are assumed to be uncontested. Yet what justifies these principles in times of radical dispute is the superiority of one construction of the tradition, including its first principles, over alternative attempts to characterise the tradition of inquiry.[19] A second observation on the status of tradition-constituted inquiry is that past history is crucial to an understanding of the present state of the tradition. In this respect, there is a sharp distinction from the pre-Enlightenment ahistorical model of moral inquiry in which the circumstances surrounding the emergence of moral standards and doctrines are irrelevant to their rational assessment. Hence the bulk of the two sequels to *After Virtue* is taken up with descriptions of particular historical episodes in moral inquiry.

From a theologian's perspective, the most interesting and perhaps most elusive aspect of MacIntyre's philosophical project is his rehabilitation of Thomism. How does MacIntyre advance from Aristotelianism to Thomism, and on what basis is the latter to be defended? It is clear from his discussion of Augustinianism that he perceives four crucial differences between the Christian moral theory of Augustine and the paganism of Aristotle. First, the scope of morality is extended beyond selected groups within the *polis* to include all human beings. This is reinforced by theological conceptions about divine laws and a created nature which can know these. Second, the reality of sin and grace for Augustine entails a radical shift in moral psychology in which the will occupies a central place in determining human action. The explanatory role assigned to the will would have been unintelligible to Plato and Aristotle. Third, Augustine's taxonomy of the virtues differs from that of Aristotle on account of this alternative moral psychology. The most fundamental sin is that of pride, its correlative virtue being that of humility. Fourth, the *telos* of human life is now to be described theologically and not merely in terms of a life style within the *polis*. The moral life requires some overriding notion of the end of life and this can only be made sense of in a theistically ordered universe. The moral life, therefore, can only be fulfilled in the religious.[20] MacIntyre's description of Augustine probably represents his own position.

Jesus points us toward that immutable form of justice in God which we first directly apprehended within our own minds, but toward a clearer apprehension of which we continually move, as we come to love God more and more, as He is revealed in Jesus Christ.[21]

In the later writings of Thomas Aquinas, we see an overcoming of the conflict between Augustinian Christianity and Aristotelian philosophy. Aquinas, by virtue of his education was able to inhabit both traditions and thus to reform Augustinian Christianity by accommodating the best insights, concepts, and arguments of Aristotelianism. For MacIntyre, Aquinas provides not only an illustration of a dynamic tradition of rational inquiry, but also the most adequate tradition available for resolving the moral problems of modernity.[22] How does MacIntyre justify this claim?

The vindication of Aquinas' synthesis lies not in any demonstrable refutation of the leading alternatives from agreed first principles. Instead its rationality resides in its ability to accommodate the best insights of its rivals while setting these within a new framework which alone is capable of resolving the difficulties faced by those rivals.

> What justifies his representation of the order of things over against its Averroist, Neoplatonist, and Augustinian rivals is its ability to identify, to explain, and to transcend their limitations and defects, while preserving from them everything that survives dialectical questioning in a way which those rivals are unable from their philosophical resources to provide any counterpart.[23]

To the objection that, for Aristotle and Aquinas, rational justification is a matter of deduction from self-evident first principles, MacIntyre makes the following response. Although there are some principles which are so fundamental as to be undeniable, their application is not uncontroversial. Thus, while the good is that which we ought to seek – the most fundamental law of practical reason – the nature of goodness remains contested in relation to our biological, social, and rational ends. Moreover, attaining recognition of those ends is a work of 'dialectical construction'. It is only as we understand the implications of first principles that we come to recognise their truth, and to deepen our apprehension of them.[24] There is thus a sense in which the fullest discovery of the first principles of right action is the *telos* of the moral life, an account of rationality which MacIntyre claims places Aquinas at odds with Descartes, Hume, and Kant.

How is Aquinas able to integrate Augustinian and Aristotelian traditions and what makes his reshaped tradition persuasive? MacIntyre is here elusive, at best suggestive.[25] He claims that in the early stages of his career Aquinas developed conceptions of truth and being in the opening sections of the *Quaestiones Disputatae de Veritate* and in the *De Ente et Essentia*, which enabled him to develop a metaphysic capable of reconstructing both Aristotelian and Augustinian traditions. At the heart of this metaphysic is a concept of a reality which is necessary and self-explanatory, and which constitutes the final *telos* of all other beings. How other particular goods are to be organised and related to the ultimate good is a complex matter for human reflection and for Christian faith. Debate on this question is ongoing. Thus, 'every article in the *Summa* poses a question whose answer depends upon the outcome of an essentially uncompleted debate'.[26]

The concept of truth is handled in a way that is both participatory and critically realist. In a craft such as furniture-making, fishing, or farming, the mind of the participant must become adequate to an independent good. The embodied mind must therefore seek to correspond to the object which is sought through practice, and this is achieved through the intellectual and moral virtues.[27] Yet the progressive nature of the moral life is such that this correspondence of embodied mind to object is partial, incomplete, and open to revision.

Aquinas' conception of rational inquiry is, in an important sense, both holistic and eclectic. In the *Summa*, every single article finds its place within a larger whole and makes a corresponding contribution to that whole. At the same time, in the exploration of each question Aquinas draws upon an array of sources including the biblical writers, Greek and Roman philosophers, Arab and Jewish thinkers, and Christian theologians from across the centuries. 'The length and details of the *Summa* are not accidental features of it, but integral to its purpose and more particularly to providing both Aquinas himself and his readers with the assurance that the arguments adduced for particular articles were the strongest produced so far from any known point of view.'[28]

It is clear from *Three Rival Versions of Moral Enquiry* that MacIntyre advocates something like a post-modern reading of Thomas Aquinas. The role of philosophy as a craft is strongly emphasised. As such, philosophy is not primarily an epistemological project to which all rational inquirers have immediate and equal access. It is a practice, the art of which one must learn through teaching, discipline, acknowledgement of authority, and a realisation of the good which is sought therein. To learn the craft requires that the practitioner finds his or her identity within the history of the craft, and his or her participation in the development of that history.[29] On this reading, Aquinas' *Summa* becomes a way of instructing the reader into the crafts of philosophy and theology rather than the setting out of an epistemology on the basis of perspicuous first principles. The

Thomism of Cajetan and *Aeterni Patris* (1879) is thus preferred by MacIntyre to that of Suarez and Kleugten. Aquinas is read not as someone who provides an answer to the epistemological questions raised by Descartes and his successors. Aquinas' work cannot be understood except in relation to traditions of inquiry which include those of the classical philosophers and the Church Fathers. According to the encyclical *Aeterni Patris*, the exercise of reason is not a free-standing activity which should take place without reference to the Christian faith. Only within this context can the errors and obscurity of unaided reason be avoided. Even the great philosophers of antiquity fell into appalling error.

A wise man, therefore, would not accuse faith and look upon it as opposed to reason and natural truths, but would rather offer heartfelt thanks to God, and sincerely rejoice that, in the density of ignorance and in the flood-tide of error, holy faith, like a friendly star, shines down upon his path and points out to him the fair gate of truth beyond all danger of wandering.[30]

MacIntyre proceeds to interpret Thomas Aquinas' ethics in a manner similar to that outlined in chapter 3. The section on natural law cannot be read except in the context of the search for the good and the necessity of the virtues. The cardinal virtues cannot be properly exercised except with the gift of the theological virtues. In this holistic reading of Aquinas, it becomes impossible to extract his teaching on natural law as characterising the moral reasoning of every rational person irrespective of tradition and training.

The role here ascribed to history and tradition contrasts sharply with the classical liberalism which MacIntyre inveighs against and which he sees exemplified in the ninth edition of the *Encyclopaedia Britannica*. Here the history which has given rise to the statement of a set of rational principles is merely a prologue irrelevant to the task of rational assessment. Sidgwick's remark that 'Principles will soon be everything, and tradition nothing' epitomises the spirit of the encyclopaedia. In the moral theory, expounded by Sidgwick in his article on 'Ethics' and subsequently in *Outlines of the History of Ethics*, moral principles have come to be recognised, since the Reformation, as dictated by

the common experience and reason of human beings.[31] Moral
principles have now become disengaged from superstition,
ritual, and other irrational trappings. The 'ought' of moral
obligation is not reducible to any non-moral concept. There is
rational consensus regarding moral conduct throughout the
civilised world. Moral principles are therefore self-evident and
detachable from any particular understanding of human
nature, history, or God. Practical reason obliges us to seek both
the general and also our own personal happiness. According to
MacIntyre, the implausibility of this account is evident in
several ways. The potential for conflict between the twin goals
of universal and egoistic happiness is endless. Moral claims
become vulnerable to those of prudential self-interest. This
cannot be resolved while the moral 'ought' is radically divorced
from its context in a system of rules and beliefs. Moreover, the
fragmentedness of the discipline of moral philosophy and the
radical nature of subsequent moral disagreement disconfirm
Sidgwick's thesis about the emergence of rational moral principles independent of tradition. 'Thus post-Sidgwickian moral
philosophy, judged by the standards of the Ninth Edition and of
Sidgwick himself, has turned out to be a dubious type of
activity.'[32]

At the same time, MacIntyre's realism emerges in his attack
on the genealogist who deconstructs the encyclopaedist's quest
of truth as masking only the will to power within a particular
social class, and who attacks the tradition-constituted model of
inquiry for its oppressiveness and innate conservatism. The
genealogist may correctly perceive that the encyclopaedist has a
social context in which powerful interests suppress the notion
that tradition, background, or prejudice are germane to rational inquiry. Nietzsche thus understood academic discourse to
mask repressed and repressive sentiments behind a mask of
pure objectivity.[33] Yet the genealogist's deconstruction of the
notions of rationality and truth are rejected in MacIntyre's
tradition-based approach. The problems for the genealogist are
those problems which typically beset the opponents of
realism.[34] Its subversive use of language cannot recognise the
manner in which meaning is delimited by social conventions.

Without such delimitation, language acquisition and communication would be impossible. The identity, unity, and continuity of the self who performs the activity of intellectual deconstruction cannot be made sense of in terms of the position that is being advanced. Finally, the narrative presented by the genealogist, which seeks to expose the illicitness of other narratives, demands exemption from an otherwise universal scepticism. Again this presupposes a location of the narrator which is unexplained in terms of the philosophy being promulgated. The exponent of a tradition-based concept of rationality will not deny that every thesis, argument, or doctrine must be understood as situated within a history of inquirers whose lives have been shaped by particular practices, narratives, and methods of education. None the less, the direction and meaning of the tradition derives from a conception of truth as independent of that tradition. Its success or failure is to be assessed in terms of a realist understanding of what it is that makes our utterances true. This concept of truth is denied by the genealogist in such a manner as to lead to self-referential incoherence.

So confronted by the incommensurability of the genealogist's theses about the self with metaphysical and theological claims about accountability, we can enquire whether in telling the tale of how he or she came to advance those claims, the genealogist does not have to fall back into a mode of speech in which the use of personal pronouns presupposes just that metaphysical conception of accountability which genealogy disowns. Or to put this question another way: can the genealogist legitimately include the self out of which he speaks in explaining himself within his or her genealogical narrative? Is the genealogist not self-indulgently engaged in exempting his or her utterances from the treatment to which everyone else's is subjected?[35]

It transpires from all this that MacIntyre is, in some sense, both a communitarian and a realist, and that the only tenable combination of these resides in the Aristotelian–Thomist tradition. The attractions of this for contemporary theology are considerable but require careful and judicious assessment. A range of difficulties in MacIntyre's position is now becoming apparent from the burgeoning secondary literature that it has elicited. These difficulties might be identified as afflicting both his realism and his communitarianism respectively.

The problem of perspectivism arises through claims that traditions deal with problems in terms of criteria of rationality which are, in an important sense, internal to those traditions. How then is it possible to adjudicate rival claims of traditions without assuming the Archimedean point which MacIntyre claims to be illusory? Are traditions not sheerly incommensurable in the absence of any tradition-transcendent criteria capable of resolving disagreement? MacIntyre's problem arises in part from his desire to explain the impervious nature of our modern disagreements without abandoning realism by assuming the role of the genealogist. His response to the charge of perspectivism is that traditions are indirectly commensurable by virtue of one tradition's ability both to accommodate the insights of another while also resolving new problems which are incapable of resolution in the rival account. MacIntyre provides parallels from the history of science to justify this claim. A new scientific theory succeeds not only by accommodating the recalcitrant data that its rivals faced, but also by explaining why its predecessor could succeed within its own limits. Galileo, for example, succeeds over against his predecessors in part because he is able to explain their successes and failures. His own account not only can improve upon earlier versions, but also can make sense of their achievements. 'The contributions of Plato, Aristotle, the scholars of Merton college, Oxford and at Padua, the work of Copernicus himself all fall into place. Or, to put matters in another and equivalent way: the history of late medieval science can finally be cast into a coherent narrative.'[36]

How this response avoids perspectivism without abandoning the tradition-centred model of rationality can be seen by considering MacIntyre's views on incommensurability and radical translation. Although traditions are in some measure incommensurable, translation is possible from the discourse of one tradition to that of another. It is by attempting such translation and acknowledging its shortcomings that one learns that what can be said in one language cannot be said in another. The inhabitant of two traditions and the speaker of two languages (with the fluency of a native) can come to the realisation that certain things can be thought and spoken of in one tradition or language but not another. In this respect, the recognition of incommensurablity can be achieved without lapsing into perspectivism or assuming that one holds an Archimedean position.[37]

It is worth noticing that the prospect of translation and the recognition of its occasional impossibility presuppose a belief in a shared environment and low-level standards of rationality, including those of formal logic.[38] It also implies a theory of reference by which exponents of rival traditions of inquiry can agree that they are referring to the same subject-matter and attempting to characterise it in different ways.[39] Indeed, elsewhere, MacIntyre can plead for recognition of the large measure of agreement about standards across traditions.[40]

Yet the suggestion that a tradition is like a language with its distinctive concepts which cannot exactly be translated into the concepts of another language may imply an exaggerated level of homogeneity and incommensurability. It is never entirely clear where one tradition breaks off and another begins, and in contemporary debate all traditions incorporate variations which are in part the result of influences from without. On the issue of translatability, MacIntyre has shown how difficult it can be to express in one language what is said in another. The translator of ancient texts soon becomes aware of the impossibility of an exact one-to-one translation between the terms of an ancient language and those of a modern language. The anthropological concepts of classical Hebrew, for instance, cannot adequately be captured by the conceptuality of classical Greek. This conceptual difference reflects disparities in belief and practice. Yet does this problem of translation entail incommensurability? Stout has argued that, despite difficulties in translation, any belief embedded in another culture can be rendered intelligible with sufficient explanation and digression in another language.[41] The lack of

conceptual resources to provide an adequate simple translation can itself be explained in another language. This is a
necessary condition of drawing the sorts of comparisons
between traditions that MacIntyre believes will advance rational debate. A similar criticism is offered by Jürgen Habermas, who argues in Davidsonian fashion that MacIntyre's
ability to show the disparity between linguistic resources
presupposes a standpoint of 'flexible identity'. Through comparing and contrasting meanings in rival traditions, MacIntyre
assumes the position of one who is 'bilingually extended'.[42]
This criticism echoes MacIntyre's own attack upon the
posture of the genealogist which is inexplicably immune from
the criticism made of all other postures. On the other hand,
MacIntyre can make the rejoinder that, while translation of
this sort into 'trans-Atlantic and trans-Pacific English' is
possible, the detachment of concepts from the cultural and
historical context in which they originally derived their intelligibility makes corruption inevitable. Only an imaginative
inhabitation of this context would enable the translator to
begin to understand its concepts.

Related to the issue of perspectivism is the even more
pressing problem for the realist of relativism. By setting rational
inquiry in the context of a tradition with its principles and
presuppositions, has MacIntyre relativised the concept of truth?
If truth is to be evaluated in terms of the 'best theory so far',
does this not lead to the substitution of 'warranted assertibility'
for a correspondence notion of truth? What is true is determined by the most coherent organisation of data within the
most successful tradition. The criteria of truth are given by the
constraints and organisational success of traditions. MacIntyre's
response to this problem of relativism is that a tradition-centred
model of rationality cannot avoid a realist conception of truth
which must be perceived as distinct from the concept of
'warranted assertibility'. The latter can be a property of statements generated by the basic criteria of a tradition, but the
need in times of epistemological crisis to revise those criteria
themselves can only be understood in terms of a realist notion
of what is adequate to the way things are. Thus it is the

correspondence theory of truth which is presupposed in this account of how traditions themselves flourish or wither.

> The concept of warranted responsibility always has application only at some particular time and place in respect of standards then prevailing at some particular state in the development of a tradition of enquiry, and a claim that such and such is warrantedly assertible always, therefore, has to make implicit or explicit references to such times and places. The concept of truth, however, is timeless. To claim that some thesis is true is not only to claim for all possible times and places that it cannot be shown to fail to correspond to reality in the sense of 'correspond' elucidated earlier but that the mind which expresses its thought in that thesis is in fact adequate to its object.[43]

The charge of relativism is thus met by emphasis upon the defeasibility of translation, the ability of participants to inhabit several traditions, the possibility of one tradition defeating its rivals in virtue of its greater explanatory power, the incoherence of genealogical accounts of the concept of truth, and the ineluctably realist nature of truth. 'To claim truth for an expression is to presuppose that this is the way things are irrespective of how they appear from whatever point of view.'[44]

The emphasis upon tradition, practice, community, and authority as necessary conditions for the apprehension of truth has also prompted the criticism that MacIntyre's neo-Thomism is seriously oppressive. The communitarian thrust of *Whose Justice? Which Rationality?* has resulted in a much more hostile reception than *After Virtue* encountered. Before considering this reception, it is worth asking in what sense MacIntyre's philosophy can be characterised as communitarian. The concluding sections of *After Virtue* appeared to recommend the cultivation of a variety of small-scale communities which enabled their inhabitants to develop those virtues that were appropriate to their shared practices and beliefs. This proposal seemed to endorse the ideal of a variety of local communities which could coexist and interrelate in modern liberal societies. Such an ideal might be construed as a form of neo-Aristotelian communitarianism. By contrast, the Thomism of MacIntyre's latest work appears to advocate the ideal of one civic order which strives to organise the goals, practices, beliefs, and institutions of justice amongst its members. Within certain limits, the authority of this way of life must be secured by the use of sanctions. It is this strand of MacIntyre's philosophy which has evoked the wrath of Martha Nussbaum who discerns the spectre of an oppressive church riding roughshod over diverse and discrete local traditions while invoking the doctrine of original sin in support of its own necessary authority.[45]

This last point, however, provides an opportunity for a rejoinder on MacIntyre's behalf. He fully acknowledges that the creation of a society within the Thomist tradition is unattainable under present constraints. The most that can be realised are more local sub-groups which seek to foster the traditions and practices which produce Christian virtues. It is clear, moreover, that this tradition can only manifest its rationality through encounter and confrontation with rivals. This seems to require the condition of a polity in which different traditions are tolerated and brought together in dialogue. The progress of reason thus requires the peaceful coexistence of rival traditions which can debate and argue their most fundamental differences. MacIntyre's description of a tradition presupposes ongoing development and debate. It recalls John Henry Newman's dictum that claims about the meaning of human life 'are not placed in a void, but in the crowded world, and make way for themselves by interpenetration, and develop by absorption'.[46] In this respect, MacIntyre's position may have more in common with liberalism than is usually recognised. Indeed, in his own academic career he has frequently found himself tilting against a range of established positions. In playing out the role of the dissident, he has depended upon an academic culture in which there is scope for radical disagreement and dissent.[47] The modern university is advocated as a forum within which competing traditions may engage. The university should be a 'place of constrained disagreements'.[48] The rationality of the most superior tradition can only be evinced through confrontation, dialogue, and a testing of assumptions and counter-assumptions. Jean Porter has accordingly argued that if a tradition survives and prospers by engagement with its rivals, then a condition of tradition-constituted inquiry must be the

maintenance of tolerance, pluralism, and openness to change
within our societies. And these, of course, are amongst the
central values of liberalism.[49]

Further clarification of MacIntyre's position is given in a
recent interview in *Kinesis*. The difficulty in a variety of voluntary associations pursuing their own goods is that this merely
weakens any commitment to and articulation of a common
good within society.

What I'm talking about, by contrast, is the kind of local community in
which the variety of goods that people pursue – in the workplace, in
their leisure, in the schools, in clinics and hospitals, in a variety of
activities – are integrated into the life of an overall community, a
community that is able to recognize that it has a life of its own and to
celebrate that life by things that it does together, in a ceremonial and
festive way.[50]

On the other hand, the current political impossibility of
creating such a monolithic society seems to imply the need, on
an interim basis, for the cultivation of more local forms of
community. This remains part of MacIntyre's strategy for
moral survival in a post-liberal age.[51] Here we find a criticism
of other forms of communitarianism which is crucial to the
shape of MacIntyre's present position. As we shall see in the
following chapter, 'communitarian' is an adjective that he
rejects, in part because he perceives amongst so-called communitarians a desire for the state to embrace some vision of the
common good. This, however, is fraught with dangers of
distortion and authoritarianism, for the nation state is essentially an inadequate vehicle for the formation of the common
good.

What must emerge from this is an interim commitment to a
pluralist polity. The nation state cannot reform itself. To
attempt such a reform is to court fascism. Therefore, it is better
in the interim if the state continues to assume as best it can its
principled neutrality between competing conceptions of the
good. Communitarianism for the present must develop in local
ways and at grassroots level. For MacIntyre *qua* Thomist, it is
presumably the church rather than the state which is best
placed to develop such community.

In this regard, what is required is a theory of church and state which distinguishes these on the grounds that the former is a free association of those who confess a common good, whereas the latter accommodates within its perimeters individuals and groups of differing persuasions. While, as MacIntyre has shown, there will be acute difficulties establishing a moral basis upon which such a polity is established and the limits of moral disagreement permitted, it seems that for the time being accommodation must be made to some such polity. Yet it is not clear that his moral philosophy can say much about how a pluralist society can be organised or what the disposition of the Thomist should be towards it. In this respect, other critics have found his proposals of little positive application. Brian Barry argues that any attempt to model the societies we currently inhabit on the basis of Thomism is a non-starter. It makes no sense to reconstruct our world in such a way as would entail rolling back not only the Enlightenment but also the Reformation. 'The problem is akin to that of "keeping 'em down on the farm after they've seen Paree" but on a *much, much* bigger scale.'[52]

It is precisely because there is no present prospect of widespread agreement upon the ends of human life, social goods, and the ordering of the virtues, that liberals typically argue for a polity that is based upon fundamental procedural rules of freedom and equality. Ronald Dworkin claims that political decisions must be, so far as is possible, independent of any conception of the good life. Citizens will differ in their conceptions, so it is incumbent upon government to treat all equally by refusing to give preference to any one. The scheme of civil rights in the USA is interpreted as ensuring that citizens are not discriminated against in this way, and for the most part Dworkin judges this successful.[53] The fear of the totalitarian imposition of a very specific conception of the common good may lead us to prefer a social order which construes freedom and equality around the idea of legitimate non-interference.[54] MacIntyre's criticism of liberalism suggests that such procedural rules are too thin and rootless to sustain social life and its institutions of justice. None the less, one might be tempted to conclude that, in the absence of any alternative proposal in MacIntyre for the organisation of a pluralist society, we have to make the best of liberalism.

Yet MacIntyre's notion of moral inquiry is fundamentally at odds with liberal claims that there are moral norms which transcend all traditions, societies, and cultures. His hostility to the only contemporary candidate for a universal moral discourse – the language of human rights[55] – confirms this. For some theological critics, this is a principal weakness of his moral theory.[56] The Christian tradition has persistently claimed that there are laws of morality which are known outwith the visible church and which Christians share with all other human beings. MacIntyre's philosophy, however, despite its frequently combative style may be able to accommodate such claims. It is incumbent upon any prosperous tradition to explain the best insights of its rivals, and MacIntyre provides resources for this in his redescription of natural law theory. It is already a feature of his account of a practice in *After Virtue* that practitioners are necessarily committed to the virtues of justice, courage, and honesty. 'We have to learn to recognize what is due to whom; we have to be prepared to take whatever self-endangering risks are demanded along the way; and we have to listen carefully to what we are told about our own inadequacies and to reply with the same carefulness for the facts.'[57] Anyone who wishes to learn a practice to achieve those goods towards which it is directed must espouse justice, courage, and honesty. The social nature of the goods we seek entails a commitment to these virtues in one form or another. We thus find here a minimalist account of human nature which presupposes the necessity of some set of rules governing all forms of human conduct aimed at the good. This can be combined with the recognition that 'different societies have and have had different codes of truthfulness, justice and courage'.[58] A commitment to the indispensability of basic moral rules is even more apparent in his recent writing. The achievement of our human good is dependent upon observance of principles, respect for which is a necessary condition of social well-being. In particular, the negative precepts of the natural law must govern every genuine ethical practice.

[A] first primitive conception of each of the virtues that we need to acquire, if we are to achieve our good, can be articulated only through a set of rules which turn out to be another application of the primary precepts of the natural law. We can only learn what it is to be courageous or temperate or truthful by first learning that certain types of action are always and exceptionlessly such as we must refrain from if we are to exemplify those virtues.[59]

Such features of his Thomism are well placed to recognise and explain why a Kantian, for instance, should assert the primacy and universality of moral principles concerning honesty and respect in one's dealing with others *qua* human beings. The natural law reveals to us exceptionless negative precepts which must govern our lives. The examples offered are those of not committing murder and not telling lies. While human reason needs to be instructed and corrected by divine revelation, none the less these negative precepts have the character of fundamental rules governing all ethical behaviour worthy of the name. Failure to respect them is destructive of those very forms of life which make any virtuous life possible.[60]

The perception that there are fundamental moral norms governing human life is not limited, according to MacIntyre, to Thomist Christianity. In his recent discussion of the work of the Danish philosophical theologian, Knud Løgstrup, MacIntyre insists that all interaction between human beings requires a basic trust.[61] In the encounter with the other person, I become aware of some fundamental moral claims upon me – here a further comparision with Levinas is drawn. I am under a demand to do what is best for the other in so far as it lies within me. This may provide at least some minimal moral norms even for a pluralist society beset with disagreement about the ends of human life. There is no return to foundationalism or a thick moral code independent of a particular tradition. None the less, MacIntyre's philosophy, despite its onslaught upon liberalism, may possess resources for acknowledging on non-liberal grounds the importance of tolerance, individual freeeedom, respect for persons, and the maintenance of a pluralist polity.

THEOLOGICAL ISSUES

There has been considerable theological interest in MacIntyre's moral philosophy and especially its recent Thomist turn. Its theological significance might be viewed in relation to one of the main theological options today, post-liberalism. As has been argued, this offers modern theology a way of asserting both the distinctiveness of the church and the truthfulness of its faith. There are some striking similarities between the tradition-constituted model of rational inquiry and the cultural–linguistic model of religion. The denouncing of liberalism, the rejection of foundationalism, the assertion of incommensurability, the denial of radical translation, the epistemological indispensability of a community – all these are shared features of MacIntyre's philosophical and Lindbeck's theological programme. Moreover, the criticisms of relativism, perspectivism, non-cognitivism, and sectarianism have been directed at both. A similarity less obvious is a shared ambivalence surrounding liberal themes. While both MacIntyre and Lindbeck are apparently hostile to liberalism and vociferous exponents of some form of communitarianism, their writings display a commitment to realism and a recognition of the pluralist context within which Christian theology must be conducted.[62]

As MacIntyre claims that a tradition will evince its rationality by demonstrating an ability to cope with new situations and problems, so Lindbeck speaks about applicability as futurology. 'A theological proposal is adjudged both faithful and applicable to the degree that it appears practical in terms of an eschatologically and empirically defensible scenario of what is to come.'[63] Alongside applicability, Lindbeck cites intelligibility as a further possible mark of a religion. This rational intelligibility is not the result of some demonstrative argument, but is rather the accumulation of positive tests, checks, and arguments from within a living tradition. The current imperative for the Christian community is to socialise its members into a distinctive form of life. This alone can provide a vision of social co-operation and service which will provide an alternative to the individualism of acquisitive theories of justice and rights entitlements.

One disanalogical feature in Lindbeck is the apparent absence of any notion of translatability in the presentation of the cultural–linguistic model of religion. This absence prevents due attention being devoted to the possibility of cross-fertilisation between traditions and to the influencing of a tradition by external forces. Lindbeck's accommodation of 'relevant data'[64] must refer not to raw empirical information, but to the insights of other communities, associations, and traditions. Yet the modern Christian citizen will find herself typically belonging to various forms of social organisation through the workplace, leisure pursuits, and voluntary commitments, and these it must be assumed will have some influence upon her understanding of the forms of the Christian life. A communitarian theology must therefore be able to accommodate the insights that will be gleaned from diverse places, and which must be pressed into the service of the Christian faith. The greater emphasis upon realism, conversation, and partial translatability in MacIntyre may thus enhance aspects of Lindbeckian post-liberalism.

What finally of MacIntyre's understanding of God? Here he is uncharacteristically reticent. He has much to say about the fusion of Augustinian Christianity with Aristotelianism, but why one should ever adopt the former standpoint is not entirely explained. What is it that makes Thomism a more viable option than some form of neo-Aristotelianism? This is the root of Nussbaum's complaint. MacIntyre shows how Aquinas was able to accommodate Aristotelianism within Augustinian Christianity. Yet why should an Aristotelian assent to Augustinian Christianity? 'The astonishing fact is that, in this lengthy book about Aristotelianism and rational justification, this question is never seriously asked . . . We are simply transported into the Christian era.'[65]

The most extensive discussion of this problem is that offered in John Milbank's *Theology and Social Theory.*[66] According to Milbank, MacIntyre's presentation is too rationalist in attempting to argue on philosophical grounds from Aristotelianism to Thomism. The discontinuity between a secular and a Christian moral vision is not adequately accounted for in MacIntyre's arguments for the rational superiority of Thomism. There can be no refutation of the secularist. 'Hence there is a question-ableness about every switch of tradition, which escapes dialec-tical adjudication.'[67] The only possibility is an out-narrating of other traditions by the persuasive power of the Christian *mythos*.

Milbank has accurately pointed to a lack of theological development in MacIntyre's position. Yet the switching of traditions, according to MacIntyre's account, is never an action to which one is compelled on grounds of rational contem-plation. One may have some sense of the inadequacies of one's position and the possibility of a better one through rational scrutiny, but the full realisation of another alternative takes place only through something akin to conversion. One must learn to inhabit the new tradition, to see oneself and the world in its terms, to acknowledge its authorities in order properly to understand its greater adequacy. Rational persuasion, for Mac-Intyre, can take place only from inside another way which is created by divine grace. Moreover, his philosophy seeks to explain how one may fail to see one's tradition as inadequate by contrast with another which is rationally superior. '[S]ome at least of the adherents of a defeated set of positions may remain unable to recognize that defeat.'[68]

For MacIntyre, the notions of truth, realism, and rational justification stand or fall together. In this respect, his insistence upon one position being capable of rational justification even in the presence of intractable disagreement is a corollary of his realism. The concept of 'truth' cannot be reduced to any operational or pragmatist alternative without our practices of assertion, commendation, and argument becoming seriously distorted. In order to avoid perspectivism and relativism, our moral theory is committed to the view that this is how things are and not merely how they appear from this particular standpoint. In making this claim about how things are in distinction from how they appear one is also committed to the view that one's position can be rationally justified. At the very least, this includes the assumption that arguments advanced for rival positions are unsound in some respect or other. What MacIntyre's critics have not always recognised is that his account of rational justification is entailed by his realism rather

than by any covert foundationalism. Conversely, any abandonment of this notion of rational justification entails a retreat for
him into a perspectivism or relativism which is finally incoherent.[69] It is not clear, in any case, that one can appropriate
and commend to one's public MacIntyre's arguments against
post-Enlightenment liberalism without assuming that these are
rationally persuasive.[70]

The distance that Milbank perceives between the Christian
mythos and MacIntyre's understanding of tradition-centred rationality may be exaggerated by virtue of the former's instrumentalist construction of science which tends towards the type
of perspectivism that MacIntyre seeks to avoid. MacIntyre's
own account of the history of science is explicitly critical of any
attempt to substitute the realist conception of truth with a
functionalist alternative. A problem may also be generated by
Milbank's criticism of MacIntyre's account of (partial) translatability and incommensurability. The claim that we may 'hold
inside our heads several subjectivities'[71] may be psychologically
true, but it does not in itself exclude the possibility that we can
reflect upon these and compare them. This possibility is all that
MacIntyre's philosophy requires.

MacIntyre's position has the capacity to recognise that dependence upon divine revelation for Christian perception is not
incompatible with a certain style of apologetic argument. For
example, he argues that the moral psychology of Christianity
employs notions of the will, sin, and grace which are lacking in
classical philosophy but which are adequate to our moral
predicament. The irrational and flawed aspects of human
nature – which are powerfully attested to in modernity – are
signs of a disorder which Christian psychology has long recognised. Yet the fullest acknowledgement of such disorder comes
for the Christian only in the recognition of his or her true end
as revealed by God's grace. The following sentence in MacIntyre is remarkable for its theological potential.

The self-revelation of God in the events of the scriptural history and
the gratuitous grace through which that revelation is appropriated, so
that an individual can come to recognize his or her place within that
same history, enable such individuals to recognize also that prudence,

justice, temperateness, and courage are genuine virtues, that the apprehension of the natural law was not illusory, and that the moral life up to this point requires to be corrected in order to be completed but not displaced.[72]

This brings us to the second claim that MacIntyre advances for theism, its teleology. The ordinary moral life requires to be understood in Aristotelian terms as a series of projects which individually and collectively aim at the good. 'What is the good life?', is the question that each of us must ask himself or herself. This question in turn raises further issues about the ordering of goods, the complex set of relationships into which we must enter, and an account of what it is to succeed or to fail finally in one's moral endeavour. Such an account can only be provided if the universe itself is teleologically ordered.

[T]he only type of teleologically ordered universe in which we have good reason to believe is a theistic universe. Hence, the moral progress of the plain person towards her or his ultimate good is always a matter of more than morality . . . The moral progress of the plain person is always the beginning of a pilgrim's progress.[73]

This is not an argument which can compel the moralist to become a believer. It does not remove the need for grace and conversion. Yet it does show how the inadequacies of the moral life may find their resolution in the Christian life. MacIntyre's long-standing commitment to Aristotelianism requires a theological setting and this is best supplied by some form of Thomism. A future task is to defend the view that 'the predicaments of contemporary philosophy, whether analytic or deconstructive, are best understood as arising as a long-term consequence of the rejection of Aristotelian and Thomistic teleology at the threshold of the modern world'.[74]

None the less, a theological criticism not dissimilar to those of Milbank and Banner can be registered. MacIntyre approaches Aquinas primarily as a resource to complement and correct an Aristotelian moral philosophy. Yet, if the Christian life is viewed merely as the correction of the moral life, the radical nature of God's grace – a theme in the Augustinian Christianity not only of the Reformation but of Aquinas also – is threatened.[75] MacIntyre mentions the forgiveness of sins and the nature of redemption, yet is it not significant that his reading of *Veritatis Splendor* takes its point of departure from the middle rather than the beginning of the encyclical? Little attention is devoted in the structure of his argument to the notion of our union with Christ – a gift that is given by grace prior to any works of obedience – as the context and presupposition of Christian discipleship. The emphases in *Veritatis Splendor* upon the Christian life as one of response and witness, as lived within the body of Christ and enabled by the sacraments, are strangely muted in MacIntyre's neo-Thomism. Perhaps this is because it is approached from the perspective of moral philosophy rather than theology. Our love of God is more often stressed as the goal of the moral life, than God's unconditional love for us is presented as its presupposition. For all that the context of Aquinas' discussion of the virtues is emphasised for interpreting his natural law theory, not enough is said about the nature and presuppositions of *caritas* which reorients the moral life within a religious life enabled by the work of Christ and the action of the Holy Spirit. The setting of the Christian life as a response to God's prevenient love for us in Christ is, I suspect, unintentionally lost in passages such as the following.

Grace often corrects, as well as completes, what we have so far taken to be conclusions of reason, but, when grace does so correct us, it is always because we have in some way failed as reasoners.

But unless we can understand and obey the law adequately, we will be unable to recognize the truth concerning our own natures and to realize their potentiality for an exercise of rational freedom through which we can perfect our individual and communal lives.[76]

The Christian ethos of the moral life is not adequately captured in such remarks. The way in which moral activity within the Chritian life is determined by a range of conceptions including the divine command, obedience, grace, justification, the body of Christ, sanctification, and response to God's action *extra nos* seem somehow to be missing. These shape not only the moral perception of the Christian, but also the moral seriousness, commitment, and motivation which characterise a life of faith.

This Protestant query notwithstanding, MacIntyre's work is of major significance in reintroducing the discourse of the Christian faith to moral philosophy at the highest level. In this respect, he has achieved more than any theologian. The theological deficiencies of his work are more in the nature of lacunae than fatal flaws. We see as yet only the outline of a theological position. But, if MacIntyre can continue to advance and develop his argument, one of the benefits to theology will ironically be a more prominent place in public debate.

CHAPTER SIX

Communitarianism and its critics

COMMUNITARIAN THEMES

MacIntyre's philosophy has frequently been identified with the movement known as 'communitarianism'. It is often set in contradistinction to liberalism. This is hardly surprising given the assault on liberalism that one finds in his and others' writings. I shall argue, however, that despite the legitimacy of this attack on liberalism many of its characteristic themes need to be accommodated within theological ethics. While there may be no common theory shared by all citizens within a pluralist society, there may none the less be some common ground which needs to be articulated in the terms of rival theories.[1]

Communitarian approaches to ethics typically begin with criticisms of the project of liberalism which seeks to provide a moral basis for societies in the absence of any shared conception of the good. This basis is usually articulated in terms of the rights of individual citizens to various freedoms and to equality of treatment. The critics of liberalism argue that not only is the justification for such a moral basis elusive without some governing notion of the good, but also that this basis is too thin to sustain the polity of a pluralist society. Both the self and the social units to which it belongs require to be situated in the context of a thicker morality which expresses a substantive conception of human nature and those goods which are to be sought. These will tend to be social in so far as they cannot be achieved except in relationships of co-operation and friendship with other human beings. Having begun with a critique of liberalism, the communitarian programme seeks to promote human flourishing through the fostering of those forms of association without which we cannot achieve well-being. The importance of moral training within the home and the school is frequently emphasised. However, in the absence of any single overriding conception of the common good in modern pluralist societies, many communitarians are anxious to promote local groups and voluntary associations within a polity that promotes diversity.[2]

Although I shall argue that the differences between communitarians and liberals become blurred upon closer inspection, the main lines of debate have been drawn in the following terms. Liberalism asserts the right of each person to free and equal treatment. Since modern societies comprise citizens with divergent notions of the good life, the state should adopt a position of relative neutrality with respect to these. Its function is to maintain the equality and freedom of each citizen. In this respect, the right may be said to precede the good. The communitarian, by contrast, is more impressed by the essentially social nature of the human being. The self is formed by its roles, attachments, and relationships with other people, institutions, communities, and traditions. Conceptions of what is right and how society should be organised always presuppose some vision of the common good. In this respect, the good presupposes the right. Modern societies, although not united by any commonly agreed conception of the good, should none the less seek to promote those civic ties, communities, and institutions through which alone the self is formed and can find fulfilment.

The above delineation presents the contrasting emphases of communitarianism and liberalism. In many books and articles, these are presented as mutually exclusive alternatives. This creates an impression that to be communitarian is to be anti-liberal and that to be liberal one cannot recognise the importance of shared social goods. Charles Taylor, however, has argued that the terms liberalism and communitarianism are too unrefined to be of much use in contemporary debate.[3] As overworked portmanteau terms, they conceal two distinct but related problems. The first is what he calls the ontological problem of how the self is to be characterised. Here there is a debate between atomists and holists, a debate which has been raging for three centuries. The atomist will tend to explain social structures and conditions in terms of the properties of individuals; the holist will appeal to larger social units in terms of which individual identities are, at least in part, defined. A second issue is the advocacy issue of what policies one supports. Here there is a dispute between individualists and collectivists concerning the relative importance assigned to individual rights and freedoms on the one side, and communities on the other. 'At one extreme we would find people like Nozick and Friedman and other libertarians; at the other, Enver Hodja's Albania, or the Red Guards of the cultural revolution define the ultimate benchmarks.'[4] Although there are connections between these two issues, Taylor's distinction none the less provides a useful means of examining the rise of communitarianism in the 1980s and 90s.

Communitarianism is sometimes dated from the publication of a series of works by MacIntyre, Sandel, Walzer, and Taylor himself which appear to attack liberal atomism.[5] In this sense, it is concerned with the ontological question of the constitution of the self. According to Sandel, the self is already shaped by its social attachments and situation prior to any choices that it makes. These attachments inevitably determine subsequent choices. Thus, built into John Rawls' conception of the original position is a faulty doctrine of the unencumbered self. The self must be understood as a rational agent who transcends any particular choices or commitments. There is no possibility here of the self being constituted by its attachments. 'No role or commitment could define me so completely that I could not understand myself without it. No project could be so essential that turning away from it would call into question the person I am.'[6]

Taylor criticises atomistic accounts of the self for their failure to make sense of common goods that are more than a concatenation of individual ones. At a trivial level, my conversation with my neighbour about the weather is a way of our acknowledging that this is a matter that we share. It is something that we attend to together. Our conversation is a common action which is informed by linguistic conventions and phatic utterances.[7] It is a means of affirming that there are certain goods that are valued by us together rather than by each of us as individuals. In the republican ideal, citizens are committed to the laws of the state through a sense of shared or common values. This is not to be analysed in terms of enlightened self-interest, but in terms of the virtue of patriotism.

In the sociological work of Robert Bellah and his co-authors, the corrosive effects of individualism in American society are carefully explored. *Habits of the Heart*, in Toquevillean fashion, points towards the social disintegration and sense of *anomie* caused by the decline in traditional forms of community life and voluntary association. The stress on independence and self-reliance at the expense of civic concerns for shared goods impoverishes national discourse 'by the monotones of a strident and ultimately destructive individualism'.[8] A community which nurtures moral commitment and shared goods is defined in contradistinction to a life-style enclave. The community is a group of people who are socially interdependent, share certain practices, and whose lives are thereby shaped. By contrast, the enclave merely reflects a similar private life through common appearance, consumption, and leisure activities. The community generally owns a history which the enclave lacks.[9] The main thesis of *Habits of the Heart* regarding the deleterious erosion of forms of community life is restated by other social theorists and philosophers.

Robert Putnam has produced the striking example of the increase of the number of persons who now bowl alone. At a time (1980–93) when the total number of bowlers in America increased by 10 per cent, league bowling decreased by 40 per cent. This poignant image of 'bowling alone' is interpreted as signifying a decline in social capital, those 'features of social life – networks, norms, and trust – that enable participants to act together more effectively to pursue shared objectives'.[10] Whether or not the bowling example is empirically accurate, there seem to be wider indicators of this decline in communal activities. Membership of groups as diverse as the PTA, the Elks club, the Red Cross, trade unions and bowling leagues has been steadily declining by 25 per cent–50 per cent over the last thirty years. Of all the possible causes suggested for this decrease in civic activity, none is more significant or banal than that of TV watching which comes at the 'expense of nearly every social activity outside the home, especially social gatherings and informal conversations'.[11]

In the UK, a similar diagnosis has been advanced by the Chief Rabbi, Jonathan Sacks, though with greater emphasis upon the decline of social capital within family life. In his Reith Lectures, Sacks laments the decline of the family as an institution of moral formation. Marriage is a covenant in which the partners bind themselves in mutual loyalty and trust. It provides the basis for the upbringing of children to whom religious and social traditions are handed down. The family is thus crucial to our moral development and understanding. 'It lies behind our ideas of individual dignity and freedom, of social kinship and concern, and our sense of continuity between the future and the past.'[12] Elsewhere, he argues that the family is the best means we have discovered for the nurturing of successive generations. Its influence is deeper and more lasting than that of teachers, schools, politicians, or the media. There are three functions of the family that are vital to our subsequent progress as moral agents. We learn about welfare through the care of dependants; we discover education through the transmission of wisdom to the next generation; and we encounter what he calls 'ecology', a concern with and investment in the future of the world beyond our own lifetime. All this leads to a negative verdict on contemporary trends. The temporary attachments and random encounters which increasingly substitute for marriage are, he claims, disastrous for the nurture of children.[13]

Underpinning Sacks' description is the philosophical claim that a consumerist notion of the individual has now invaded discourse about personal relationships. The gratification of the individual's interests is the criterion by which marriage and the family are to be evaluated. In the absence of such gratification, divorce and desertion can be justified. The rhetoric of the market-place has now invaded the home, despite Adam Smith's attempt to distinguish these on moral grounds. The fundamental defect, therefore, in the moral chaos of our private lives, is a faulty understanding of what it is to be a person. The person is not an individual with interests to be satisfied. He or she is a person whose identity and fulfilment are inextricably bound up with relations and communities. Other people are constitutive of rather than instrumental to my identity and well-being as a person.

This pessimistic analysis of contemporary trends is supported by some medical and sociological evidence. Dennis and Erdos claim that, whenever the data make assessment possible, the lack of a father's commitment in each social class generally disadvantages a child.[14] They go on to point out that, even where there is an extended family which provides support, this reposes upon the practice of long-term marriage. Grannies and grandpas, uncles and aunts, are likewise dependent upon the same institution. 'When marriage is weakened, the whole network of kin is weakened, and the present generation of one-parent families, where they are fortunate enough to be able to depend on kinsfolk, are depending upon a wasting asset.'[15]

These sociologists offer a similar philosophical analysis to that of the Chief Rabbi. The threat comes from a rampant individualism which permits the egregious injustice of men fathering children for whom the state alone must make subsequent provision. A. H. Halsey, renowned for his work on ethical socialism, argues that this may ironically be perceived as an effect of Thatcherism, despite its incantation of traditional family values.

[B]y an irony of history, while Mrs Thatcher forbore to extend the ethic of individualism into domestic life, and tacitly accepted that the family was the one institution that properly continued to embrace the sacred as distinct from the contractual conception of kinship, those who denounced her doctrines of market-controlled egoism with the greatest vehemence were also those who most rigorously insisted on modernizing marriage and parenthood along her individualistic and contractual lines.[16]

LIBERAL REJOINDERS

It is possible to concede this analysis while also recognising that there are other relevant considerations which need to be taken into account. There is a danger of constructing the past as a golden age from which present standards have declined. Commentators have been swift to point to the oppressive conditions under which families and communities existed in the past. Evidence shows that couples were often locked into oppressive and loveless relationships through economic necessity or the threat of social disgrace.[17] Hang-ups about sex abound in English literature, and it is doubtful if the fear of detection, infection, or conception did very much for the cause of sexual fulfilment. The family, moreover, has been the locus for physical violence and sexual abuse, the latter only coming to light in recent times. Many commentators have noticed destructive forces at work within traditional family life, and have argued that there is no way back to the past. The economic unity of the family in pre-industrial times has now been destroyed. The members of a family have different employers, and go their own separate ways in terms of education and work, if they are fortunate to have such. MacIntyre has criticised Sacks for paying insufficient attention to the workplace in his argument for the regeneration of the family. Fufilment in the home is closely linked to fulfilment in the workplace. Where people are threatened with unemployment or meaningless work for low wages, the family will inevitably suffer as a consequence.[18]

Other critics of communitarianism have criticised its latent oppressiveness. In his sociological study, Derek Philips concludes that strong expressions of communitarian sentiment have historically been accompanied by dislike, contempt, and even hatred of outsiders. He cites the examples of the Puritan settlement in early Boston, the German home-towns of the seventeenth and eighteenth centuries, classical Athens, and Nazi Germany.[19] Others argue that the pluralist culture of our modern cities needs to be preserved to avoid the imposition of the standards of one community upon all others. The voluntary forms of association which characterise urban life are to be cherished in the interests of a politics of difference. It is the rich social differentiations of the city which facilitate new patterns of relationship and promote fresh cultural experiences.[20] These can only be maintained where no single overriding conception of the common good is imposed upon the entire community.

The impossibility of imposing upon a modern pluralist society any one local conception of the common good provides the impetus to recent defences of procedural ethics. One of the most significant is that found in the writings of Jürgen Habermas. Writing in a neo-Kantian vein, Habermas claims that the very nature of moral communication logically requires a commitment to certain procedures of speech and action. It is these and these alone which form the fabric of morality. Conceptions of the good can be debated ethically, but must be undergirded with procedural rules of justice which apply by virtue of the rational nature of moral agreement and disagreement. All communicative action depends upon the intersubjective recognition of validity claims.[21] When I make an assertion about a state of affairs to another speaker, it is assumed that I am making a sincere truth claim which can be supported by reasons. In an analogous way, a claim or command to act rightly depends upon the common observance of various norms. The social currency of any norm depends upon its acceptance as valid within the group to which it is addressed. Habermas thus offers the Kantian formulation that a 'moral principle is so conceived as to exclude as invalid any norm that could not meet with the qualified assent of all who are or might be affected by it'.[22] This establishes a principle of universalisation according to which all affected can accept the consequences for the satisfaction of everyone's interests of a general observance of a norm. Arising out of this logical condition of practical discourse are social requirements concerning impartiality, consensus, and compromise. Against the charge of promoting an empty formalism, Habermas responds that he has sought to provide a procedure for assessing those norms which arise from particular forms of life and which constitute the stuff of moral debate.[23] These procedures of justice, however, are more fundamental than notions of human goods whose discussion they regulate. It is impossible under the conditions of modernity to permit any substantive account of the good life to dominate moral discourse. With the collapse of sacred canopies, the world has become disenchanted. Pluralism is now an inescapable feature of modern societies. The moral perspective must continue to function as a means of impartial adjudication between competing claims. Each should put himself or herself in the place of the other in assessing the fairness of a proposed norm.

While this procedural ethic has some appeal in a modern pluralist polity, it suffers from serious defects which have been exposed from the MacIntyrian perspective outlined in the preceding chapter. There are two in particular. One is the difficulty of showing why the logical shape of moral discourse creates an obligation on each citizen to respect the principle of universalisability. Here the problem of the grounding of Kant's categorical imperative re-emerges. Does a commitment to the well-being of every citizen make sense except on the basis of substantive convictions about the worth of each individual life? Can this be replaced by considerations relating to mere rational consistency? This leads to a second and related problem of whether a substantive and thick notion of the human good must underlie the procedural rules of justice. The sense of importance that attaches to moral obligation does not seem to be captured by considerations about the logical form of moral judgments. What is good or valuable about these norms, or why they should command assent seems altogether to be missing on a purely procedural approach. Without some reference to those goods which are to be valued above all others, the significance of morality cannot be articulated. Charles Taylor points to a 'strange pragmatic contradiction' in which procedural ethics is caught.[24] In order to prevent parochial oppression in the name of one culture or tradition, the rules of justice are exalted over conceptions of the good life. This move is itself based upon ideals of freedom, altruism, and universalism, the 'hypergoods' of modern culture. Yet commitment to these very goods causes the procedural ethicist to deny that the rules of justice are based upon any substantive conception of what is good.

Some recent liberal theories have responded to this type of attack by arguing that the real issue at stake is not that of metaphysical individualism or rational consistency, but rather state neutrality. In a society which is composed of different moral communities and competing conceptions of the good life, the state must adopt a relatively detached position which permits citizens to make their own choices about which goods to adopt. Within such a society, some moral consensus is necessary. John Rawls has argued that his own theory of justice is best understood as outlining principles of justice and equality which can command consensus support in constitutional democracies. In this respect, his proposal is political rather than metaphysical. It remains open for anyone accepting his theory to argue that the self can only attain its good through social attachments and shared practices. Yet the variety of goods sought within modern cosmopolitan societies requires that citizens be granted the space within which they can pursue their chosen projects. Rawls' advocacy of principles of equality and distribution of wealth are an attempt to articulate what might be acceded to by different moral doctrines. In this respect, it is best viewed as a pragmatic consensual proposal rather than a metaphysical theory.[25] The neutrality of the state is, of course, relative in practice to some notional moral consensus that obtains within civil society. Rawls claims that a partially comprehensive consensus about values is sufficient to establish agreement about the priority of certain political values in a pluralist society. These political values will express 'the terms of fair cooperation consistent with mutual respect between citizens regarded as fair and equal'.[26]

Other liberal rejoinders to communitarianism have been willing to concede that the self cannot be understood apart from its social roles and attachments. Any fulfilled life is one in which the self is committed to goods that are essentially social in nature. According to Will Kymlicka, the point of liberalism is to enable the self to articulate and to choose which social goods it wishes to pursue. The self is not unencumbered, but it can and should make choices about whether it wishes to stick with the roles that have been assigned to it and the community in which it has been reared. 'We do indeed find ourselves in various roles and relationships, but we may not like what we find. The roles and relationships may be oppressive or demeaning, they "may be experienced as suffocating rather than embracing".'[27] The liberal ideal is not the evasion of all social roles but the protection of the space within which one can endorse, revise, or even reject the commitments with which one finds oneself. The importance of communities is not neglected here. In a sense it is affirmed. Moreover, in an effort to provide socially embedded persons with a worthwhile range of possible attachments, one can argue for proper welfare provisions and government subsidies for the arts, leisure, and sport.

Seyla Benhabib has provided a reading of Habermas' communicative ethics which recognises the legitimacy of communitarian criticisms. Over against the strong deontological thesis of Habermas' ethics, she sets a weaker interpretation by which his universalist and communicative model may be construed as a moral strategy for dealing with the plurality of conceptions of goodness we find in our societies. Assent to this model of ethics will doubtless rest upon varying substantive presuppositions. We should not conceal the discrete attachments and ends that constitute our moral selves, and which we bring to moral discourse. These will be the basis upon which we commit ourselves to procedures which are essential to the regulation of modern society. On the other hand, communicative ethics requires that we are willing reflectively to distance ourselves from our social roles. The communitarians are correct to recognise the ways in which traditions, communities, and practices shape our identities. Yet this should not preclude an ability to criticize, challenge, and question the content of these identities and the practices they prescribe. Without the facility of this reflective distance, which is a central liberal concern, communitarians 'are hard put to distinguish their emphasis upon constitutive communities from an endorsement of social conformism, authoritarianism, and, from the standpoint of women, of patriarchalism'.[28] The value of communicative ethics does not depend upon its ability to provide a single, integrated moral scheme. However, it may none the less maximise the participation in democratic processes of those who are committed to more specific and provincial ends. Its ability to make a participationist contribution to problems inherent in modernity is judged to be the abiding value of Habermas' ethical work.[29]

What we have here has been described as 'the communitarianization' of liberalism.[30] Trends in recent political thought indicate ways in which communitarian concerns are compatible with liberal themes of state neutrality and individual choice. When coupled with the residual liberalism of communitarianism which we noted earlier, we have a case for a possible convergence of what were taken to be mutually exclusive positions. There are, of course, other forms of liberalism which offer a more radical individualism, for example that found in the writings of Robert Nozick. The salient point, however, is simply that it is possible for liberal theorists to accommodate within their thinking assumptions about the significance of social attachments and shared goods.

Much feminist literature should be located within this context as mediating between forms of liberalism and communitarianism. It does not seek to deny the extent to which human beings are shaped by their social roles and attachments. Nor does it deny that it is within particular types of relationship that shared goods are to be pursued. What it does stress, however, is that many of the attachments and social models which we inherit need to be subject to closer inspection, criticism, and reform.[31] One finds here a preference for fostering those communities of voluntary association that are typically present in the modern urban environment. Patriotism, family values, and those communities of memory referred to in Bellah's *Habits of the Heart* are viewed with suspicion. Yet social networks which nurture and support those damaged by more traditional communities are to be affirmed and cultivated.[32]

The argument towards a convergence of liberal and communitarian themes can be reinforced by considering in more detail

certain advocacy issues. 'The Responsive Communitarian Platform: Rights and Responsibilities' was first drafted by Amitai
Etzioni and after amendment was issued in 1991.[33] It is the
charter of the new communitarian quarterly, *The Responsive
Community: Rights and Responsibilities*. The statement claims that
individual and social goods are correlative, and that individuals
cannot prosper except within a network of social environments.
Individual rights and social obligations similarly require correlation. There are no rights which do not produce corresponding
obligations upon some person or agency. The communitarian
perspective is against neither rights nor individuals. It does,
however, demand that greater political attention be accorded
'the social side of human nature; the responsibilities that must
be borne by citizens, individually and collectively, in a regime of
rights; the fragile ecology of families and their supporting
communities; the ripple effects and long-term consequences of
present decisions'.[34]

Etzioni and his colleagues are clearly sensitive to two criticisms levelled against communitarianism. Communitarianism
is not majoritarian. It does not suppress the identity and claims
of minority groups and cultures. The community must be
responsive to all its members, and not merely some majority
group. To do this it must develop moral values that are applied
equally to all members, and which are accessible and understandable to all. The expression of a need for a common
definition of justice upon which all citizens can draw has a
curiously Rawlsian ring to it.[35] Secondly, it is denied that
communitarianism is anti-liberal. It is only by defending the
social units which preserve individuals rights and liberties that
anarchy and the subsequent threat of coercive government are
avoided. The overemphasis upon the interests and rights of
individuals in political and moral discourse is threatening to
destroy the communal structures without which these cannot be
met. The current danger in western democracies is not totalitarianism but anarchy. If we are to avoid further social dissolu-
tion and fascist calls for strong-armed leadership, we must
devote greater attention to the communitarian agenda. Communitarianism is thus presented as an ally of liberalism against

state coercion. With respect to advocacy issues, it is again governed by key liberal tenets.[36]

The policy goals outlined in the communitarian platform include a reinforcing of the institution of the family as the primary moral community. This is to be achieved through a reform – possibly a tightening – of divorce laws, but also through a recognition that fathers need to be more deeply involved in the upbringing of their children. Educational institutions from kindergartens to universities are to be more concerned with character formation and moral education. To the question as to whose morals are to be taught in these institutions the following answer is given.

We ought to teach those values Americans share, for example, that the dignity of all persons ought to be respected, that tolerance is a virtue and discrimination abhorrent, that peaceful resolution of conflicts is superior to violence, that generally truth telling is morally superior to lying, that democratic government is morally superior to totalitarianism and authoritarianism, that one ought to give a day's work for a day's pay, that saving for one's own and one's country's future is better than squandering one's income and relying on others to attend to one's future needs.[37]

Further social goals include national service, enabling citizens to become better informed of public affairs, wider participation in voting and jury service, a reduction of the role of private money in public life, stronger legislation on public safety and health, and laws curbing gun ownership. One problem with all this is that most of us will probably warm to some of the programme but not to all of it. Gun control, the regulation of the funding of political parties, and public health measures might command broad support within some sectors of society. Many of us, however, might be less sure about the desirability of national service and the tightening of divorce laws. It is arguable, particularly in modern liberal societies, that people will select from the communitarian programme whatever appeals to them personally. Whatever convergence there is between liberals and communitarians at the philosophical level, debates will continue about the likely effects on human well-being of particular communitarian proposals. One could acknowledge this, however, while also recognising that the shift of attention to social goods and civic responsibilities is a welcome corrective in political debate.

Ironically, it is on account of this apparent convergence between liberalism and communitarianism that several writers have become wary of adopting the label 'communitarian'. Here some significant theological issues arise. MacIntyre, despite being frequently identified with it, has wasted no opportunity to distance himself from the communitarian movement. His fundamental objection is that the modern nation state cannot sustain the common good. By virtue of its presumed neutrality and its attempt to mediate between irreconcilables, the state lacks the moral commitment and resources to facilitate the common good.

> The modern nation-state, in whatever guise, is a dangerous and unmanageable institution, presenting itself on the one hand as a bureaucratic supplier of goods and services, which is always about to, but never actually does, give its clients value for money, and on the other as a repository of sacred values, which from time to time invite one to lay down one's life on its behalf . . . it is like being asked to die for the telephone company.[38]

To pretend that the nation state can deliver is to court fascism. On the other hand, to encourage a polity in which smaller voluntary associations can pursue their own goods is to lose any commitment to a common good. MacIntyre's endgame is a society in which the variety of goods that are sought are integrated into the life of the whole. These should then be celebrated in ceremonial fashion.[39]

While closely associated with the communitarian movement, Robert Bellah has expressed reservations about the value of merely reviving small-scale local communities.[40] The danger inherent in this strategy is that it leaves unchecked the wider structures of political and economic power. It is not sufficient to engage in rhetoric urging men to be faithful to their wives and to support their children. Nor is it enough to encourage people to leave their TV sets more often to form face-to-face groups within their local communities. The economic and political pressures on family life need to be addressed. We need to recognise that voluntary activity in the community is generally correlated with income, education, and occupation. Many local forms of associations are designed merely to enhance the quality of life of more affluent sectors of society. Yet many of the forces that undermine community life at every level derive from neo-capitalism. The pressures of a global market economy, for example, are producing a 'deracinated elite' which has seceded from society 'into guarded, gated residential enclaves and ultra-modern offices, research centers, and universities'.[41] In its wake, there is an increasingly anxious middle class concerned about its future job security and an impoverished underclass in inner-city areas that have been evacuated by the better-off. Only if these forces can be tempered by strong government intervention and the influence of other social factors can the deleterious effects of individualism be overcome.[42] Communitarianism, therefore, cannot be the panacea for our social ills if it remains at the level of individual moral exhortation and enthusiasm for small-scale forms of voluntary association.

Stanley Hauerwas likewise has similar difficulties with recent communitarianism. Where the church seeks to be a part of a moral consensus, it imperils the distinctiveness of its own witness. Where Christians assume that they inhabit common ground with other groups in a civil society, they risk compromise. Here one can detect several misgivings. Appeals to shared moral values which are a part of the communitarian platform mask genuine conflicts about which goods are to be sought and on what basis.[43] They do not provide us with the resources to deal with issues in medical ethics, warfare, and the distribution of wealth. Where the church is lured into becoming part of a pragmatic moral consensus it may already have disowned its inheritance. This is said not in the interest of withdrawal from secular life, but in the interests of making a more distinctive contribution. The church is called upon to expose the tribal prejudices and distortions of American culture. It can do so only by refraining from the easy option of collaborating in a comfortable consensus.[44] Calls for a religious contribution to the civic life of the nation are more likely to lead to the subordination of Christian imperatives to a violent nationalism.[45]

A further theological difficulty which can be identified in communitarian proposals concerns the reinvigoration of groups of people with a common moral purpose. It is not sufficient merely to point to the harmful social effects of a rampant individualism. Unless there are other options capable of sustaining and commanding the allegiance of communities, there is little alternative but to acquiesce in some of these individualist trends. The church will not be revitalised by the observation that civil religion has a socially cohesive role to exercise. Nor will its polity be maintained simply because it is morally efficacious in organising the lives of its adherents. Its reinvigoration is dependent upon persons becoming convinced that it points to 'the way, the truth and the life'. Without the presence of such convictions manifest in thought and action, there can be no maintaining or renewing of the church. In a similar connection, Taylor makes the point that Bellah's communitarianism elides distinct issues of social efficacy and meaning.[46] The loss of meaning in our culture is a discrete problem and one that is not solved by demonstrating the functional value of religion. For the church, this is a theological matter which cannot be solved by a nostalgic recollection of the historic role of religion in shaping our society. The sociological thesis of Bellah thus needs to be matched philosophically and theologically by something akin to MacIntyre's rehabilitation of Thomist Christianity.

This last point can be illustrated by further consideration of Rawls' advocacy of a partially comprehensive consensus about political values. He claims that this is sufficient to establish the primacy of political values concerning fairness, tolerance, and practical reasonableness. Yet the commitment that we have to these political values will tend to repose upon some conception of the human good. Their sustenance will tend to depend upon our ability to provide some description of the goals of human life from which a commitment to fairness etc. derives.[47] This reveals the need for some substantive conception of the good which can command our intellectual and practical allegiance. In the absence of some vision of the common good which mobilises persons, the commitment to the politics of fairness is

hard to sustain. There may be non-theological ways of articulating such a vision, but a religion which presents human life as
a gift held in trust, as having a purpose conferred upon it, and
as capable by grace of achieving a measure of goodness is likely
to have an important social role to exercise.

THE INCIPIENT LIBERALISM IN THEOLOGY

One might agree that the temptation to make an easy alliance
with liberal society is all too apparent. This is exposed in the
South African Kairos document's description of 'church theology' and its espousal of neutrality. 'Neutrality enables the status
quo of oppression (and therefore violence) to continue. It is a
way of giving tacit support to the oppressor, a support for brutal
violence.'[48] There are times when a position of neutrality
between competing ideological forces is inadmissible. One
should not underestimate the ease with which one can collude
with a liberal polity from a position of privilege. The security
one can find in academic pursuits may be more fragile and
questionable than is often realised. The words of John Courtney
Murray remain cautionary. 'It is a Christian theological intuition, confirmed by all of historical experience, that man lives
both his personal and his social life always more or less close to
the brink of barbarism, threatened not only by the disintegra-
tions of physical illness and by the disorganizations of mental
imbalance, but also by the decadence of moral corruption and
the political chaos of formlessness or the moral chaos of
tyranny.'[49]

Yet, currently, there are secular ideals which cannot be
gainsaid. Although the commitment to freedom, human
dignity, universal justice, and universal benevolence may often
be observed in the breach, these cannot be dismissed. They
have contributed to the spread of democracy and to greater
equality between sexes, races, and social classes. They have
helped to bring about the abolition of slavery, universal adult
suffrage, comprehensive education, and systems of social security. While we need to hear about the ways in which our
societies distort and manipulate these standards, and how we

are often myopic in our perception of their application, we cannot dismiss them merely as relative or as having ulterior motivation. As Taylor remarks in his impressive defence of these moral imperatives, 'it is too easy just to make the intellectual gesture of wiping this aside as a bit of prideful illusion'.[50] The need for an ecclesial recognition of secular norms is expressed in the following remarks of Eberhard Jüngel.

[T]he church may be thankful that its spiritual goods now exist in secular form. For example, the secular respect for freedom of conscience, the secular assertion of the inviolability of the dignity of the person, the secular commitment to protect handicapped human life, universal schooling and many other achievements of the modern constitutional state are secularised church treasures, and not least of the Protestant Church – treasures which were often recognised in their full significance only when they had been secularised.[51]

The stake that the church has in liberal societies can be shown by reference to the necessary distinction yet co-ordination of church and civil society. There are at least three arguments for maintaining both a differentiated yet positive relationship between the common good that is sought by the Christian community and those principles on which civil organisation is founded. Each of these recalls arguments that have been advanced in the history of theology to correlate the provinces of church and state. First, the church is a community to which one belongs not by social coercion but by one's free consent. This applies even where the practice of infant baptism is acknowledged. The baptised belong to the body of Christ, yet they are not held there against their wills. Their freedom may be constrained by the action of the Holy Spirit, yet it ought not to be restricted by any civil polity. There ought to be no compulsion either for or against belonging to the community of the church. This creates a theological obligation upon the state to recognise and maintain the space within which the individual can confess the Christian faith by belonging to the church. One can find historical support for this position. For Luther and Calvin, despite their differences, the church and the state are generally to be distinguished both by the scope of their jurisdiction and by the methods they employ to exercise their respective functions. Yet the church and the state are to be perceived in relation to one another as under the rule and serving the good purposes of God.[52] Oliver O'Donovan has written recently of the 'social space' required by the mission of the church. Secular authority is authorised by the Word of God to provide and ensure that space.[53]

Second, there is embedded within this distinction between church and state a theological recognition of the individual's entitlement to an area of moral and social freedom. The state should not coerce the dissident to membership of a particular religious polity, nor, by the same token, should it prevent the dissident from exercising choice. This stress upon the integrity of the individual can be seen in Old Testament injunctions to respect the stranger in one's midst. In the teaching and ministry of Jesus, the solitary individual is an object of God's grace. As such, she or he is worthy of respect irrespective of religious status or group affiliation.[54]

It might be countered that the purpose of God's grace in the ministry and parables of Jesus is to include the marginalised individual within a community. Similarly, there is to be a place accorded the stranger in the house of Israel. In this respect, these biblical themes cannot be construed as support for a political theory which establishes the rights of the individual as logically prior to the existence and well-being of a community. It is precisely against such false prioritising that communitarians inveigh. The individual must finally be understood in terms of his or her having an appointed place in the kingdom of God. The community under the rule of God is thus the goal of each individual life. The relationships in which it exists both to God and others are essential to its theological identity. This response raises a possible theological objection to liberal individualism and, indeed, also to any easy embrace of a radical pluralism. The concept of the kingdom of God situates each individual within a specific polity. In so far as this is a polity under the divine sovereignty, it is religiously particular. The rule of God, moreover, is closely linked in the New Testament to the lordship of Christ which will be universally acknowledged at the end of the world (Phil. 2:9–11; Rev. 5:13).

This rejoinder, however, provides a third argument for a theological accommodation of liberal ideals. The kingdom of God is ultimately an eschatological reality not to be confused with any penultimate political state. The church may bear witness to the kingdom through its own polity, but it is not to be identified with it. The church is a penultimate reality to be distinguished from the heavenly *polis* of Revelation 22. In the meantime, we must reckon with human weakness and failing within the world and the church. As Courteny Murray argues on the basis of the American experience, neither the privilege of theocratic power nor persecution are to be actively sought. The state must position itself between these two damaging options in relation to the church.[55] Attempts to bring about the common good are inevitably obstructed and corrupted by the particular interests of individuals and groups. In this situation, the state has the ameliorative role of protecting its citizens from abuses. Here again, there is a theological rationale for the protection of individuals against forces which infringe their legitimate freedom. The conclusions of a theological reflection upon the relationship between church and state may thus resonate with secular claims about the dignity of the person and the rights of each individual.[56]

The foregoing considerations do not imply that standard liberal theories can simply be annexed by Christian theology. We have here another instance of common ground without common theory. The assumptions on which ideals of individual freedom and equality are founded do not reflect, in this case, a commitment to any doctrine of the unencumbered self, or a procedural ethic such as that found in Habermas. They are instead essential elements of a theology which must distinguish yet correlate the provinces of the church and the state.[57] Their articulation may, none the less, differ in some respects from the description of freedom and equality of liberal individualism. For example, the importance of participation in the economic and social life of the community may be a more significant feature of the rights of each person for a philosophy or theology which stresses the importance of community for the moral formation and fulfilment of the self.[58] Thus a theological rationale for liberalism yields a conception of the civil state which is not wholly equivalent with classical liberal individualism. The degree of commensurability should not be overstated.

For the church to function as a community which bears witness to the kingdom of God within a wider civil polity, some doctrine of the state is necessary. The church demands from the civil community space within which to practice. In this respect, it seeks something like a social consensus concerning religious toleration and freedom. It requires tolerance not because religious convictions do not matter or are merely matters of private taste, but because the church seeks a polity which will respect the conditions under which it can worship and witness. While the church may survive impressively under oppressive regimes, this is none the less the condition that it seeks for its own well-being. Thus, even the Reformers – sometimes accused of theocratic tendencies – could argue that the state was ordained by God for the maintenance of peace and order within its geographical bounds but that its function and jurisdiction were distinct from that of the church. This provides a situation in which the church can support and affirm the value of the state and civil society, although this support is always critical and provisional. This attitude of critical support is doubtless perpetually in danger of lapsing into either assimilation or separatism. However, there is little alternative for Christians but to attempt to live accordingly. With the greater moral and religious diversity of our societies, the arguments for relative state neutrality apply *a fortiori*. For the time being at least, there must be compromise, consensus, and the kind of pragmatic moral bricolage that Jeffrey Stout describes. This may rightly make us uneasy, but the alternatives appear too bad to contemplate. The civil polities that most of us live under require both our criticism and qualified support.[59] Unless something better is on offer, anarchy is not an option. For all that he is accused of sectarianism, fideism, and imperialism Karl Barth still has something to say in this regard. In his coordination of church and state, he claims that neither an absolute heterogeneity nor an absolute equating of state and church is possible.

The only possibility that remains – and it suggests itself compellingly – is to regard the existence of the state as a parable, as a correspondence and an analogue to the Kingdom of God which the church preaches and believes in. Since the state forms the outer circle, within which the church, with the mystery of its faith and gospel, is the inner circle, since it shares a common center with the church, it is inevitable that, although its presuppositions and its tasks are its own and different, it is nevertheless capable of reflecting indirectly the truth and reality which constitute the Christian community.[60]

If we are tempted to discern here an outmoded and complacent European ideal of a Christian society, we should remember that this was written shortly after the time of the German church struggle. The state may not command our absolute allegiance, yet we do not have the right to withhold support from every civil government. Despite the impressive gains of MacIntyre's tradition-centred rationality, the criticisms of communitarian thinkers, and Hauerwas' suspicion of a sell-out, the church has a more positive stake in the articulation of a social consensus and the defence of state neutrality than is conceded. Some theological sense needs to be made of our social institutions prior to the eschaton, and those within the church who find themselves involved in communities other than the Christian one may need greater encouragement than that found in wholesale denunciations of liberalism.

CHAPTER SEVEN

Conclusion

The preceding discussion has attempted to review some of the leading disputes on the interface between theology and moral philosophy. It has been preoccupied with the role of community in moral formation and the defence of moral realism. These coexist in some tension. The stress on the formative role of community may suggest a commitment to relativism in which virtues are embedded in the particular practices, traditions, and forms of life espoused across time by one group of people. There is no possibility here of appeal to a standard which transcends the particularities of one moral tribe. Thus there is no independent criterion by which one may be judged more true or false than another. By contrast, moral realists, drawing on analogies from sense perception, typically present moral perception in terms as universal and constant as our knowledge of medium-sized physical objects. Moral knowledge, according to Kantians, utilitarians, and intuitionists, is available to any sincere and rational agent irrespective of context. Realism thus appears at odds with a communitarian emphasis upon the formative role of a specific moral society.

Arguments for moral realism tend to claim that the phenomena of moral (dis)agreement, argument, conversion, and evaluation together with the measure of moral consensus found in pluralist societies presuppose that notions of objectivity and truth ineluctably apply in ethical discourse. This ontological realism about moral truth can, however, be combined with an epistemology which stresses the significance of tradition, community, and practice for moral perception. Moral truth, although not created by a tradition, is knowable only in terms of the language, virtues, practices, and beliefs of a tradition. This position need not collapse into perspectivism where traditions are seen as mobile, partially commensurate, in conversation with one another, and capable of attaining a degree of consensus with other positions.

I have argued for a neo-Barthianism in which the Christian life has a distinctive ethos on account of its understanding of human action as determined by the prior, ongoing, and future action of the triune God. This establishes a strong notion of Christian distinctiveness and gives high priority to the *polis* of the church which bears witness by the Spirit in manifold ways to the action of God. At the same time, since distinctiveness is derived from God primarily and acknowledged by the church secondarily, there is an open possibility of human action outside the church also being determined by God. This meshes with philosophical arguments for moral realism and theological recognition of values shared in part with liberalism. It is a theological attempt to make sense of Walzer's notion that different thick moralities may share thin precepts, there being common moral ground in the absence of common moral theory.

It is, of course, possible for a tough-minded theologian to maintain this ontological realism with a more radical form of epistemological relativism, and thus to eschew the strategy of identifying common moral ground. In MacIntyrean terms, one might construe this position by claiming that the genealogist rather than the Aristotelian is the most appropriate philosophical partner for theology. This position strikes me as implausible for a range of reasons. It ignores the extent to which any moral community must be governed by some precepts concerning the telling of truth and the keeping of promises. More specifically, it cannot make much sense of the type of moral consensus that Stout identifies as platitudinous in liberal societies.[1] Furthermore, it ignores the typical claim of the Christian tradition that God does not abandon the creation to the consequences of its worst excesses but is present, active, and faithful to creatures beyond the domain of the church. Without some such claim, it becomes difficult to understand how or why common cause might be made with other forces, agencies, and communities. It is hard to see also how, if the arguments of the genealogists are accepted as valid, the terms used in Christian moral discourse can suddenly become exempt from deconstruction.[2]

In maintaining the criticisms levelled against post-Enlightenment moral philosophy, I have sought to defend the significance of the ecclesial community in theological ethics, yet without jettisoning realism. This works in several ways. The Kantian claim that there are moral principles perspicuous to all rational persons irrespective of particular ends, desires, or practices can be called into question in different respects. Are these principles not more likely to seem perspicuous to someone schooled in a particular tradition such as Lutheranism?[3] The stress upon the constitutive principle of respect for persons assumes substantive convictions about the sanctity of human life. These are difficult to make sense of except in theistic terms. The detachment of moral principles from all hypothetical imperatives is also problematic. Can an understanding of what is right be so firmly divorced from our understanding of what is good, of how human nature can be fulfilled, of the sorts of people we should become, and of the goals of human life? The formal and thin moralities which modernity has spawned can neither be made sense of nor command our allegiance in the absence of many of these background assumptions. Without attention to the thicker language of virtue, narrative, community, and tradition the categorical imperative lacks both form and content.

As a protest against the inherent difficulties of post-Enlightenment thought, the arguments of MacIntyre, Hauerwas *et al.* are well made. The setting of moral theory in historical context has brought much of the discussion into sharper relief, and has given a more adequate account of the actual processes by which moral formation takes place. Beyond this, their work has enabled Christian ethics to affirm the distinctiveness of ecclesial convictions about the purposes of life, human nature, society, and the centrality of the story of the life, passion, and resurrection of Christ. This recovery of distinctiveness meshes with claims found in Lindbeck's post-liberal model of religion which asserts the formative significance of biblical narratives in relation to communal speech, action, and experience. It is part of the attraction of this approach that it enables greater Christian authenticity in more secular and pluralist societies. The social witness of the church is here more closely tied to its worship, fellowship, and theology than in other paradigms.

Yet the commitment to realism remains central to most writers who emphasise the formative role of community. A central claim of Hauerwas is that it is not community in general which is morally significant, but the church in particular which bears witness to the being and action of God as these give a particular shape to Christian character. This view is held together, albeit in some tension, with claims that there is genuine moral perception outwith the church. The church, moreover, may have much to learn about its own distinctive themes from such extra-ecclesial insight. When coupled with MacIntyre's insistence upon the development of traditions in conversation and disagreement with one another, the position becomes more fluid. A measure of translation and commensurability is required for conversation to take place across traditions. In MacIntyre's more recent writings, this is supplemented by a commitment to a version of natural law theory. According to this, any moral pursuit requires the observance of some minimal rules requiring truthfulness and justice from all participants. Although this is insufficient for the moral foundations of a pluralist society, it none the less implies a universal commitment to the basic norms of practical reason.

In emphasising the possibilities of genuine moral perception outwith the church and conversation across moral traditions, I have sought to articulate the incipient liberalism in much of this literature. Values of tolerance, respect, equality, and freedom are part of the Christian moral tradition and can be given theological legitimation. There is a sense, therefore, in which the church has a stake in the maintenance of the pluralist societies to which liberals are so committed. Attention to the significance of relative state neutrality as the background to Enlightenment epistemological projects in moral theory should remind us of the importance of ensuring that disagreements are conducted with civility.[4]

There is an important theological task facing any attempt to square this incipient liberalism with an ecclesial ethic which claims that moral standards are embedded within particular convictions, narratives, and forms of life. In the past, concepts of natural law, the orders of creation, and common grace were employed by Catholic and Protestant theologians to explain the common moral ground between Christian and non-Christian. Moral perception and action, although clouded by sin and error, were possible outside the province of the church. A range of moral precepts, perhaps those contained in the Decalogue, were available to all rational persons who could thus be held accountable for their actions. These precepts provided a basis upon which the civil state could legitimately rule, where necessary through the exercise of force.

Yet the arguments that have been rehearsed against liberal projects to establish the validity of moral principles independently of any particular tradition will tend also to destroy the more substantive and free-standing formulations of natural law theory or the doctrine of the orders of creation. The way in which moral claims are situated within the context of theories of human nature, forms of life, and configurations of the virtues tells against ecclesial attempts to maintain a realm of moral life which is independent of substantive theological convictions.

One resolution of this problem is to provide a theological rationale for Michael Walzer's distinction between thick and thin moralities. According to this, each thick morality with its substantive claims also tends to yield a thin morality which it judges to be required of all rational persons irrespective of whether they are committed to this particular thick account. It is not possible to articulate the contents of this thin morality except in the most general of terms, yet we can find global examples of different thick moralities converging upon thin considerations. Walzer uses this distinction to explain why it is possible for persons of different moral outlooks to rejoice collectively over the destruction of the Iron Curtain in Eastern Europe or the abolition of apartheid in South Africa. The measure of moral agreement is limited but is none the less significant. Even allowing for elements of sentiment, detachment, and hypocrisy in our reaction to international events, one can discern some common moral elements in widespread international reaction to contemporary events. Walzer argues that, although every minimal morality is grounded and leads inevitably to a thicker and more local morality, we can designate its likely content.

There is no neutral (unexpressive) moral language. Still, we can pick out from among our values and commitments those that make it possible for us to march vicariously with the people in Prague. We can make a list of similar occasions (at home, too) and catalogue our responses and try to figure out what the occasions and the responses have in common. Perhaps the end product of this effort will be a set of standards to which all societies can be held – negative injunctions, most likely, rules against murder, deceit, torture, oppression, and tyranny.[5]

Walzer's distinction suggests a way in which there can be common moral ground without common moral theory. Each particular theory has its own account of why there is common ground and where it is to be located. What is needed in Christian theology, therefore, is a theological explanation of why there might be common ground in the absence of common theory. This explanation will itself be context-dependent. None the less, from within one tradition it will seek to account for a measure of moral agreement across traditions. While there may be no free-standing natural theology governed by presuppositions to which all rational inquirers can in principle give their assent, it remains possible to offer a theology of nature which explains why moral perception and agreement can be found across traditions, cultures, and communities.

Drawing upon the ethics of Barth, I suggested earlier that one might seek to provide theological explanation for moral discernment outside the circle of faith in terms of all three articles. The character of the world as created and redeemed by God in Jesus Christ, as the arena for the action of the Holy Spirit, and as moving towards an eschatological identity already revealed, provides a basis for explaining moral activity everywhere. What we have here is a critical standard – Jesus Christ as attested in Scripture – by which all such activity is measured. This may include a partial criticism of all ecclesial activity and selected affirmation of much non-ecclesial activity, yet without implying a moral theory which is independent of, and undetermined, by positive theological claims. A theology which emphasises the action of the triune God in creation, history, and the eschaton can seek to understand moral perception and practice critically yet positively. By appeal to how we are made, what God has done for us, and the destiny that awaits us we can measure extra-ecclesial activity by the standards of Christ. This might be viewed as a theological expression of the commitment to ontological realism and epistemological contextualism that was earlier outlined. By emphasising the universal significance of God's action in Christ from which the polity of the church derives, ecclesial isolationism may be avoided.

There are two broad issues which emerge from this discussion which must at least be registered. Although fuller discussion is impossible, several comments may be ventured. One unavoidable problem is the legitimacy of the language of human rights. In MacIntyre's philosophy, human rights discourse is too closely bound up with the inadequate claims of liberalism to be of much use as a common moral language in a pluralist society. It lacks grounding in any theory of the good, and is incapable of resolving significant moral disagreements. As it becomes increasingly debased, it functions as a means of asserting the interests of particular groups of individuals. The proliferation of rights language confirms this. A similar critique is made from a theological perspective by Joan Lockwood O'Donovan.[6] In patristic and medieval traditions, she argues, one finds the notion of right located in God's establishing of a natural and moral order. Deriving from this order are notions of the common good, political authority, justice, and obligations. By contrast, in the more recent tradition stemming from late-medieval nominalism, God establishes discrete rights which are possessed primarily by individuals and only derivatively by communities. With the gradual divorce of rights language from these theological roots, there emerged the notion

of the individual subject possessing rights over body and property, and with the right to exercise his or her freedom except
where there is clear justification for its curtailment. In contrac-
tualist theories of rights, as opposed to theories of natural rights,
the role of civil government is understood only in terms of
supplying those services and commodities for which contracting
citizens have taken on social obligations. Elsewhere the sovereignty of market forces is permitted. O'Donovan counsels
against any facile theological appropriation of this mode of
discourse through glib appeals to innate human dignity or
human life as created in the image of God. The modern
rhetoric of human rights is too closely thirled to a philosophy of
liberal individualism to be of much use to Christian theology.
We should have the courage to abandon it, and to attempt to
rehabilitate an older discourse about the divine order, the
covenant, the nature of community, the common good, and
principles of justice and charity apprehended through God's
law.

This criticism of rights language coheres with the earlier
criticism of liberalism, and yet it is not clear that the concept of
human rights is necessarily tethered to the assumptions of
liberal individualism. One might attempt to appropriate rights
language while stressing its limitations and the need to root it in
some substantial moral theory. There are good reasons for
doing this. The language of human rights is the only plausible
candidate for a global moral language. It is the fundamental
concept in the United Nations Declaration (1948); it is used by
international courts such as the European Court for Human
Rights; and it is increasingly a language employed in interfaith
dialogue. To abandon it because of its inadequacies is to make
the perfect the enemy of the good. The language of rights has
an important function in articulating a moral consensus against
some of the most flagrant abuses in our time. The work of
Amnesty International illustrates this. It uses a vocabulary of
human rights to advocate the cause of (non-violent) political
prisoners, to repudiate torture, and to oppose detention without
a fair trial. It draws support from a wide cross-section of
populations, many of whom would use different thick discourses

and many of whom would have difficulty articulating in any way the reason for their commitment to the principles of Amnesty.[7] If it is possible to recognise common moral ground in the absence of common moral theory, it ought to be possible for Christian theology to appropriate for specific tasks the language of human rights.

A commitment to human rights can be articulated in terms of the minimum conditions necessary for membership of a moral community. Here one can derive a notion of rights that are owed to persons on the basis of a substantive notion of the common good. If the goods required by persons are irreducibly social, human well-being requires as its necessary condition full participation in a community. Rights language can specify some of the general demands of social justice in this context.[8] The minima for full membership of a community in which one's personal good is realised include the right not to be tortured or murdered, the right to a fair trial, to freedom of speech, to a share in the material prosperity of one's society, and partici- pation in its economic life. These rights, derived from the notion of membership of a community, include both negative immunities and positive empowerments. Despite MacIntyre's hostility to rights discourse, this construal is consonant with his recent description of what is involved in natural law theory. The natural law concerns those fundamental rules which must govern any genuine moral community. Only therein can human well-being be achieved. The notion of 'rights' might be utilised in this context to specify what it is that citizens owe to one another by virtue of belonging to the same community. This, however, does not signal a return to a free-standing natural law theory since its assumptions are based upon convictions about the nature and ends of the human person in relation to social goods.

A second issue which lurks behind the discussion of much of this book concerns the relationship of church to civil society. Recent ecclesial ethics is in danger of silencing the voice of the church in public debate. This is one of its paradoxes given its insistence on the church speaking with a distinctive voice. If Christian action only makes sense on the basis of commitment to a particular community with its shared practices and narratives, it is hard to see on what basis any moral appeal can be made to those who choose not to belong to that community. The church's social teaching here makes sense only where the members of a society are collectively committed to the establishment of one religion. Prior to such commitment, social witness is meaningless except in the forms of proclamation and evangelism. These, of course, are central tasks of the church, but is there not also a further calling to contribute to public debate in such a way as to influence its outcomes even where there is no collective conversion to the Christian faith? Is there not a prophetic witness which presupposes the ability of those outwith the faith to hear and to be influenced by the voice of the church?[9] The making of common cause on a range of issues works on the assumption that there is a more widespread moral recognition which can be confirmed and supported.

Where society requires the practice of civic virtue on the part of its members, it remains likely that religion will continue to play a role in the formation of citizens and the meaning of such civic virtue. Here it is beset by the dangers of capitulation to nationalist sentiment or domestication by political strategies. For these reasons, as well as to prevent exclusion of those belonging to other or no faiths, too close an alignment of church and civil society needs to be avoided. On the other hand, the total abandonment of the historic roles of shaping, promoting, and advocating the common good within society is unlikely to be of benefit to either the church or the civil community. The former will fail in the task of serving the world, not least through failing to equip and inspire its members to lead decent lives within the secular world. The latter will be denuded of the social capital that arises from a religious community which is concerned with the well-being of its host society and advocates its moral improvement.

There is clearly an uneasy and ambivalent relationship between church and state both in contemporary Britain and the USA. Although the interpretation of the First Amendment is often judged to have created a rigid wall of separation between church and state, the matter is both historically and practically more complex. The original intention behind the First Amendment was not so much a divorce of religion from the organisation of the civil state, as a refusal to allow any single confession an established status. Appealing to freedom of conscience, Madison insisted that the State should not in any way seek to coerce or influence the religious affiliation of its citizens. Yet Christianity remained the majority religion and consequently shaped the civic culture of the nation. As Thiemann points out, 'while Madison and others address the question of the *legal* establishment of Christianity, they neglected to ponder fully the consequence of Christianity's *cultural* establishment as the majority religion of the republic'.[10] Accordingly, there are significant signs of a Christian dimension to civic life. The Declaration of Independence uses theistic (perhaps deistic) language; cents, nickels, dimes, quarters, and dollar bills assert that it is 'in God we trust'; chaplains are appointed to Congress; presidents make annual thanksgiving proclamations. Meanwhile, the political rhetoric of American culture has in times of crisis regularly employed the symbolism of divine providence. What we have is a curiously ambivalent scenario in which the constitution prevents any formal mixing of religion and civil law, while fragments of popular religious culture maintain the historical role that Christian belief and practice have in shaping the American identity. These tensions have increased with the expanding pluralism of American society and concerted attempts in schools and elsewhere to eliminate any sense of the Christian religion as culturally normative. In light of this deep ambivalence, Taylor suggests that it is difficult to envisage either total separation or much greater integration in the foreseeable future.

[I]n a political system founded on common values, which had moreover their earlier canonical expression in religious terms, it is very hard just to take the road of privatization and declare religion altogether outside the public domain. If it should come to a Kulturkampf, it is clear that neither side could win. Nor would either side unequivocally deserve to.[11]

In Britain, the historical situation is strikingly different yet it yields a contemporary situation that is at least as ambivalent.

Britain has established churches north and south of the Scottish border. These are Presbyterian and Episcopalian respectively. Although they are established in different ways – a point sometimes missed by English political commentators – they function as national churches in terms of their territorial ministries, mission, and witness. On the other hand, there are probably more Roman Catholics, than Anglicans and Scottish Presbyterians combined, worshipping on any one Sunday in the UK. Declining levels of commitment to the established churches, coupled with the rise in the number of adherents to other religions (most notably Islam) deepens the complexity of this situation. There is increasing pluralism, yet a strong Christian input to most civic ceremonial events. The comments of bishops and other church leaders are reported by the media often with approval. Arguments for universal health care and the conserving of the NHS may be based on particular theological assumptions, but these are likely to resonate with the fragments and theories of other moral perspectives.[12] Services of worship not only mark royal weddings[13] and other celebrations, but also provide the focal point for national mourning following the tragedies at Hillsborough, Lockerbie, and Dunblane, and the death of the Princess of Wales.[14] To fan the embers of a dying Christian culture may seem a poor strategy for ecclesial revitalisation in the coming century. Yet the foreseeable future seems to offer our churches an enigmatic social situation which is neither establishment nor marginalisation, and which is beset with promise and danger in almost equal measure.

The strangeness of this scenario is consonant with the argument of this book which has sought to defend many of the criticisms and insights of theological communitarianism, while yet maintaining a commitment to a residual liberalism. The practical orientation that this prescribes is one whereby the church should seek to maintain its homogeneity as a moral community while acknowledging its stake in the peaceful maintenance of a pluralist society. It should expect to meet both the hostility and hospitality of alternative moral arguments since it offers a distinctive vision but one which is not lacking in connection with other convictions and aspirations. If there is a fitting epigram with which to conclude, it is an early comment of Karl Barth that the Christian task is 'to uphold God's cause in the world and yet not wage war on it'.[15]

Notes

I INTRODUCTION

1 Cf. Steve Bruce, *Religion in the Modern World: Cathedrals to Cults* (Oxford University Press, 1996).
2 Alexis de Tocqueville, *Democracy in America* (New York: Random House, 1985), Book 2, chapter 5, 407–8.
3 Robert Bellah, Richard Madsen, William M. Sullivan, Ann Swidler, and Steven M. Tipton, *Habits of the Heart* (Berkeley: University of California Press, 1985), 282.
4 *After Virtue* (London: Duckworth, 1981), 259.
5 This is a common theme in recent sociological studies of religion. For example, Steve Bruce summarises his argument in the following way. '[E]clecticism is the characteristic form of religion in the late modern period. It may not yet be the most common, but it represents in religious culture the dominant ethos of late capitalism: the world of options, lifestyles, and preferences.' *Religion in the Modern World*, 233.
6 Cf. James McClendon's study of the role of Martin Luther King and others in the shaping of our moral consciousness, *Biography as Theology* (Nashville: Abingdon Press, 1974).
7 'Community is one of those buzz words (like "meaning" or "relevance") that we should be wary of using. Study after study suggests that people in our society are searching for community. The need for "belonging" has come to be identified as one of the primary functions that religious institutions can fulfil. Members of the clergy preach sermon upon sermon, admonishing believers to find community within the church. But what does it all mean? Where will it lead in the years ahead?' Robert Wuthnow, *Christianity in the 21st Century* (Oxford University Press, 1993), 6.
8 This is explored most effectively by Arne Rasmusson, *The Church as Polis: From Political Theology to Theological Politics as Exemplified by*

Jürgen Moltmann and Stanley Hauerwas (University of Notre Dame Press, 1996).

9 'The Everlasting Gospel', from *The Complete Writings of William Blake*, Geoffrey Keynes (ed.) (London: Nonesuch Press, 1957), 758.

10 E.g. *The First Urban Christians* (New Haven: Yale University Press, 1983); *The Moral World of the First Christians* (London: SPCK, 1986); *The Origins of Christian Morality* (New Haven: Yale University Press, 1993).

11 Meeks, *The Moral World of the First Christians*, 114.

12 This is explored in detail by Gerd Theissen, *The Social Setting of Pauline Christianity* (Philadelphia: Fortress Press, 1982), 145–74.

13 'The Didache' 9.4, *The Apostolic Fathers*, J. B. Lightfoot & J. R. Harmer, (eds.), second edition, (Grand Rapids, Baker Book House, 1992), 261. Cited by Meeks, *The Origins of Christian Morality*, 97.

14 *The Moral World of the First Christians*, 96.

15 *The Moral Vision of the New Testament: A Contemporary Introduction to New Testament Ethics* (San Francisco: HarperCollins, 1996), 308.

16 Cf. Meeks, *The Origins of Christian Morality*, 104.

17 Ibid., 108.

18 *The Origins of Christian Morality*, 68.

19 Cf. Robert Grant, 'The Christian Population of the Roman Empire', *Early Christianity and Society* (San Francisco: Harper and Row, 1978), 1–12.

20 I am following here a line of argument set out by Henry Chadwick, *The Originality of Early Christian Ethics* (Oxford: Somerville College, 1990). I am also indebted to the short case studies presented in George Forrell's *History of Christian Ethics*, vol 1, (Minneapolis: Augsburg, 1979).

21 Homily XXII on Ephesians, citation from *Nicene and Post Nicene Fathers*, ed. P. Schaff (Edinburgh: T. & T. Clark, 1988), First Series, vol. 13, 159. 'A number of passages show the same awareness as we find in Augustine, that a slave in a reasonable household was far better housed, clothed and fed than a free wage labourer whose plight might be desperate', Chadwick, ibid., 4.

22 'Meeks correctly observes that the commands of others are those most frequently quoted by the Apologists. But are we to believe that these surfaced only gradually during the first Christian century? Do they tell us nothing about the "origins of Christian morality"?' A. E. Harvey, 'Review of Meeks', *The Origins of Christian Morality*, *Journal of Theological Studies*, 46 (1995), 301.

23 Brevard Childs, *Biblical Theology of the Old and New Testaments* (London: SCM, 1992), 667.

24 This tension between 'normal moral virtues' and the 'judgment of absolute demands' is seen as the setting for New Testament ethics by W. D. Davies, 'The Relevance of the Moral Teaching of the Early Church', in *Neotestamentica et Semitica*, E. E. Ellis and M. Wilcox (eds.) (Edinburgh: T. & T. Clark, 1969), 30–49. For a discussion of Davies' approach see J. I. H. McDonald, *Biblical Interpretation and Christian Ethics* (Cambridge University Press, 1993), 144ff.

25 *The Body in Society* (New York: Columbia University Press, 1988), 44.

26 Cf. W. D. Davies, 'The Relevance of the Moral Teaching of the Early Church', 44–5. The way in which the church both supported and criticised the secular state is explored by Oscar Cullmann in *The State in the New Testament* (New York: Charles Scribner's Sons, 1956).

27 Cf. The discussion of appeals to natural law in Eric Osborn, *Ethical Patterns in Early Christian Thought* (Cambridge University Press, 1976).

28 E.g. W. D. Davies, 'The Relevance of the Moral Teaching of the Early Church', 36.

29 Justin Martyr, *First Apology*, chapter 7. Cf. *Morality and Ethics in Early Christianity*, Jan L. Womer (ed.) (Philadelphia: Fortress Press, 1987). For further discussion see John Mahoney, *The Making of Moral Theology* (Oxford, Clarendon Press, 1987), chapter 3.

30 Rowan Greer, *Broken Lights and Mended Lives: Theology and Common Life in the Early Church* (University Park: Pennsylvania State University Press, 1986), 141ff. In what follows I am indebted to Greer.

31 'Epistle to Diognetus', chapter 5. Citation from *Ante-Nicene Fathers*, Philip Schaff (ed.) (Grand Rapids: Eerdmans, 1981), vol. 1, 26–7.

32 Greer, *Broken Lights and Mended Lives*, 156. See also the account of the relationship between church and state in Augustine in R. A. Markus, *Sacred and Secular* (Aldershot: Variorum, 1994), chapter 4, 'Refusing to Bless the State: Prophetic Church and Secular State', 372–9.

33 *City of God*, Book XIX, 13. Citation from Marcus Dods' translation (New York: Random House, 1950), 691.

34 E.g. 'The Morals of the Catholic Church', chapters 15ff., in *Basic Writings of Augustine*, Whitney J. Oates (ed.) (New York: Random House, 1948), vol. 1, 331ff.

35 E.g. 'The Morals of the Catholic Church', chapter 30, ibid., 348.

36 *City of God*, Book XIX, 17, 696.

37 Cf. John Barclay, *Jews in the Mediterranean Diaspora from Alexander to Trajan (323 BCE – 117 CE)* (Edinburgh: T. & T. Clark, 1996).

2 CHRISTIAN ETHICAL DISTINCTIVENESS

1 Karl Barth, *Ethics* (New York: Seabury Press, 1981), ed. Dietrich Braun, trans. Geoffrey Bromiley.

2 *Church Dogmatics* II/2 (Edinburgh: T. & T. Clark, 1957), 510.

3 Barth, *Ethics*, 13.

4 *Church Dogmatics* II/2, 632f.

5 In his recent study of the fragmentary materials of *Church Dogmatics* IV/4, John Webster examines the ways in which human ethical action can be viewed as corresponding to God's prior action. This notion of correspondence is devoid of any trace of repetition or substitution. *Barth's Ethics of Reconciliation* (Cambridge University Press, 1995), esp. chapter 3.

6 *The Christian Life* (Edinburgh: T. & T. Clark, 1981), 265.

7 This criticism is developed by Robert Willis, *The Ethics of Karl Barth* (Leiden: E. J. Brill, 1971), 170ff.

8 This handling of the ethical norms found in Scripture is already present in Barth's *The Epistle to the Romans* (London: Oxford University Press, 1933), 461. For discussion of this section see Bruce McCormack, *Karl Barth's Critically Realistic Dialectical Theology* (Oxford University Press, 1995), 274–80.

9 George Hunsinger has described 'actualism' as one of the dominant motifs of Barth's theology. 'Barth's theology of active relations is therefore a theology which stresses the sovereignty of grace, the incapacity of the creature, and the miraculous history whereby grace grants what the creature lacks for the sake of love and freedom,' *How to Read Karl Barth* (Oxford University Press, 1991), 30ff.

10 *Church Dogmatics* II/2, 678.

11 William Werpehowski has argued against critics of Barth that his ethics can avoid criticisms of 'intuitionism' and 'occasionalism' by stressing the way in which agents take their place in a history of relationship with God. 'Command and History in the Ethics of Karl Barth', *Journal of Religious Ethics*, 9 (1981), 298–320.

12 *Church Dogmatics* III/4, 7ff. Nigel Biggar argues that this is a misconception of casuistry and shows how Barth's own method of ethical deliberation contains many features of casuistry properly understood. *The Hastening that Waits* (Oxford: Clarendon, Press, 1993), esp. 40ff.

13 *Church Dogmatics* II/2, 585ff.

14 Ibid., 709.

15 Ibid., 527.

16 Ibid., 530f.

17 *Barth's Ethics of Reconciliation*, 100.
18 This aspect of Barth's ethics is analysed by William Werpehowski in 'Narrative and Ethics in Barth', *Theology Today*, 43 (1986/7), 334–53. For the criticism that Barth's treatment of character suffers because of his preoccupation with command and decision, see Stanley Hauerwas, *Character and the Christian Life* (San Antonio, Trinity University Press, 1975), 176. 'By describing the Christian life primarily in terms of command and decision, Barth cannot fully account for the kind of growth and deepening that he thinks is essential to the Christian's existence.'
19 *Church Dogmatics* II/2, 524ff. Cf. the similar treatment of this theme in *Ethics*, 27ff.
20 E.g. *Church Dogmatics* II/2, 522.
21 *Church Dogmatics* IV/3, 493ff. This is explored in greater depth by Nigel Biggar, *The Hastening that Waits*, 146ff.
22 E.g. *Christian Life*, 20ff.
23 *Church Dogmatics* IV/3, 38–165.
24 *Church Dogmatics* II/2, 569.
25 Ibid., 542.
26 *Church Dogmatics* III/1, 43. The relationship between creation and covenant in Barth is discussed by Webster, *Barth's Ethics of Reconciliation*, 59ff.
27 *Ethics*, 215.
28 Cf. the preface to *Ethics*.
29 For a discussion of Luther's understanding of the orders see Paul Althaus, *The Ethics of Martin Luther* (Philadelphia: Fortress, 1972), 36–42.
30 For a recent defence of this Lutheran doctrine see Carl Braaten, 'God in Public Life: Rehabilitating the "Orders of Creation"', *First Things*, 8 (1990), 32–8.
31 Barth's discussion of the relationship between law and gospel can be found in 'Gospel and Law', *Community, State and Church* (New York: Anchor Books, 1960), 71–100. For an acute analysis of Barth *vis-à-vis* Lutheranism see Eberhard Jüngel, 'Gospel and Law: The Relationship of Dogmatics to Ethics', *Karl Barth, A Theological Legacy* (Edinburgh: T. & T. Clark, 1986), 104–26.
32 *Church Dogmatics* III/4, 19ff. Barth's criticism of Brunner and Bonhoeffer is explored by Robin Lovin, *Christian Faith and Public Choices* (Philadelphia: Fortress Press, 1984), esp. 37ff.
33 *Church Dogmatics* III/4, 23.
34 Ibid., 30.
35 *Church Dogmatics* III/2, 208ff.
36 Ibid., 277.

37 E.g. Nico Horn, 'From Barmen to Balhar and Kairos', in Charles Villa-Vicencio (ed.), *On Reading Karl Barth in South Africa* (Grand Rapids: Eerdmans, 1988), 105–20.

38 George Hunsinger, 'Barth, Barmen and the Confessing Church Today', in *Barth, Barmen and the Confessing Church Today*, James Y. Holloway (ed.) (Lampeter, Edwin Mellen Press, 1995), 36. This publication also contains the German original and English translation of the Barmen Declaration. It is one of the strengths of Barmen that it is capable of providing a point of theological reference in very different social contexts. For an impressive British example of the counter-cultural force of Barthian theology see Michael Banner, *Turning the World Upside Down (and Some other Tasks for Dogmatic Christian Ethics)*, Inaugural lecture, King's College, London, 1996.

39 Hunsinger, 'Barth, Barmen and the Confessing Church Today', 292.

40 For a useful overview of post-liberalism see William Placher, 'Post-liberalism' in *The Modern Theologians*, David Ford (ed.) (Oxford: Blackwell, 1997), 343–56, and his more extensive *Unapologetic Theology* (Louisville, Westminster/John Knox, 1989).

41 *The Nature of Doctrine* (London: SPCK, 1984), 18.

42 His reflections on ten years of debate can be found in the new foreword to the German translation of his work, *Christliche Lehre als Grammatik des Glaubens* (Gütersloh: Chr. Kaiser, 1994), 16–22. This translation also contains a useful bibliography of Lindbeck's published work.

43 'Epilogue: George Lindbeck and *The Nature of Doctrine*', *Theology and Dialogue: Essays in Conversation with George Lindbeck*, Bruce D. Marshall (ed.) (Indiana, University of Notre Dame Press, 1990), 276.

44 Lindbeck notes the way in which the cultural–linguistic theory can be judged 'methodologically atheistic'. *The Nature of Doctrine*, 20. This is reiterated in the new foreword to the German translation.

45 'Lindbeck's New Program for Theology: A Reflection', *Thomist*, 49 (1985), 465.

46 *The Nature of Doctrine*, 121. Cf. Hans Frei, 'Theological Reflections on the Accounts of Jesus' Death and Resurrection', *Theology and Narrative: Selected Essays* (Oxford University Press, 1993), 45–93.

47 Lindbeck, *The Nature of Doctrine*, 132. Lindbeck's theological intentions are reflected in a range of essays prior to *The Nature of Doctrine*. E.g. 'The Sectarian Future of the Church', *The God Experience*, J. P. Whelan (ed.) (New York: Newman, 1971), 226–43.

48 *The Nature of Doctrine*, 64.

49 For an earlier version of this criticism see my 'Meaning, Truth and Realism in Bultmann and Lindbeck', *Religious Studies*, 26 (1990), 183–98.
50 *The Nature of Doctrine*, 65.
51 Ibid., 67.
52 'The Story-Shaped Church: Critical Exegesis and Theological Interpretation', in *Scriptural Authority and Narrative Interpretation*, Garret Green (ed.) (Philadelphia: Fortress Press, 1987), 164.
53 Cf. *The Nature of Doctrine*, chapter 3; '*Fides ex Auditu* and the Salvation of Non-Christians: Contemporary Catholic and Protestant Positions', *The Gospel and the Ambiguity of the Church*, Vilmos Vajta (ed.) (Philadelphia: Fortress Press, 1974), 92–123.
54 Bruce Marshall, 'Aquinas as Post-liberal Theologian', *Thomist*, 53 (1989), 353–402; George Lindbeck, 'Response to Bruce Marshall', ibid., 403–6. For a further discussion which contrasts Barth's understanding of the priority of divine action in constituting theological truth with Lindbeck's account see George Hunsinger, 'Truth as Self-Involving: Barth and Lindbeck on the Cognitive and Performative Aspects of Truth in Theological Discourse', *Journal of the American Academy of Religion*, 61 (1993), 41–55.
55 George Lindbeck, 'Response to Bruce Marshall', 403.
56 *The Nature of Doctrine*, 94.
57 Cf. the comment of Geoffrey Wainwright that, 'A subsistent trinitarian relation is being declared by Nicea and by Athanasius. It is with this substantive content that the conciliar declaration is intended to give guidance to Christian language concerning God and Jesus Christ', 'Ecumenical Dimensions of Lindbeck's *Nature of Doctrine*', *Modern Theology*, 4 (1987/8), 126.
58 *The Nature of Doctrine*, 106. This analogy itself is misleading. It fails to recognise that almost all scientists engaged in such disputes assume that they are thereby contesting 'the ways things really are'. At this point, one suspects again that the secular influences behind the cultural–linguistic theory of religion carry a bias towards a regulative account of theological truth.
59 Frei himself expresses some anxieties about the rule theory of doctrine. 'Epilogue: George Lindbeck and *The Nature of Doctrine*', 279. His own understanding of doctrine seems to be expressed in the following exposition of Barth. '[J]ustification by faith is a doctrine that functions as a rule in, let us say, orthodox Christian discourse. Not only does it function as a rule but it looks as though it were asserting something about how God deals with human beings, and to that extent it is a statement that holds true regardless of the attitude of the person or persons articulating it',

Types of Modern Theology (New Haven: Yale University Press, 1992), 42.

60 *Revelation and Theology* (Indiana: University of Notre Dame Press, 1985), 150–1. Thiemann criticises Lindbeck for devoting insufficient attention, *contra* Barth, to the way in which intratextuality derives its force only from particular assumptions about revelation. 'Response to George Lindbeck', *Theology Today*, 43 (1986/7), 377–82.

61 Mark Corner, 'Review of *The Nature of Doctrine*', *Modern Theology*, 3 (1986), 112.

62 'Lindbeck's New Program for Theology', 470.

63 This point is developed skilfully by David Kelsey, 'Church Discourse and Public Realm', in *Theology and Dialogue: Essays in Conversation with George Lindbeck*, Bruce D. Marshall (ed.), 7–34.

64 *The Nature of Doctrine*, 82.

65 'Absorbing the World: Christianity and the Universe of Truths', *Theology and Dialogue: Essays in Conversation with George Lindbeck*, ibid., 85. Ingolf Dalferth perceives a similar theological rationality in Barth. 'Karl Barth's Eschatological Realism', *Studies in Karl Barth: Centenary Essays*, S. W. Sykes (ed.) (Cambridge University Press, 1989), 14–45.

66 *The Nature of Doctrine*, 131. Lindbeck makes explicit appeal to the procedure defended by Basil Mitchell in *The Justification of Religious Belief* (London: Macmillan, 1973). This also explains why, for Lindbeck, the Christian theologian may properly belong both to church and academy though his or her place in the former remains prior. This is noted by Hans Frei, 'Both vocations are best served when theology is seen to be in service to the church first, to the academy second. Academic theology is that second-order reflection which is an appropriate, albeit very modest instrument in aid of the critical description and self-description of specific, religious–cultural communities, in our case the Christian church', 'Epilogue: George Lindbeck and *The Nature of Doctrine*', in *Theology and Dialogue: Essays in Conversation with George Lindbeck*, 278.

67 *The Nature of Doctrine*, 131–2.

68 Ibid., 128.

69 Originally coined by Gilbert Ryle, the term 'thick description' is used by Clifford Geertz for the interpretation and explanation of social life. 'Towards an Interpretive Theory of Culture', *The Interpretation of Culture* (New York: Basic Books, 1973), 3–32.

70 This may explain the enthusiastic reception of various Protestant commentators. E.g. Robin Gill, Review in *Church Times* (12

November 93); Oliver O'Donovan, 'A Summons to Reality', in *Understanding Veritatis Splendor*, John Wilkins (ed.) (London: SPCK, 1994), 41–5; Stanley Hauerwas, *Commonweal* (22 October 93), 16–18.

71 *Church Dogmatics* II/2, 613ff.

72 *Veritatis Splendor*, 10.

73 *Catechism of the Catholic Church* (Washington DC: United States Catholic Conference, 1994). Bernard Häring has remarked, 'The renewal of moral theology is also evident in the decision to treat sacramental life before the treatise on moral theology. I would remind the reader that most of the manuals of moral theology after the Council of Trent treated the sacraments after the commandments as a means to, and providing strength for, heeding all the commandments and laws of the Church. In the new *Catechism* there appears of the joy of faith and of celebration of the Christian mystery', 'More than Law and Precept: Commandments 1 to 3', in *Commentary on the Catechism of the Catholic Church*, Michael J Walsh (ed.) (London, Geoffrey Chapman, 1994), 357.

74 *Veritatis Splendor*, 19.

75 Ibid., 28.

76 Ibid., 58.

77 Ibid., 44.

78 Ibid., 64. This rather solitary reference to the significance of the virtues is seen as a weakness of the encyclical and a sign of its captivity by the language of law. Cf. Herbert McCabe, 'Manuals and Rule Books', *Understanding Veritatis Splendor*, John Wilkins (ed.), 67–8.

79 *Veritatis Splendor*, 41.

80 Ibid., 89.

81 E.g. the essays by Bernhard Häring, Richard McCormick, and Nicholas Lash in *Understanding Veritatis Splendor*.

82 E.g. Walter Moberly, 'The Use of Scripture', *Veritatis Splendor: A Response*, Charles Yeats (ed.) (Norwich: Canterbury Press, 1994), 8–24.

83 In one of the most measured discussions of the recent encyclicals, Jean Porter has argued that the pope fails to take into account both the difficulties involved in making certain types of moral judgment and the need for civil moral disagreement in our communities. These failures may be related. 'Moral Reasoning, Authority and Community in *Veritatis Splendor*', *Annual of the Society of Christian Ethics* (1995), 201–19.

84 *Veritatis Splendor*, 158.

85 John Paul II, *The Gospel of Life: Evangelium Vitae: On the Value and Inviolability of Human Life* (Washington DC: United States Catholic Conference, 1995), 20.
86 Ibid., 151
87 Oliver O'Donovan, 'A Summons to Reality', 45. Russell Hittinger, in his excellent analysis of the encyclical, points to the similarity with Karl Barth's theonomous ethics. 'Natural Law and Catholic Moral Theology', *A Preserving Grace*, Michael Cromartie (ed.) (Grand Rapids, Eerdmans, 1997), 26.
88 I am indebted here to the account of Aquinas' moral theory set out by Jean Porter, *The Recovery of Virtue* (Philadelphia: Westminster/John Knox, 1990).
89 *Summa Theologiae* ΙΙαΙΙαe, 47.13.
90 Ibid., 23.2.
91 For an account of Catholic moral theology since Vatican II, see John Mahoney, *The Making of Moral Theology: A Study of the Roman Catholic Tradition* (Oxford: Clarendon, 1987), 302–47.

3 ECCLESIAL ETHICS – STANLEY HAUERWAS

1 The term 'ecclesial ethics' is employed by Reinhold Hütter in 'Ecclesial Ethics, the Church's Vocation, and Paraclesis', *Pro Ecclesia*, 2 (1993), 433–50. I use it here in preference to 'communitarian' since Hauerwas does not wish his ethics to be sustained by the philosophical arguments for communitarianism, but rather by more exclusive theological considerations. For a more popular and wide-ranging exposition of ecclesial ethics see Robert E. Webber and Rodney Clapp, *People of the Truth* (San Francisco: Harper & Row, 1988).
2 In what follows I have drawn upon material previously published in 'Another Way of Reading Stanley Hauerwas?', *Scottish Journal of Theology*, 50 (1997), 242–9.
3 Hauerwas' criticism of liberalism can be found in 'The Church and Liberal Democracy: The Moral Limits of a Secular Polity', *A Community of Character* (University of Notre Dame Press, 1981), 72–86, and in several of the essays contained in *Christian Existence Today* (Durham: Labyrinth Press, 1988).
4 Cf. *After Christendom* (Nashville: Abingdon Press, 1991), 66ff.
5 Cf. Edmund Pincoffs 'Quandary Ethics', *Revisions*, Alasdair MacIntyre and Stanley Hauerwas (eds.) (University of Notre Dame Press, 1983), 92–112.
6 S. Hauerwas and D. Burrell, 'From System to Story: An Alternative Pattern for Rationality in Ethics', in *Why Narrative?* Stanley

Hauerwas and L. Gregory Jones (eds.) (Grand Rapids: Eerdmans, 1989), 169.

7 Ibid.

8 Hauerwas' survey of recent work in Christian ethics is written with this conclusion in view. 'On Keeping Ethics Theological', in *Revisions*, 16–42. This is reproduced in *Against the Nations* (University of Notre Dame Press, 1992), 23–50.

9 John Howard Yoder, *The Politics of Jesus* (Grand Rapids: Eerdmans, 1972), 15ff.

10 Cf. the introduction to *Against the Nations*.

11 In his response to Gloria Albrecht, he claims that 'when Albrecht . . . suggests that I resist the full implications of my epistemology for my ecclesiology, I can only say that ecclesiology is all I have', 'Failure of Communication or A Case of Uncomprehending Feminism', *Scottish Journal of Theology*, 50 (1997), 230.

12 *Character and the Christian Life* (San Antonio, Trinity University Press, 1975), 20–1. The significance of character for ethical theory is also argued by James McClendon, *Biography as Theology* (Nashville: Abingdon Press, 1974), 13–38. For a recent exploration of the centrality of character to the Old Testament Wisdom literature, see William P. Brown, *Character in Crisis* (Grand Rapids: Eerdmans, 1996).

13 *A Community of Character*, 114. Cf. Alasdair MacIntyre, 'Why is the Search for the Foundation of Ethics so Frustrating?' *Hastings Center Report* 9/4 (1979), 21–2, (cited in *A Community of Character*, 257).

14 This shift is acknowledged by Hauerwas himself in the introduction to the 1985 reissue of *Character and the Christian Life*. 'Though I had stressed the relational character of the self, this is not sufficient to indicate the centrality of a particular community called the church for the development of the kind of character required of Christians', xxxi.

15 *Community of Character*, 117.

16 'On Keeping Theological Ethics Theological', 33–4.

17 *A Community of Character*, 37.

18 *A Community of Character*, 95.

19 *Character and the Christian Life*, xxix. Robert Jenson comments on the Catholic assumptions underlying Hauerwas' epistemology in 'The Hauerwas Project', *Modern Theology*, 8 (1992), 289ff.

20 E.g. *A Community of Character*, 90.

21 'Rather the truthfulness of Christian convictions resides in their power to form a people sufficient to acknowledge the divided character of the world and thus necessarily ready to offer hospitality to the stranger', ibid., 90.

22 E.g. *In Good Company* (University of Notre Dame Press, 1995), 62. In light of this dispute concerning the reception of the Reformation, it is surprising that Hauerwas and Willimon, in surveying the responses of most of the mainstream denominations to their work, fail to mention Lutheranism.

23 Julian Hartt, 'Theological Investments in Story: Some Comments on Recent Developments and Some Proposals', *Why Narrative?* Stanley Hauerwas and Gregory Jones (eds.) (Grand Rapids: Eerdmans, 1989), 286–92.

24 'Why the Truth Demands Truthfulness: An Imperious Engagement with Hartt', ibid., 303–10.

25 In this respect, Hauerwas eschews the sharp distinction of Thiemann, Frei and others between narrative as a general hermeneutical category and narrative as the form in which the Christian gospel is given by God. Cf. William Werpehowski, 'Narrative and Ethics in Barth', *Theology Today*, 43 (1987), 350.

26 Stanley Hauerwas and David Burrell, 'From System to Story: An Alternative Pattern for Rationality in Ethics', 177.

27 'What sets the context for one's moral judgment is rather the stories we hold about the place of children in our lives, or the connection one deems ought or ought not to hold between sexuality and procreation, or some other such account', ibid., 169.

28 Ibid., 185.

29 The dominant influence at this juncture appears to be Hans Frei (and thus Karl Barth). See the frequent references to *The Identity of Jesus Christ* (Philadelphia: Fortress Press, 1975) in *A Community of Character*, chapter 2.

30 *A Community of Character*, 45.

31 *The Politics of Jesus*, 100.

32 Ibid., 222ff. Yoder cites Markus Barth's comment that 'Justification in Christ is thus not an individual miracle happening to this person or that person, which each may seek or possess for himself. Rather justification by grace is a joining together of this person and that person, of the near and far; . . . it is a social event', 225.

33 *The Peaceable Kingdom*, 91.

34 *Christian Existence Today*, 95.

35 John Howard Yoder, 'What Would You Do If?', *Journal of Religious Ethics*, 2 (1974), 90, quoted by Hauerwas, *The Peaceable Kingdom*, 125.

36 'It is my contention that Christian opposition to abortion on demand has failed because, by attempting to meet the moral challenge within the limits of public polity, we have failed to exhibit our deepest convictions that make our rejection of abortion intelligible', *A Community of Character*, 212.

37 Ibid., 226.
38 Ibid., 225.
39 Ibid., 191.
40 *Against the Nations*, 166.
41 Ibid.
42 *Suffering Presence: Theological Reflections on Medicine, the Mentally Handicapped, and the Church* (University of Notre Dame Press, 1986), 186.
43 Stanley Hauerwas and William H. Willimon, *Resident Aliens* (Nashville: Abingdon Press, 1993), 146.
44 This is a central theme in Hauerwas' reading of the recent history of theological ethics in America. Cf. 'On Keeping Ethics Theological', in *Against the Nations*, 23–50.
45 *Resident Aliens*, 74.
46 'Why Resident Aliens Struck a Chord', *In Good Company*, 58. Hauerwas and Willimon make the further point that their work elicits most enthusiasm in clergy under the age of forty-five.
47 Ibid., 45. Cf. John Howard Yoder, 'A People in the World: Theological Interpretation', in *The Concept of the Believer's Church*, James Leo Garrett, Jr. (ed.) (Scottdale, PA: Herald Press, 1969), 252–83.
48 *Resident Aliens*, 160.
49 *After Christendom* (Nashville: Abingdon Press, 1991), 100.
50 Ibid., 151.
51 'Christian vegetarianism might be understood as a witness to the world that God's creation is not meant to be at war with itself. Such a witness does not entail romantic conceptions of nature and/or our fallen creation but is an eschatological act, signifying that our lives are not captured by the old order', *In Good Company*, 196–7.
52 *Resident Aliens*, 171.
53 'The Sectarian Temptation', *Proceedings of the Catholic Theological Society of America*, 40 (1985), 84–5.
54 Cf. Wilson Miscamble, 'Sectarian Passivism?', *Theology Today* (1987/8), 69–77. Ronald Thiemann in his recent study labels Hauerwas' approach as 'sectarian communitarianism'. *Religion in Public Life: A Dilemma for Democracy* (Washington DC: Georgetown University Press, 1996), 99ff.
55 Oliver O'Donovan has rightly repudiated the charge of sectarianism levelled against Hauerwas. *The Desire of the Nations: Rediscovering the Roots of Political Theology* (Cambridge University Press, 1996), 216.
56 I suspect that Hauerwas must eschew the fascinating construction

of his position suggested by Robert Jenson in 'The Hauerwas Project', *Modern Theology*, 8.3 (1992), 285–96. Jenson claims that Hauerwas is committed to something like the view that the world exists to be included in the church's story. This is an ecclesial analogue of Barth's view that 'creation is the external basis of the covenant'. This absorption of the world into the story of the church tends to reverse Hauerwas' (and, *pace* Jenson, Barth's) continual stress upon the mission of the church in and to the world. Barth's doctrine of election renders such a co-ordination of church and world impossible.

57 H. R. Niebuhr, *Christ and Culture* (New York: Harper & Row, 1956), 81.

58 James Wm. McClendon Jr., *Systematic Theology: Ethics* (Nashville: Abingdon Press, 1986), 233. A comprehensive discussion of the sectarian charge can be found in Arne Rasmusson, *The Church as Polis: From Political Theology to Theological Politics as Exemplified by Jürgen Moltmann and Stanley Hauerwas* (University of Notre Dame Press, 1996), 231–47. Hauerwas and Willimon have remarked, 'We do not want to call Methodists out of Congress; we just want them to be there as Methodists, for heavens' sake', *In Good Company*, 60.

59 *The Church as Polis*.

60 *Systematic Theology: Ethics*, 35.

61 *A Community of Character*, 6.

62 E.g. 'On Keeping Theological Ethics Imaginative', *Against the Nations*, 59.

63 *In Good Company*, 57.

64 *Biography as Theology*, 37.

65 Article review of Stanley Hauerwas' *In Good Company; The Church as Polis*, *Scottish Journal of Theology*, 50 (1997), 225.

66 This is worked out in *The Character of our Communities* (Nashville, Abingdon Press, 1995).

67 This is accommodated in Robin Gill's formulation of the church as the 'harbinger' rather than the 'exemplar' of moral values, *Christian Ethics in Secular Worlds* (Edinburgh: T. & T. Clark, 1991), 17.

68 E.g. the criticism of Gerhard Ebeling's treatment of the *sola scriptura* principle in *Unleashing the Scripture* (Nashville: Abingdon Press, 1993), 27.

69 'Even though I do not share the liberal rejection of the classical christological formulas, the liberal concern to recover the centrality of Jesus' life strikes me as right', *A Community of Character*, 40.

70 E.g. *The Peaceable Kingdom*, 72ff.

71 I am thinking here especially of *The Peaceable Kingdom*, chapter 5, and *A Community of Character*, chapter 2.

72 Hans Frei's Barthian construction of the uniqueness and unsubstitutability of the story of Jesus become strangely attenuated in Hauerwas, other similarities notwithstanding.

73 *The Peaceable Kingdom*, 94. It is perhaps significant that one encounters a similar criticism of Anabaptist theology in Article XII of the Lutheran *Formula of Concord*. The third error condemned is 'that our righteousness before God does not consist wholly in the unique merit of Christ, but in renewal and in our own pious behaviour. For the most part this piety is built on one's own individual self-chosen spirituality, which in fact is nothing else but a new kind of monkery.' I owe this comparison to George Hunsinger.

74 Thus Bonhoeffer in *Life Together* (New York: Harper, 1954), argues that it is only in Christ that we relate to God and to others. This is understood in terms of union, justification, forgiveness, renewal, service, worship, prayer, etc. Christian ethics is here closely associated with Christian piety.

75 I am aware that I am placing a construction upon his writings which Hauerwas would eschew. None the less, there seem to be grounds at least for further clarification of his position on these issues.

76 Richard Hays, *The Moral Vision of the New Testament* (San Francisco: HarperCollins, 1996), 253ff.

77 E.g. *A Community of Character*, 70–1. One might anticipate a response, though not from Hauerwas, along the following lines. Cosmic Christologies and objective theories of the atonement do not make much sense. We should take as our standard the word and example of the historical Jesus as these can be discerned from the Synoptic Gospels. This rejoinder should not be underestimated, yet its difficulty is that it selects the moral teaching of Jesus while abandoning large tracts of the New Testament. The principle by which this selection is made is presumably its moral adequacy. This assumes some prior access to moral knowledge and thus reduces the ethical distinctiveness of Christian faith. It is thus a rehabilitation of the type of liberal Protestantism to which Hauerwas is implacably opposed.

78 *Church Dogmatics* I/1 (Edinburgh: T. & T. Clark, 1957), section 4. This Barthian criticism can also be detected in Child's comment that 'because Hauerwas has accepted a functional description of the Bible which denies any special properties in the text, his actual use of the story increasingly turns out to be an abstraction without

specific biblical content', *Biblical Theology of the Old and New Testaments* (London: SCM, 1992), 665.

79 At its best, the doctrine of election has functioned in this way in the Christian life. As far as I am aware, this plays no part in Hauerwas' theology.

80 Hauerwas himself presupposes this in his remark that 'we believe that history has already come out right and just because it has we can take the time in a world threatened by its own pretensions of control to seek patiently a truthful peace', *Against the Nations*, 166.

81 'Ecclesial Ethics, The Church's Vocation and Paraclesis', *Pro Ecclesia*, 2 (1993), 433–50; citation is from 448. It seems to me, however, that Hütter's critique has identified not so much a defective pneumatology in ecclesial ethics as a defective Christology and soteriology.

82 For Barth's criticism of Bultmann, see 'Rudolf Bultmann: An Attempt to Understand Him', *Kerygma and Myth*, II, H. W. Bartsch (ed.) (London: SPCK, 1964), 83–132; *Church Dogmatics* IV/I (Edinburgh: T. & T. Clark, 1956), 767ff.

83 *A Community of Character*, 228.

84 Ibid., 106.

85 Hauerwas is correct to point out that there is no necessary connection between the uniqueness of Christ and liberalism's penchant for finding common moral ground everywhere. My claim here is simply that, by stressing to a greater extent the uniqueness of the work of Christ over against the polity of the church, one has greater scope for affirming the action of the Spirit beyond the church.

86 *Church Dogmatics* IV/3 (Edinburgh: T. & T. Clark, 1961), 38ff. Iain Torrance has argued that Hauerwas' ecclesiology reveals some interesting similarities to Donatist exclusivism over against Augustinian catholicity. 'They Speak to Us across the Centuries: Cyprian', *Expository Times*, 108.12 (1997), 356–9.

87 Ibid., 115–16.

88 *Ethics After Babel* (Cambridge: Clarke, 1988), 214.

89 E.g. *Thick and Thin: Moral Argument at Home and Abroad* (University of Notre Dame Press, 1994).

90 Cf. The strangely undeveloped comment: 'What allows us to look expectantly for agreement among those who do not worship God is not that we have a common morality based on autonomous knowledge of autonomous nature, but that God's kingdom is wider than the church', *Christian Existence Today*, 17. Similar observations elsewhere are generally not integrated into his overall argument. 'Unity comes not from the assumption that all people

share the same nature, but that we share the same Lord. Though
certainly the fact that we have a common creator provides a basis
for some common experience and appeals', *A Community of Character*, 106.

91 Hauerwas is roundly attacked for his wide-ranging assault on
liberalism by Max Stackhouse, 'Liberalism dispatched vs. Liberalism engaged', *Christian Century*, 18, (October 1995), 962–7.

92 Hauerwas, borrowing from Stanley Fish, points to the anti-
Catholicism concealed in Milton's 'Areopagitica'. *In Good Company*,
203.

93 Stephen Toulmin, *Cosmopolis: The Hidden Agenda of Modernity* (New
York: Free Press, 1990), 104.

94 *The Nature of Doctrine*, 128.

95 Ibid., 131.

96 'Hauerwas Examined', *First Things*, 25 (1992), 51.

4 MORAL REALISM IN RECENT PHILOSOPHY

1 *Truth and Other Enigmas* (London: Duckworth, 1978), 146.

2 Cf. Crispin Wright, 'Truth Conditions and Criteria', *Aristotelian
Society Supplementary Volume*, 50 (1976), 224. For a realist counter-
blast, see P. F. Strawson, 'Scruton and Wright on Anti-Realism
Etc.', *Aristotelian Society Proceedings*, 77 (1976/7), 15–21.

3 'What is a Theory of Meaning II?', in *Truth and Meaning*, G. Evans
and J. McDowell (eds.) (Oxford: Clarendon, 1976), 71.

4 *Truth and Other Enigmas*, 362.

5 Ibid., 18.

6 Criticism of Dummett can be found in Colin McGinn, 'Truth and
Use', *Reference, Truth and Reality*, M. Platts (ed.) (London: Routledge
and Kegan Paul, 1980), 19–40; Edward Craig, 'Meaning, Use and
Privacy', *Mind*, 91 (1982), 541–64. For robust defences of global
realism see Michael Devitt, *Realism and Truth* (Oxford: Blackwell,
1984), and William P. Alston, *A Realist Conception of Truth* (Ithaca:
Cornell University Press, 1996).

7 This description of a realist philosophy of science is in part derived
from W. H. Newton-Smith's four ingredients of realism, *The
Rationality of Science* (London: Routledge and Kegan Paul, 1981), 43.

8 *Language, Truth and Logic* (Harmondsworth: Penguin, 1971), 199.

9 Cf. Newton-Smith, *The Rationality of Science*, 25.

10 *The Structure of Scientific Revolutions* (University of Chicago Press,
1970), 150.

11 This parallel is drawn by Devitt, *Realism and Truth*, chapter 9.

12 'Realism and Reference', *Monist*, 59 (1976), 321.

13 *Meaning and the Moral Sciences* (London: Routledge and Kegan Paul, 1978).

14 Michael Devitt, *Realism and Truth*, 63. For a physicist's defence of realism see John Polkinghorne, *One World* (London: SPCK, 1986), 6–25.

15 'Does Moral Philosophy rest on a Mistake?', *Moral Obligation* (Oxford: Clarendon Press, 1949), 16.

16 This problem is set out in Jonathan Dancy's 'Intuitionism', *A Companion to Ethics*, Peter Singer (ed.) (Oxford: Blackwell, 1991), 414ff.

17 The lack of clarity amongst the intuitionists regarding self-evident principles is illustrated by D. D. Raphael's inventory of intuitionist examples, *Moral Philosophy* (Oxford University Press, 1981), 44.

18 Cf. Mary Warnock, *Ethics Since 1900* (Oxford University Press, 1960), 77–8.

19 *Language, Truth and Logic*, 142.

20 *Facts and Values* (New Haven: Yale University Press, 1963), 18.

21 Ibid., 24.

22 Ibid., 30–1.

23 *Moral Philosophy*, 26ff.

24 Alasdair MacIntyre, *After Virtue* (London: Duckworth, 1981), 20.

25 In much of what follows I am indebted to the discussion of these issues in David McNaughton's *Moral Vision* (Oxford: Blackwell, 1988).

26 John McDowell, 'Aesthetic value, objectivity, and the fabric of the world', *Pleasure, Preference and Value*, Eva Schaper (ed.) (Cambridge University Press, 1983), 3.

27 For another defence of moral realism in the same vein see Sabina Lovibond, *Realism and Imagination in Ethics* (Oxford: Blackwell, 1983).

28 Cf. Iris Murdoch, *The Sovereignty of Good* (London: Routledge and Kegan Paul, 1970).

29 'Virtue and Reason', *Monist*, 62 (1979), 331.

30 Ibid., 344.

31 Ibid., 345.

32 Ibid., 346.

33 McDowell's theory has some difficulty at this juncture in coping with the phenomenon of weakness of the will. This has led to a modification of his theory of moral action in Jonathan Dancy's *Moral Reason* (Oxford: Blackwell, 1993), 53ff.

34 'Virtue and Reason', 347.

35 'Values and Secondary Qualities', in *Morality and Objectivity*,

T. Honderich (ed.) (London: Routledge and Kegan Paul, 1985), 111–12.

36 Ibid., 120.

37 Ibid., 121.

38 John McDowell, *Mind and World* (Cambridge, MA: Harvard University Press, 1994), 84.

39 *Ethics: Inventing Right and Wrong* (Harmondsworth: Penguin, 1977), 33.

40 Ibid., 37.

41 For a significant response to the Humean problem of supervenience, see Dancy, *Moral Reason*, 77ff. Dancy argues that the apparent mysteriousness of supervenience can be removed by recognising the way in which the moral features of an action result from natural ones. The notion of a resultant property is itself a commonplace of sensory perception.

42 Gilbert Harman, *The Nature of Morality* (New York: Oxford University Press, 1977), 6–9; for realist responses to Harman see McNaughton, *Moral Vision*, 101ff. and Jeffrey Stout, *Ethics After Babel*, 37ff. Stout argues that the moral features of a situation may explain why moral beliefs are held in a way that is not disanalagous to empirical realism.

43 Mackie, *Ethics: Inventing Right and Wrong*, 10–11.

44 Cf. David Wiggins' discussion of the marks of truth in moral discourse. *Needs, Values, Truth* (Oxford: Blackwell, 1987), 146ff.

45 *Spreading the Word* (Oxford: Clarendon Press, 1984), 182ff.

46 Ibid., 186.

47 Ibid., 180.

48 'Errors and the Phenomenology of Value', in *Morality and Objectivity*, T. Honderich (ed.), 11.

49 I have drawn here from David MacNaugton, *Moral Vision*, 92ff.

50 Jeffrey Stout, *Ethics After Babel*, 39ff.

51 Simon Blackburn, 'Errors and the Phenomenology of Value', 11.

52 Charles Taylor, *Sources of the Self: the Making of the Modern Identity* (Cambridge, MA: Harvard University Press, 1989), 59.

53 It is one of the strengths of Stout's defence of moral realism in *Ethics After Babel* that it pays close attention to the diversity of moral languages.

54 *Consequences of Pragmatism* (Brighton: Harvester Press, 1982), xvii. For Rorty's fuller attempt to read the history of philosophy in this way see his *Philosophy and the Mirror of Nature* (Oxford: Blackwell, 1981).

55 I am following here Rorty's description of pragmatism in 'Pragma-

tism, Relativism and Irrationalism' in *Consequences of Pragmatism*, 160–75.

56 *Contingency, Irony and Solidarity* (Cambridge University Press, 1989), 51–2.

57 Cited by Charles Guignon and David Hiley, 'Biting the Bullet: Rorty on Private and Public Morality', in *Reading Rorty*, Alan R. Malachowski (ed.) (Oxford: Blackwell, 1990).

58 'Human Rights, Rationality and Sentimentality', in *On Human Rights*, Stephen Shute and Susan Hurley (eds.) (New York: Basic Books, 1993), 133–4.

59 Cf. Alston, *A Realist Conception of Truth.*

60 'Philosophy, the "Other" Disciplines, and Their Histories: A Rejoinder to Richard Rorty', *Soundings*, 65 (1982), 138. A similar criticism is made by Bernard Williams in *Ethics and the Limits of Philosophy* (London: Collins, 1985), 137.

61 This strategy is employed by Devitt in *Realism and Truth.*

62 John Polkinghorne, *One World* (London: SPCK, 1986), 21.

63 *Ethics After Babel*, 21ff.

64 'Auto-da-Fé: Consequences of Pragmatism', *Reading Rorty*, 30.

65 Ibid., 31.

66 *Reading Rorty*, 356.

5 VIRTUE, TRADITION AND GOD – ALASDAIR MACINTYRE

1 'What distinguishes Professor MacIntyre is not the number of beliefs he has doubted, but the number of beliefs he has embraced. His capacity for doubt we share or surpass; it is his capacity for faith which is distinctive and perhaps unrivalled', Ernest Gellner, *The Devil in Modern Philosophy* (London: Routledge and Kegan Paul, 1974), 193, cited by John Horton and Susan Mendus (eds.), *After MacIntyre* (Oxford: Polity Press, 1994), 1.

2 This approach to the discipline has evoked the criticism that the history of ideas is being conflated with moral philosophy. Cf. William K Frankena's review of *After Virtue*, *Ethics*, 93 (1983), 579–87.

3 *Marxism: An Interpretation* (London: SCM 1953), 62. In a recent interview, MacIntyre has commented on his indebtedness to Marx. 'There are two points in which I remain very much at one with the Marxist tradition of thought. The first of these is in general wanting to understand reasoning, especially practical reasoning, as giving expression to forms of social practice . . . Secondly, I think that Marxists have much that was relevant to say about the nature and the function of the nation-state, and the

Marxist critique of the modern nation-state as a form of government is one which I accept, though in fact I have (*sic*) to think that the Marxist critique is insufficiently radical', Thomas D Pearson, 'Interview with Alasdair MacIntyre', *Kinesis*, 20.2 (1994), 35.

4 His criticism of the narrow focus of the analytic tradition would probably apply to much of the debate between McDowell and his critics. 'Analytic philosophy's strengths and weaknesses both derive from its exclusive focus on a rigorous treatment of detail, one that results in a piecemeal approach to philosophy, isolable problem by isolable problem. Its literary genres are the professional journal article and the short monograph', 'Nietzsche or Aristotle', *The American Philosopher*, Giovanna Borrodori (ed.) (University of Chicago Press, 1994), 144.

5 The explicit conclusion of *After Virtue* (London: Duckworth, 1981) reveals a strong affinity with earlier positions. 'My own conclusion is very clear. It is that on the one hand we still, in spite of the efforts of three centuries of moral philosophy, and one of sociology, lack any coherent rationally defensible statement of a liberal individualist point of view, and that, on the other hand, the Aristotelian tradition can be restated in a way that restores intelligibility and rationality to our moral and social attitudes and commitments', 259.

6 *Philosophy*, 33 (1958), 1–19, reprinted in *Ethics, Religion and Politics: Collected Philosophical Papers*, vol. 3 (Oxford: Blackwell, 1981), 26–42. MacIntyre's affinity with Anscombe is already apparent in a 1959 essay on Hume reprinted in *Against the Self Images of the Age* (London: Duckworth, 1971), 109–24.

7 *After Virtue*, 110–11.

8 Basil Mitchell, *Morality: Religious and Secular* (Oxford: Clarendon, 1984), 63.

9 Ibid., 95.

10 For MacIntyre's summary of Aristotelian ethics see *After Virtue*, 146–64.

11 Ibid., 184.

12 'An Aristotle whose Ethics is read for the most part apart from his Politics, and both as though his theology did not exist, is much more unlike Aquinas than Aristotle in fact was', *Whose Justice? Which Rationality?* (London: Duckworth, 1988) 166.

13 *After Virtue*, 187ff.

14 Ibid., 216.

15 Ibid., 222f.

16 Ibid., 263.

17 MacIntyre states that his early work was marked by insufficient

attention to the points of discontinuity in the chronological transition from one line of thought to another. 'The fundamental shifts in central concepts and in basic principles are reported, but they appear as pure facts, unscrutinized and not at all understood', 'Nietzsche or Aristotle', 144.

18 *Whose Justice? Which Rationality?*, 8ff.

19 Ibid., 8.

20 Cf. 'Plain Persons and Moral Philosophy: Rules, Virtue and Goods', *American Catholic Philosophical Quarterly*, 56 (1992), 1–19.

21 *Whose Justice? Which Rationality?*, 154. That this is now MacIntyre's own position is confirmed by his remarks about the emergence of a theological conception of justice in the move from Aristotle to Aquinas in 'Which God Ought We To Obey and Why?', *Faith and Philosophy*, 3.4 (1986), 369.

22 The 'Unresolved Tension between the Purported Goals' of *Whose Justice? Which Rationality?* is commented upon by Thomas S. Hibbs, 'MacIntyre, Tradition and the Christian Philosopher', *The Modern Schoolman*, 68 (1991), 211–23.

23 *Whose Justice? Which Rationality?*, 172.

24 Ibid., 174–5.

25 The lack of explanation here is described as 'one of the most egregious gaps in MacIntyre's reading of Thomas' by Hibbs, 'MacIntyre, Tradition and the Christian Philosopher', 221.

26 *Whose Justice? Which Rationality?* 171–2.

27 *Three Rival Versions of Moral Enquiry* (London: Duckworth, 1990), 68.

28 Ibid.

29 Ibid., 65ff.

30 *Aeterni Patris*, Para. 9, in Claudia Carlen (ed.), *The Papal Encyclicals* (Raleigh: McGrath, 1981), 20.

31 This is discussed by MacIntyre in *Three Rival Versions of Moral Enquiry*, 176ff.

32 Ibid., 189.

33 Ibid., 39.

34 Ibid., 207ff.

35 Ibid., 210.

36 'Epistemological Crises, Narrative and Philosophy of Science,' *Why Narrative?* , Stanley Hauerwas and L. Gregor Jones (eds.) (Grand Rapids, Eerdmans, 1989), 145.

37 This appears to be the gist of MacIntyre's response to John Haldane in 'A Partial Response to my Critics', in *After MacIntyre*, John Horton and Susan Mendus (eds.) (Polity Press, Oxford, 1994), 295–6.

38 Cf. *Whose Justice? Which Rationality?* 351.
39 'Incommensurability, Truth and the Conversation between Confucians and Aristotelians about the Virtues', in *Culture and Modernity: East–West Philosophic Perspectives*, Eliot Deutsch (ed.) (Honolulu: University of Hawaii Press, 1991), 109.
40 *Three Rival Versions of Moral Enquiry*, 231–2.
41 *Ethics After Babel* (Cambridge: Clarke, 1988), 60ff. Cf. the useful discussion of this problem by Stephen Fowl in 'Could Horace talk with the Hebrews? Translatability and Moral Disagreement in MacIntyre and Stout', *Journal of Religious Ethics*, 19 (1991), 1–20. For a discussion which affirms a greater measure of incommensurability, see John Milbank, *Theology and Social Theory* (Oxford: Blackwell, 1990), chapter 11.
42 Jürgen Habermas, *Justification and Application: Remarks on Discourse Ethics* (Cambridge, MA: MIT Press, 1993), 103–4.
43 *Whose Justice? Which Rationality?*, 363.
44 'Incommensurability, Truth and the Conversation between Confucians and Aristotelians about the Virtues', 113.
45 Martha Nussbaum, 'Recoiling from Reason', *New York Review of Books*, 19 (1989), 36–41. A similar charge of oppressiveness is levelled against MacIntyre by Ian Markham, 'Faith and Reason: Reflections on MacIntyre's Tradition-Constituted Enquiry', *Religious Studies*, 27 (1991), 259–67.
46 John Henry Newman, An Essay on the Development of Christian Doctrine (Garden City, NY: Doubleday Image, 1960), 189. I owe this reference to David Hollenbach, 'A Communitarian Reconstruction of Human Rights: Contributions from Catholic Tradition', in *Catholicism and Liberalism: Contributions to American Public Philosophy*, David Hollenbach and R. Bruce Douglas (eds.) (Cambridge University Press, 1994), 143.
47 Jeffrey Stout comments, 'When MacIntyre complains that one of the "most striking facts" about our society is its lack of "institutionalized forums within which . . . fundamental disagreement can be systematically explored and charted", I have trouble squaring his complaint with the facts of his career or the existence of this journal', 'Homeward Bound: MacIntyre on Liberal Society and the History of Ethics', *The Journal of Religion*, 69 (1989), 232.
48 *Three Rival Versions of Moral Enquiry*, 233. The practicality of this view is questioned by Stanley Hauerwas and Charles Pinches, *Christians Among the Virtues : Theological Conversations with Ancient and Modern Ethics* (University of Notre Dame Press, 1997), 191–2.
49 'Openness and Constraint: Moral Reflection as Tradition-guided

Inquiry in Alasdair MacIntyre's Recent Works', *Journal of Religion*, 73 (1993), 523.

50 Thomas D. Pearson, 'Interview with Alasdair MacIntyre', *Kinesis*, 20.2 (1994), 36.

51 Ibid., 42.

52 Brian Barry, 'The Light That Failed', *Ethics*, 100 (1989), 160–8.

53 Ronald Dworkin, 'Liberalism' in *Public and Private Morality*, Stuart Hampshire (ed.) (Cambridge University Press, 1978), 113–43.

54 The leading exponent of this notion is probably Isaiah Berlin. Cf. *Four Essays on Liberty* (London: Oxford University Press, 1969). For a theological application of Berlin's ideas see George Newlands, *Generosity and the Christian Future* (London: SPCK, 1997), chapter 10.

55 Cf. 'Community, Law and the Idiom and Rhetoric of Rights', *Listening*, 26 (1991), 96–110.

56 Cf. Max Stackhouse's complaint that in MacIntyre 'there is not a single reference to Moses, the Torah, the Old Testament, the Ten Commandments, or any prophetic standards of judgment in this entire corpus of work on Ethics in the West (let alone any treatment of Solon, Justinian, Manu, Confucius, Muhammad, etc.)! It is as if the idea of a universal moral law, present in the mind of God, established over all creation, and written on the hearts of all people had never been discussed, except as an absurd speculation.' 'Alasdair MacIntyre: An Overview and Evaluation', *Religious Studies Review*, 18 (1992), 207.

57 *After Virtue*, 191.

58 Ibid., 192.

59 'Plain Persons and Moral Philosophy: Rules, Virtues and Goods', *American Catholic Philosophical Quarterly*, 66 (1992), 10. In another context MacIntyre appears to concede a way in which an Aristotelian could recognise the language of human rights as 'enabling provisions, whereby individuals could claim a place within the life of some particular community', 'The Return to Virtue Ethics', *The Twenty-Fifth Anniversary of Vatican II*, Russell E. Smith (ed.) (Braintree: The Pope John Centre, 1990), 247.

60 This is most apparent in 'How can we Learn what *Veritatis Splendor* has to Teach', *The Thomist*, 58 (1994), 171–95. It can be argued that the defence offered here of the exceptionless negative precepts fails to deal adequately with cases of moral conflict and regret. This criticism is developed by Fergus Kerr, who contrasts the modernity of *After Virtue* with MacIntyre's later work. 'Moral Theology After MacIntyre: Modern Ethics, Tragedy and Thomism', *Studies in Christian Ethics*, 8 (1995), 33–44.

61 Alasdair MacIntyre and Hans Fink, Introduction to Knud Ejler

Løgstrup, *The Ethical Demand* (University of Notre Dame Press, 1997), xv–xxxviii.

62 This also emerges in Lindbeck's review of Stout's *After Babel*. 'Liberal pluralism is anything but a utopian social order. It constitutes a fragile and messy environment within which wheat and tares both grow. Its advantage is that it is more open than any other kind of polity to criticism and correction from within', *Theology Today*, 46 (1989), 60.

63 *The Nature of Doctrine* (London: SPCK, 1984), 125.

64 Ibid., 131.

65 'Recoiling from Reason', 40. John Haldane, addressing a similar problem, remarks that MacIntyre's recent trilogy requires to become a tetralogy including a study on 'The Truth in Thomism'. 'MacIntyre's Thomist Revival: What Next?', *After MacIntyre*, 92. This lacuna in MacIntyre's philosophy is reinforced by the claims of Bernard Williams and Simon Blackburn *inter alios* that the initial implausibility of theistic assumptions necessitates the development of entirely different positions.

66 Milbank's analysis of MacIntyre is discussed and generally endorsed by Stanley Hauerwas and Charles Pinches, *Christians Among the Virtues: Theological Conversations with Ancient and Modern Ethics* (University of Notre Dame Press, 1997), 61ff.

67 *Theology and Social Theory* (Oxford: Blackwell, 1990), 346. The 'interruptive' nature of the Christian life is further emphasised in Milbank's recent collection, *The Word Made Strange: Theology, Language, Culture* (Oxford: Blackwell, 1997). A similar criticism of MacIntyre is advanced by Michael Banner, *Turning the World Upside Down (and Some other Tasks for Dogmatic Christian Ethics)*, Inaugural lecture (King's College, London, 1996), 66. Yet, in suggesting that MacIntyre's rational ethics requires a 'secure bridgehead from which knowledge of good and evil can advance', his criticism appears to construe MacIntyre as a quasi-foundationalist. 'Dogmatic ethics . . . does not need to live in a world where there is a knowledge of the good and the right on which it can build, or to which it can appeal', ibid. In a similar vein, Hauerwas and Pinches seem to suggest that MacIntyre's dialectical method commits him to the view that truth can be attained by methods of philosophical reasoning which are universally accessible, *Christians Among the Virtues*, 61–2. This is hardly fair, especially if one is happy to enlist MacIntyre's arguments against post-Enlightenment liberalism in support of one's own theological position.

68 'Moral Relativism, Truth and Justification', *Moral Truth and Moral*

Tradition: Essays in Honour of Peter Geach and Elizabeth Anscombe, Luke Gormally (ed.) (Dublin: Four Court Press, 1994), 24.

69 These connections are perhaps most apparent in 'Moral Relativism, Truth and Justification', ibid.

70 Ian Markham uses something like this argument to criticise Milbank for deploying arguments relating to the history of sociology, the force of which cannot easily be explained by his account of rationality. *Plurality and Christian Ethics* (Cambridge University Press, 1994), 146. On the other hand, Markham's attempt to argue on the basis of natural theology – especially the cosmological argument – that only theology can save critical realism from collapsing into nihilism, thus protecting the liberal discourse of tolerance, is problematic. Is the apologetic force of the cosmological argument not itself relative to theistic traditions configured by the doctrine of creation? Is a critical realist likely to convert to nihilism on account of doubts about Leibniz's principle of sufficient reason?

71 *Theology and Social Theory*, 341.

72 *Three Rival Versions of Moral Enquiry*, 140.

73 'Plain Persons and Moral Philosophy: Rules, Virtues and Goods', 19.

74 *First Principles, Final Ends and Contemporary Philosophical Issues* (Milwaukee: Marquette University Press, 1990), 58.

75 Milbank argues that Christian (as opposed to Aristotelian) virtue has the character of divine gift'. Cf. 'Can Morality be Christian?', *The Word Made Strange*, 227.

76 'How can we Learn what *Veritatis Splendor* has to Teach?', 175 and 190.

6 COMMUNITARIANISM AND ITS CRITICS

1 In this chapter I draw on material previously published as 'Communitarianism and Liberalism: Towards a Convergence?', *Studies in Christian Ethics*, 10 (1997), 32–48.

2 For a clear overview of the differences between liberalism and communitarianism see David Hollenbach, 'Liberalism, Communitarianism, and the Bishops' Pastoral Letter on the Economy', *The Annual of the Society of Christian Ethics* (1987), 19–40.

3 'Cross-Purposes: The Liberal–Communitarian Debate', in *Liberalism and the Moral Life*, Nancy L. Rosenblum (ed.) (Cambridge, MA: Harvard University Press, 1989), 159–82.

4 Ibid., 160.

5 E.g. Stephen Mulhall and Adam Swift, *Liberals and Communitarians*;

Daniel Shapiro, 'Liberalism and Communitarianism', *Philosophical Books*, 36.3 (1995), 145.

6 Michael Sandel, 'The Procedural Republic and the Unencumbered Self', in *Communitarianism and Individualism*, Shlomo Avineri and Avner De-Shalit (eds.) (Oxford University Press, 1992), 19.

7 Charles Taylor, 'Cross-Purposes: The Liberal–Communitarian Debate', 167–8.

8 Robert Bellah, Richard Madsen, William M. Sullivan, Ann Swidler, and Steven M. Tipton, *Habits of the Heart: Individualism and Commitment in American Life* (Updated edition, Berkeley: University of California Press, 1996), x.

9 Ibid., 333ff.

10 Robert D. Putnam, 'Tuning In, Tuning Out: The Strange Disappearance of Social Capital in America', *Political Science* (1995), 664–5.

11 Ibid., 679.

12 Jonathan Sacks, *The Persistence of Faith* (London: Weidenfeld and Nicolson, 1991), 55.

13 *Faith in the Future* (London: Darton, Longman and Todd, 1995), 27.

14 Norman Dennis and George Erdos, *Families Without Fatherhood* (London: IEA Health and Welfare Unit, 1992), 36.

15 Ibid., 70.

16 Ibid., xii.

17 Cf. Lawrence Stone's study of marriage in England in the eighteenth century, *Broken Lives: Separation and Divorce in England 1660–1857* (Oxford University Press, 1993). 'The most striking feature of married life in eighteenth-century England was the theoretical, legal, and practical subordination of wives to their husbands, epitomized in the concept of patriarchy. . . Even worse than the condition of the unhappily married, however, was the lot of those women who were separated or divorced', 26.

18 Alasdair MacIntyre, 'Part of the Answer but not enough for a Cure: Review of Jonathan Sacks' 'The Politics of Hope', *Tablet* (26 April 1997), 540–1.

19 Derek Philips, *Looking Backward: A Critical Appraisal of Communitarian Thought* (Princeton University Press, 1993), 165.

20 Cf. Iris Marion Young, 'The Ideals of Community and the Politics of Difference', in *Feminism and Postmodernism*, Linda J. Nicholson (ed.) (London: Routledge, 1990), 300–23.

21 I am expounding here the position Habermas sets out in 'Discourse Ethics: Notes on a Program of Philosophical Justification', *Moral Consciousness and Communicative Action* (Cambridge, MA: MIT Press, 1990), 43–115.

22 Ibid., 63.
23 Ibid., 103.
24 Cf. Charles Taylor, *Sources of the Self* (Cambridge, MA: Harvard University Press, 1989), 88.
25 E.g. 'Justice as Fairness: Political not Metaphysical', *Philosophy and Public Affairs*, 14 (1985), 246. This article is reproduced in *Communitarianism and Individualism*, Shlomo Avineri and Avner de-Shaht (eds.) (Oxford University Press, 1992), 186–204.
26 *Political Liberalism* (New York: Columbia University Press, 1993), 158.
27 Will Kymlicka, *Liberalism, Community and Culture* (Oxford University Press, 1989), 54.
28 Seyla Benhabib, *Situating the Self: Gender, Community and Postmodernism in Contemporary Ethics* (New York: Routledge, 1992), 74.
29 Ibid., 76ff.
30 Daniel Bell, *Communitarianism and its Critics* (Oxford Clarendon Press, 1993), 8.
31 This is the thrust of Kymlicka's rejoinder to Bell. Ibid., Appendix 1, 'Some Questions about Justice and Community', 208–21.
32 E.g. Marilyn Friedman, 'Feminism and Modern Friendship: Dislocating the Community', *Ethics* (1989), 286ff.
33 It is reprinted in Amitai Etzioni, *The Spirit of Community: Rights, Responsibilities and the Communitarian Agenda* (London: Fontana, 1995) 251ff.
34 Ibid., 254.
35 Ibid., 256.
36 Ibid., xii.
37 Ibid., 258–9.
38 'A Partial Response to my Critics', *After MacIntyre*, John Horton and Susan Mendus (eds.) (Oxford: Polity Press, 1994), 303.
39 Cf. Thomas D. Pearson, 'Interview with Alasdair MacIntyre', *Kinesis*, 20.2 (1994), 36. In his open letter to *The Responsive Community* (Summer, 1991), 91, MacIntyre writes, 'In spite of rumours to the contrary, I am not and never have been a communitarian. For my judgement is that the political, economic and moral structures of advanced modernity in this country, as elsewhere, exclude the possibility of realising any of the worthwhile types of political community which at various times in the past have been achieved, even if always in imperfect forms. And I also believe that attempt to remake modern societies in systematically communitarian ways will always be either ineffective or disastrous.' Cited by Daniel Bell, *Communitarianism and Its Critics*, 17.
40 Cf. The introduction to the updated edition of *Habits of the Heart*.

For a full discussion of Bellah's communitarianism see Bruce Frohnen, *The New Communitarians and the Crisis of Modern Liberalism* (Lawrence, Kansas: University Press of Kansas, 1996).

41 *Habits of the Heart*, xii.

42 The ways in which the market economy now tyrannises individuals rather than serving their needs is explored in Robert N. Bellah, Richard Madsen, William M. Sullivan, Ann Swidler, and Steven M. Tipton, *The Good Society* (New York: Alfred A. Knopf, 1991), 82–110.

43 E.g. 'Communitarians and Medical Ethicists: Or Why I am None of the Above', *Dispatches from the Front* (Durham: Duke University Press, 1994), 158.

44 E.g. *Where Do Resident Aliens Live?* (Nashville: Abingdon Press, 1996), 35.

45 This is the burden of Hauerwas' criticism of Bellah. Cf. 'A Christian Critique of Christian America', in *Community in America: The Challenge of Habits of the Heart*, Charles H. Reynolds and Ralph V. Norman (eds.) (Berkeley: University of California Press, 1988), 250–65.

46 Taylor, *Sources of the Self*, 509.

47 I owe this criticism of Rawls to John Haldane, 'The Individual, the State and the Common Good', in *The Communitarian Challenge to Liberalism*, Ellen Frankel Paul, Fred D. Miller, Jr., and Jeffrey Paul (eds.) (Cambridge University Press, 1996), 59–79. Haldane shows how Rawls' own description of what is practically reasonable is loaded with assumptions that are far from uncontentious.

48 *Kairos: Three Prophetic Challenges to the Church*, Robert McAfee Brown (ed.) (Grand Rapids: Eerdmans, 1990), 45. For a discussion of Kairos with reference to the relationship between church and civil society see Duncan Forrester, *Beliefs, Values, Policies* (Oxford: Clarendon Press, 1989), 50–64.

49 John Courteny Murray, *We Hold These Truths: Catholic Reflections on the American Proposition* (New York: Sheed and Ward, 1960), 13.

50 Taylor, *Sources of the Self*, 397.

51 Eberhard Jüngel, 'The Gospel and the Protestant Churches of Europe: Christian Responsibility for Europe from a Protestant Perspective', *Religion, State and Society*, 21 (1993), 141–2.

52 Cf. *Luther and Calvin on Secular Authority*, Harro Höppfl (ed.) (Cambridge University Press, 1991). One might have to qualify this description by pointing to the way in which the scope of the jurisdiction of church and state tends to converge in Calvin's writings.

53 *The Desire of the Nations* (Cambridge University Press, 1996), 146.

54 For a striking defence of theological arguments for tolerance, openness, and generosity, see George Newlands', *Generosity and the Christian Future* (London: SPCK, 1997).

55 J. Courteny Murray, *We Hold These Truths*, 74.

56 This is particularly apparent in Roman Catholic social teaching. For the argument that there is a theological basis for some convergence of liberal and communitarian themes, see David Hollenbach, 'Liberalism, Communitarianism, and the Bishops' Pastoral Letter on the Economy'.

57 A similar appreciation of liberal society is advanced by Oliver O'Donovan in ways that are distinctively theological. The church may thus have a stake in a liberal polity if not in standard liberal political theory, *The Desire of the Nations*, 252ff.

58 'To be a person is to be a *member* of society, active within it in many ways through numerous sets of relationships. The key contribution that the bishops' letter makes to the liberal/communitarian debate lies in conceptualizing justice in terms of this link between personhood and the basic prerequisites of social participation', ibid., 34.

59 This may well be consistent with MacIntyre's proposal that the most adequate response for the moment is at the level of remaking local co-operative institutions such as schools, clinics, and work-places. 'Community, Law and Rhetoric of Rights', *Listening*, 26 (1991), 110.

60 Karl Barth, 'The Christian Community and the Civil Community', *Against the Stream*: *Shorter Post-War Writings, 1946–52* (New York: Philosophical Library, 1954), 32–3.

7 CONCLUSION

1 I am indebted here also to Basil Mitchell, 'Is There a Distinctive Christian Ethic?', *How to Play Theological Ping-Pong: And Other Essays on Faith and Reason* (London: Hodder and Stoughton, 1990), 42–56.

2 Michael Banner has sought to enlist the support of the genealogists to point to the radical insecurity of human knowledge outwith the apprehension of divine revelation. This, however, is in some tension with his highly impressive argument for an apologetic and public role for dogmatic Christian ethics. Can one deploy, as I would wish, his 'rich range of argumentative strategies and objectives' in public debate if one perceives that arena in Nietzschean terms? Cf. *Turning the World Upside Down (and Some other Tasks for Dogmatic Christian ethics)*, Inaugural lecture, King's College, London, 1996, 54ff.

3 Alasdair MacIntyre, *A Short History of Ethics* (London: Routledge and Kegan Paul, 1967), 196.

4 Jean Porter has drawn attention to the danger of a lack of civility in recent ecclesial ethics. 'Moral Reasoning, Authority and Community in *Veritatis Splendor*', *Annual of the Society of Christian Ethics* (1995), 201–19.

5 *Thick and Thin: Moral Arguments at Home and Abroad* (University of Notre Dame Press, 1994), 9–10. Walzer makes the further point that in moral discourse 'thinness and intensity go together, whereas with thickness comes qualification, compromise, complexity, and disagreement', 6.

6 E.g. 'The Concept of Rights in Christian Moral Discourse', in *A Preserving Grace: Protestants, Catholics and Natural Law*, Michael Cromartie (ed.) (Grand Rapids: Eerdmans, 1997), 143–56; 'Historical Prolegomena to a Theological Review of "Human Rights"', *Studies in Christian Ethics*, 9.2 (1996), 52–65.

7 It is this inarticulate consensus which gives some plausibility to Richard Rorty's comment that the question whether human beings really have their rights enumerated in the Helsinki Declaration is not worth raising. 'Human Rights, Rationality and Sentimentality', in *On Human Rights*, Stephen Shute and Susan Hurley (eds.), 116. Walzer appeals to the example of Amnesty International as an example of a group deliberately restricting its aims to elements of a thin morality which can command widespread support. *Thick and Thin*, 49.

8 I am indebted here to David Hollenbach's 'A Communitarian Reconstruction of Human Rights: Contributions from Catholic tradition', in *Catholicism and Liberalism: Contributions to American Public Philosophy*, R. Bruce Douglas and David Hollenbach (eds.) (Cambridge University Press, 1994), 127–50.

9 The differences between the tasks of evangelism and social criticism are captured by Jürgen Moltmann's distinction between the qualitative and quantitative missions of the church, *The Church in the Power of the Spirit* (London: SCM, 1977), 150ff.

10 Ronald Thiemann, *Religion in Public Life: A Dilemma for Democracy* (Washington, DC: Georgetown University Press, 1996), 28. For a British perspective on the relationship between religion and civil society in the USA, see Ian Markham, *Plurality and Christian Ethics* (Cambridge University Press, 1994), 83–106.

11 Charles Taylor, 'Religion in a Free Society', in *Articles of Faith, Articles of Peace*, J. D. Hunter and O. Guinness (eds.) (Washington: Brookings Institution, 1990), 108.

12 This example is developed in an American context by Thiemann, *Religion in Public Life*, 157ff.

13 Ironically, the prospect of the heir to the throne remarrying has recently triggered a public debate on the desirability of (dis)establishment.

14 Following the Lockerbie memorial service, the *Times* reproduced on its front page the complete text of the sermon preached by the Moderator of the General Assembly, James Whyte. The sermon reflected upon suffering based upon the grief of Jesus at the tomb of Lazarus. It is reprinted in James Whyte, *Laughter and Tears* (Edinburgh: St Andrew Press, 1993), 92–5.

15 'Gottes Sache in der Welt vertreten and doch nicht gegen die Welt Krieg führen.' Cited by Georg Merz, *Priesterlicher Dienst in kirchlichen Handeln* (Munich: Chr. Kaiser, 1952), 13.

Select bibliography

Albrecht, Gloria, *The Character of our Communities*, Nashville: Abingdon Press, 1995.

Article Review of Stanley Hauerwas' 'In Good Company', *Scottish Journal of Theology*, 50 (1997), 219–27.

Alston, William P., *A Realist Conception of Truth*, Ithaca: Cornell University Press, 1996.

Althaus, Paul, *The Ethics of Martin Luther*, Philadelphia: Fortress Press, 1972.

Anscombe, Elizabeth, 'Modern Moral Philosophy', *Philosophy*, 33 (1958), 1–19.

Aquinas, Thomas, *Summa Theologiae*, Blackfriars translation, Garden City, New York: Image Books, 1969–.

Augustine, *Basic Writings of Augustine*, New York: Random House, 1948.

City of God, M. Dods (translator), New York: Random House, 1950.

Avinei Sholomo, and De-Shalit, Avner (eds.), *Communitarianism and Individualism*, Oxford University Press, 1992.

Ayer, A. J., *Language, Truth and Logic*, Harmondsworth: Penguin, 1971.

Banner, Michael, *Turning the World Upside Down (and Some Other Tasks for Dogmatic Christian Ethics)*, Inaugural lecture, King's College, London, 1996.

Barclay, John, J*ews in the Mediterranean Diaspora from Alexander to Trajan (323 BCE–117 CE)*, Edinburgh: T. & T. Clark, 1996.

Barry, Brian, 'The Light that Failed', *Ethics*, 100 (1989), 160–8.

Barth, Karl, *The Epistle to the Romans*, London: Oxford University Press, 1933.

Against the Stream: Shorter Post-War Writings, 1946–52, New York: Philosophical Library, 1954.

Church Dogmatics I–IV, Edinburgh: T. & T. Clark, 1957–69.

Community, State and Church, New York: Anchor Books, 1960.

Ethics, New York: Seabury Press, 1981.

The Christian Life, Edinburgh: T. & T. Clark, 1981.

206

'Rudolf Bultmann: An Attempt to Understand Him', *Kerygma and Myth*, H. W. Bartsch (ed.) (London: SPCK, 1964).

Bell, Daniel, *Communitarianism and its Critics*, Oxford: Clarendon, 1993.

Bellah, Robert, Richard Madsen, William M. Sullivan, Ann Swidler and Steven M. Tipton, *The Good Society*, New York: Alfred A. Knopf, 1991.

Habits of the Heart: Individualism and Commitment in American Life, updated edition, Berkeley: University of California Press, 1996.

Benhabib, Seyla, *Situating the Self: Gender, Community and Postmodernism in Contemporary Ethics*, New York: Routledge, 1992.

Berlin, Isaiah, *Four Essays on Liberty*, London: Oxford University Press, 1969.

Biggar, Nigel, *The Hastening that Waits*, Oxford: Clarendon Press, 1993.

Blackburn, Simon, *Spreading the Word*, Oxford: Clarendon Press, 1984.

'Errors and the Phenomenology of Value', *Morality and Objectivity*, T. Honderich (ed.), London: Routledge and Kegan Paul, 1985, 1–22.

Blake, William, 'The Everlasting Gospel', *The Complete Writings of William Blake*, London: Nonesuch Press, 1957, 758.

Bonhoeffer, Dietrich, *Life Together*, New York: Harper, 1954.

Braaten, Carl, 'God in Public Life: Rehabilitating the "Orders of Creation" ', *First Things*, 8 (1990), 32–8.

Brown, Peter, *The Body in Society*, New York: Columbia University Press, 1988.

Brown, Robert McAfee (ed.), *Kairos: Three Prophetic Challenges to the Church*, Grand Rapids: Eerdmans, 1990.

Brown, William P., *Character in Crisis: A Fresh Approach to the Wisdom Literature of the Old Testament*, Grand Rapids: Eerdmans, 1996.

Bruce, Steve, *Religion in the Modern World: Cathedrals to Cults*, Oxford University Press, 1996.

Carlen, Claudia (ed.), *The Papal Encyclicals*, Raleigh: McGrath, 1981.

Chadwick, Henry, *The Originality of Early Christian Ethics*, Oxford: Somerville College, 1990.

Childs, Brevard, *Biblical Theology of the Old and New Testaments*, London: SCM, 1992.

Chrysostom John, 'Homily XXII on Ephesians', *Nicene and Post-Nicene Fathers*, First Series, vol. XIII, Philip Schaff (ed.), Edinburgh: T. & T. Clark, 1988, 157–63.

Corner, Mark, 'Review of *The Nature of Doctrine*', *Modern Theology*, 3 (1986), 112.

Craig, Edward, 'Meaning, Use and Privacy', *Mind*, 91 (1982), 541–64.

Cromartie, Michael (ed.), *A Preserving Grace: Protestants, Catholics and Natural Law*, Grand Rapids: Eerdmans, 1997.

Cullmann, Oscar, *The State in the New Testament*, New York: Charles Scribner's Sons, 1956.

Dalferth, Ingolf, 'Karl Barth's Eschatological Realism', *Studies in Karl Barth: Centenary Essays*, S. W. Sykes (ed.), Cambridge University Press, 1989, 14–45.

Dancy, Jonathan, *Moral Reason*, Oxford: Blackwell, 1993.

'Intuitionism', *A Companion to Ethics*, Peter Singer (ed.), Oxford: Blackwell, 1991, 411–20.

Davies, W. D., 'The Relevance of the Moral Teaching of the Early Church', *Neotestamentica et Semitica*, E. E. Ellis and M. Wilcox (eds.), Edinburgh: T. & T. Clark, 1969, 30–49.

Dennis, Norman and George Erdos, *Families without Fatherhood*, London: Institute of Economic Affairs, 1992.

Devitt, Michael, *Realism and Truth*, Oxford: Blackwell, 1984.

Douglas, R. Bruce and David Hollenbach (eds.), *Catholicism and Liberalism: Contributions to American Public Philosophy*, Cambridge University Press, 1994.

Dummett, Michael, 'What is a Theory of Meaning II?', *Truth and Meaning*, G. Evans and J. McDowell (eds.), Oxford: Clarendon Press, 1976, 67–137.

Truth and Other Enigmas, London: Duckworth, 1978.

Dworkin, Ronald, 'Liberalism', *Public and Private Morality*, Stuart Hampshire (ed.), Cambridge University Press, 1978, 113–43.

Etzioni, Amitai, *The Spirit of Community: Rights, Responsibilities and the Communitarian Agenda*, London: Fontana, 1995.

Fergusson, David, 'Meaning, Truth and Realism in Bultmann and Lindbeck', *Religious Studies*, 26 (1990), 183–98.

'Communitarianism and Liberalism: Towards a Convergence?', *Studies in Christian Ethics*, 10 (1997), 32–48.

'Another Way of Reading Stanley Hauerwas?', *Scottish Journal of Theology*, 50 (1997), 242–9.

Forrell, George, *History of Christian Ethics*, vol. 1, Minneapolis: Augsburg, 1979.

Forrester, Duncan, *Beliefs, Values and Policies*, Oxford: Clarendon, 1989.

Fowl, Stephen, 'Could Horace Talk with the Hebrews? Translatability and Moral Disagreement in MacIntyre and Stout', *Journal of Religious Ethics*, 19 (1991), 1–20.

Frankena, William K., 'Review of Alasdair MacIntyre, *After Virtue*', *Ethics*, 93 (1983), 579–87.

Frei, Hans, *The Identity of Jesus Christ*, Philadelphia: Fortress Press, 1975.

Types of Modern Theology, New Haven: Yale University Press, 1992.

Theology and Narrative: Selected Essays, Oxford: Oxford University Press, 1993.

Friedman, Marilyn, 'Feminism and Modern Friendship: Dislocating the Community', *Ethics*, 99 (1989), 275–90.

Frohnen, Bruce, *The New Communitarians and the Crisis of Modern Liberalism* (Lawrence, Kansas: University of Kansas Press, 1996.

Garrett, James Leo Jr., *The Concept of the Believer's? Church*, Scottdale, PA: Herald Press, 1969.

Geertz, Clifford, *The Interpretation of Culture*, New York: Basic Books, 1973.

Gill, Robin, *Christian Ethics in Secular Worlds*, Edinburgh: T. & T. Clark, 1991.

'Review of *Veritatis Splendor*', *Church Times* (12 November 93).

Grant, Robert, *Early Christianity and Society*, San Francisco: Harper & Row, 1978.

Green, Garret (ed.), *Scriptural Authority and Narrative Interpretation*, Philadelphia: Fortress Press, 1987.

Greer, Rowan, *Broken Lights and Mended Lives: Theology and Common Life in the Early Church*, University Park: Pennsylvania State University Press, 1986.

Gustafson, James, 'The Sectarian Temptation', *Proceedings of the Catholic Theological Society of America*, 40 (1985), 83–94.

Habermas, Jürgen, *Moral Consciousness and Communicative Action*, Cambridge, MA: MIT Press, 1990.

Haldane, John, 'The Individual, the State and the Common Good', *The Communitarian Challenge to Liberalism*, Ellen Frankel Paul, Fred D. Miller Jr., and Jeffrey Paul (eds.), Cambridge University Press, 1996, 59–79.

Harman, Gilbert, *The Nature of Morality*, New York: Oxford University Press, 1977.

Harvey, A. E., 'Review of Wayne Meeks', *The Origins of Christian Morality*', *Journal of Theological Studies*, 46 (1995), 301.

Hauerwas, Stanley, *Character and the Christian Life*, San Antonio: Trinity University Press, 1975.

A Community of Character, University of Notre Dame Press, 1981.

The Peaceable Kingdom, University of Notre Dame Press, 1983.

Suffering Presence: Theological Reflections on Medicine, the Mentally Handicapped, and the Church, University of Notre Dame Press, 1986.

Christian Existence Today, Durham: Labyrinth Press, 1988.

After Christendom, Nashville: Abingdon Press, 1991.

Against the Nations, Indiana: University of Notre Dame Press, 1992.

In Good Company, University of Notre Dame Press, 1995.

Dispatches from the Front, Nashville: Abingdon Press, 1996.

'Review of *Veritatis Splendor*', *Commonweal* (22 October 93), 16–18.

'Failure of Communication or a Case of Uncomprehending Feminism', *Scottish Journal of Theology*, 50 (1997), 228–39.

Hauerwas, Stanley and Gregory Jones (eds.), *Why Narrative?*, Grand Rapids: Eerdmans, 1989.

Hauerwas, Stanley and Charles Pinches, *Christians among the Virtues: Theological Conversations with Ancient and Modern Ethics*, University of Notre Dame Press, 1997.

Hauerwas, Stanley and William H. Willimon, *Resident Aliens*, Nashville: Abingdon Press, 1993.

Hauerwas, Stanley and William Willimon, *Where Do Resident Aliens Live?*, Nashville: Abingdon Press, 1995.

Hays, Richard, *The Moral Vision of the New Testament*, San Francisco: HarperCollins, 1996.

Hibbs, Thomas S., 'MacIntyre, Tradition and the Christian Philosopher', *The Modern Schoolman*, 68 (1991), 211–23.

Hollenbach, David, 'Liberalism, Communitarianism, and the Bishops' Pastoral Letter on the Economy', *The Annual of the Society of Christian Ethics* (1987), 19–40.

Höppfl, Harro (ed.), *Luther and Calvin on Secular Authority*, Cambridge University Press, 1991.

Horton, John and Susan Mendus (eds.), *After MacIntyre*, Oxford: Polity Press, 1994.

Hunsinger, George, *How to Read Karl Barth*, Oxford University Press, 1991.

'Barth, Barmen and the Confessing Church Today', *Barth, Barmen and the Confessing Church Today*, James Y. Holloway (ed.), Lampeter: Edwin Mellen Press, 1995, 15–50.

'Truth as Self-Involving: Barth and Lindbeck on the Cognitive and Performative Aspects of Truth in Theological Discourse', *Journal of the American Academy of Religion*, 61 (1993), 41–55.

Hütter, Reinhold, 'Ecclesial Ethics, the Church's Vocations, and Paraclesis', *Pro Ecclesia*, 2.4 (1993), 433–50.

Jenson, Robert, 'The Hauerwas Project', *Modern Theology*, 8.3 (1992), 285–95.

'Hauerwas Examined', *First Things*, 25 (1992), 49–51.

John-Paul II, *Veritatis Splendor*, Washington, DC: US Catholic Conference, 1993.

The Gospel of Life: Evangelium Vitae: On the Value and Inviolability of Human Life (Washington, DC: United States Catholic Conference, 1995).

Jüngel Eberhard, *Karl Barth: A Theological Legacy*, Edinburgh: T. & T. Clark, 1986.

'The Gospel and the Protestant Churches of Europe: Christian

Responsibility for Europe from a Protestant Perspective', *Religion, State and Society*, 21 (1993), 137–49.

Kerr, Fergus, 'Moral Theology after MacIntyre: Modern Ethics, Tragedy, and Thomism', *Studies in Christian Ethics*, 8 (1995), 33–44.

Kuhn, Thomas *The Structure of Scientific Revolution*, University of Chicago Press, 1970.

Kymlicka, Will, *Liberalism, Community and Culture*, Oxford University Press, 1989.

Lindbeck, George, *The Nature of Doctrine*, London: SPCK, 1984.

  Christliche Lehre als Grammatik des Glaubens, Güterloh: Chr. Kaiser, 1994.

  'The Sectarian Future of the Church', *The God Experience*, J. P. Whelan (ed.), New York: Newman, 1971, 226–43.

  '*Fides ex Auditu* and the Salvation of Non-Christians: Contemporary Catholic and Protestant Positions', *The Gospel and the Ambiguity of the Church*, Vilmos Vajta (ed.), Philadelphia: Fortress Press, 1974, 92–123.

  'Response to Bruce Marshall', *Thomist*, 53 (1989), 403–6.

  'Review of Jeffrey Stout, *Ethics After Babel*', *Theology Today*, 46 (1989), 59–61.

Lovin, Robin, *Christian Faith and Public Choices*, Philadelphia: Fortress Press, 1984.

MacIntyre, Alasdair, *Marxism: An Interpretation*, London: SCM, 1953.

  A Short History of Ethics, London: Macmillan, 1966.

  Against the Self Images of the Age, London: Duckworth, 1971.

  After Virtue, London: Duckworth, 1981.

  Whose Justice? Which Rationality?, London: Duckworth, 1988.

  First Principles, Final Ends and Contemporary Philosophical Issues, Milwaukee: Marquette University Press, 1990.

  Three Rival Versions of Moral Enquiry, London: Duckworth, 1990.

  'The Return to Virtue Ethics', *The Twenty-Fifth Anniversary of Vatican II*, Russell E. Smith (ed.), Braintree: The Pope John Centre, 1990, 239–49.

  'Incommensurability, Truth and the Conversation between Confucians and Aristotelians about the Virtues', *Culture and Modernity: East-West Philosophic Perspectives*, Eliot Deutsch (ed.), Honolulu: University of Hawaii Press, 1991, 104–22.

  'Nietzsche or Aristotle', *The American Philosopher*, Giovanna Borrodori (ed.), University of Chicago Press, 1994, 137–52.

  'Moral Relativism, Truth and Justification', *Moral Truth and Moral Tradition: Essays in Honour of Peter Geach and Elizabeth Anscombe*, Luke Gormally (ed.), Dublin: Four Court Press, 1994, 6–24.

'Why is the Search for the Foundation of Ethics so Frustrating?', Hasting Center Report, 9/4 (1979), 16–22.

'Philosophy, the "Other" Disciplines, and Their Histories: A Rejoinder to Richard Rorty', *Soundings*, 65.2 (1982).

'Which God Ought We To Obey and Why?', *Faith and Philosophy*, 3.4 (1986), 359–71.

'Community, Law and the Idiom and Rhetoric of Rights', *Listening*, 26 (1991), 96–110.

'Plain Persons and Moral Philosophy: Rules, Virtues and Goods', *American Catholic Philosophical Quarterly*, 66 (1992), 3–19.

'How can we Learn what Veritatis Splendor has to Teach', *Thomist*, 58 (1994), 171–95.

'Part of the Answer but not enough for a Cure: Review of Jonathan Sacks', *The Politics of Hope*', *Tablet* (26 April 1997), 540–1.

MacIntyre, Alasdair and Hans Fink, 'Introduction' to Knud Loegstrup, *The Ethical Demand*, Indiana: University of Notre Dame Press, 1997.

MacIntyre, Alasdair and Stanley Hauerwas (eds.), *Revisions*, Indiana: University of Notre Dame Press, 1983.

Mackie, J. L., *Ethics: Inventing Right and Wrong*, Harmondsworth: Penguin, 1977.

Mahoney, John, *The Making of Moral Theology: a Study of the Roman Catholic Tradition*, Oxford: Clarendon Press, 1987.

Malachowski, Alan R. (ed.), *Reading Rorty*, Oxford: Blackwell, 1990.

Markham, Ian, *Plurality and Christian Ethics*, Cambridge University Press, 1994.

'Faith and Reason: Reflections on MacIntyre's Tradition-Centred Enquiry', *Religious Studies*, 27 (1991), 259–67.

Markus, R. A., *Sacred and Secular*, Aldershot: Variorum, 1994.

Marshall, Bruce D., 'Aquinas as Post-Liberal Theologian', *Thomist*, 53 (1989), 353–402.

Marshall, Bruce D. (ed.), *Theology and Dialogue: Essays in Conversation with George Lindbeck*, Indiana: University of Notre Dame Press, 1990.

McClendon, James, *Biography as Theology*, Nashville: Abingdon Press, 1974.

Systematic Theology: Ethics, Nashville: Abingdon Press, 1986.

McCormack, Bruce, *Karl Barth's Critically Realistic Dialectical Theology*, Oxford University Press, 1995.

McDonald, J. I. H., *Biblical Interpretation and Christian Ethics*, Cambridge University Press, 1993.

McDowell, John, 'Aesthetic value, objectivity, and the fabric of the world', *Pleasure, Preference and Value*, Eva Schaper (ed.), Cambridge University Press, 1983, 1–16.

'Values and Secondary Qualities', *Morality and Objectivity*, T. Honderich (ed.), London: Routledge and Kegan Paul, 1985, 110–29.

'Virtue and Reason', *Monist*, 62 (1979), 331–50.

McGinn, Colin, 'Truth and Use', *Reference, Truth and Reality*, M. Platts (ed.), London: Routledge and Kegan Paul, 1980, 19–40.

McNaughton, David, *Moral Vision*, Oxford: Blackwell, 1988.

Meeks, Wayne, *The First Urban Christians*, New Haven: Yale University Press, 1983.

The Moral World of the First Christians, London: SPCK, 1986.

The Origins of Christian Morality, New Haven: Yale University Press, 1993.

Milbank, John, *Theology and Social Theory*, Oxford: Blackwell, 1990.

The Word Made Strange: Theology, Language, Culture, Oxford: Blackwell, 1997.

Miscamble, Wilson, 'Sectarian Passivism?', *Theology Today*, 44 (1987/8), 69–77.

Mitchell, Basil, *The justification of Religious Belief*, London: Macmillan, 1973.

Morality: Religious and Secular, Oxford: Clarendon, 1984.

How to Play Theological Ping-Pong and Other Essays on Faith and Reason, London: Hodder and Stoughton, 1990.

Moltmann, Jürgen, *The Church in the Power of the Spirit*, London: SCM, 1977.

Mulhall, Stephen and Adam Swift, *Liberals and Communitarians*, Oxford: Blackwell, 1992.

Murdoch, Iris, *The Sovereignty of Good*, London: Routledge and Kegan Paul, 1970.

Murray, John Courtney, *We Hold These Truths: Catholic Reflections on the American Proposition*, New York: Sheed and Ward, 1960.

Newlands, George M., *Generosity and the Christian Future*, London: SPCK, 1997.

Newton-Smith, W. H., *The Rationality of Science*, London: Routledge and Kegan Paul, 1981.

Niebuhr, H. R., *Christ and Culture*, New York: Harper & Row, 1956.

Nussbaum, Martha, 'Recoiling from Reason', *New York Review of Books*, 19 (1989), 36–41.

O'Donovan, Joan Lockwood, 'Historical Prolegomena to a Theological Review of "Human Rights"', *Studies in Christian Ethics*, 9.2 (1996), 52–65.

O'Donovan, Oliver, *Desire of the Nations: Rediscovering the Roots of Political Theology*, Cambridge University Press, 1996.

Osborn, Eric, *Ethical Patterns in Early Christian Thought*, Cambridge University Press, 1976.

Pearson, Thomas D., 'Interview with Alasdair MacIntyre', *Kinesis*, 20.2 (1994), 34–47.

Philips, Derek, *Looking Backward: A Critical Appraisal of Communitarian Thought* (Princeton University Press, 1993).

Placher, William, *Unapologetic Theology*, Louisville: Westminster/John Knox, 1989.

  'Post-liberalism', *The Modern Theologians*, David Ford (ed.), Oxford: Blackwell, 1997, 343–56.

Polkinghorne, John, *One World*, London: SPCK, 1986.

Porter, Jean, *The Recovery of Virtue*, Philadelphia: Westminster/John Knox Press, 1990.

  'Openness and Constraints: Moral Reflection as Tradition-guided Inquiry in Alasdair MacIntyre's Recent Works', *Journal of Religion*, 73 (1993), 514–36.

Prichard, H. A., *Moral Obligation*, Oxford: Clarendon Press, 1949.

Putnam, Hilary, *Meaning and the Moral Sciences*, London: Routledge and Kegan Paul, 1978.

Putnam, Robert D., 'Tuning In, Tuning Out: The Strange Disappearance of Social Capital in America', *Political Science* (1995), 664–83.

  'Bowling Alone: America's Declining Social Capital', *Journal of Democracy*, 6.1 (1995), 65–78.

Raphael, D. D., *Moral Philosophy*, Oxford University Press, 1981.

Rasmusson, Arne, *The Church As Polis: From Political Theology to Theological Politics as Exemplified by Jürgen Moltmann and Stanley Hauerwas*, University of Notre Dame Press, 1996.

Rawls, John, *Political Liberalism*, New York: Columbia University Press, 1993.

  'Justice as Fairness: Political not Metaphysical', *Philosophy and Public Affairs*, 14 (1985), 223–51.

Reynolds, Charles H. and Ralph V. Norman (eds.), *Community in America: The Challenge of Habits of the Heart*, Berkeley: University of California Press, 1988.

Rorty, Richard, *Philosophy and the Mirror of Nature*, Oxford: Blackwell, 1981.

  Consequences of Pragmatism, Brighton: Harvester Press, 1982.

  Contingency, Irony and Solidarity, Cambridge University Press, 1989.

  'Realism and Reference', *Monist*, 59 (1976), 321–40.

  'Human Rights, Rationality and Sentimentality', *On Human Rights*, Stephen Shute and Susan Hurley (eds.), New York: Basic Books, 1993, 111–34.

Rosenblum, Nancy (ed.), *Liberalism and the Moral Life*, Cambridge, MA: Harvard University Press, 1989.

Sacks, Jonathan, *The Persistence of Faith*, London: Weidenfeld and Nicolson, 1991.

Faith in the Future, London: Darton, Longman and Todd, 1995.

Sandel, Michael, 'The Procedural Republic and the Unencumbered Self', *Communitarianism and Individualism*, Shlomo Avineri and Avner De-Shalit (eds.), Oxford University Press, 1992, 12–28.

Shapiro, Daniel, 'Liberalism and Communitarianism', *Philosophical Books*, 36 (1995), 145–55.

Stackhouse, Max, 'Alasdair MacIntyre: An Overview and Evaluation', *Religious Studies Review*, 18 (1992), 203–8.

'Liberalism dispatched vs. Liberalism engaged', *Christian Century*, (October, 1995), 962–7.

Stevenson, C. L., *Facts and Values*, New Haven: Yale University Press, 1963.

Stone, Lawrence, *Broken Lives: Separation and Divorce in England 1600–1857*, Oxford University Press, 1993.

Stout, Jeffrey, *Ethics After Babel*, Cambridge: Clarke, 1988.

'Homeward Bound: MacIntyre on Liberal Society and the History of Ethics', *Journal of Religion*, 69 (1989), 220–32.

Strawson, P. F. 'Scruton and Wright on Anti-Realism Etc.', *Aristotelian Society Proceedings*, 77 (1976/7), 15–21.

Taylor, Charles, *Sources of the Self*, Cambridge, MA: Harvard University Press, 1989.

'Religion in a Free Society', *Articles of Faith: Articles of Peace*, Hunter, J. D. and O. Guinness (eds.), Washington: Brookings Institution, 1990, 93–113.

Theissen, Gerd, *The Social Setting of Pauline Christianity*, Philadelphia: Fortress Press, 1982.

Thiemann, Ronald, *Revelation and Theology*, University of Notre Dame Press, 1985.

Religion in Public Life: A Dilemma for Democracy, Washington, DC: Georgetown University Press, 1996.

'Response to George Lindbeck', *Theology Today*, 43 (1986/7), 377–82.

Tocqueville, Alexis de, *Democracy in America*, New York: Random House, 1985.

Torrance, Iain, 'They Speak to Us across the Centuries: Cyprian', *Expository Times*, 108.12 (1997), 356–9.

Toulmin, Stephen, *Cosmopolis: The Hidden Agenda of Modernity*, New York: Free Press, 1990.

Tracy, David, 'Lindbeck's New Program for Theology: A Reflection', *Thomist*, 49 (1985), 460–72.

Villa-Vicencio, Charles, *On Reading Karl Barth in South Africa*, Grand Rapids: Eerdmans, 1988.

Wainwright, Geoffrey, 'Ecumenical Dimensions of Lindbeck's Nature of Doctrine', *Modern Theology*, 4 (1987/8), 121–32.

Walsh, Michael J. (ed.), *Commentary on the Catechism of the Catholic Church*, London: Geoffrey Chapman, 1994.

Walzer, Michael, *Thick and Thin: Moral Argument at Home and Abroad*, University of Notre Dame Press, 1994.

Warnock, Mary, *Ethics Since 1900*, Oxford University Press, 1960.

Webber, Robert E. and Rodney Clapp, *People of the Truth*, San Francisco: Harper & Row, 1988.

Webster, John, *Barth's Ethics of Reconciliation*, Cambridge University Press, 1995.

Werpehowski, William, 'Command and History in the Ethics of Karl Barth', *Journal of Religious Ethics*, 9 (1981), 298–320.

'Narrative and Ethics in Barth', *Theology Today*, 43 (1986/7), 334–53.

Whyte, James A., *Laughter and Tears*, Edinburgh: St Andrew Press, 1993.

Wiggins, David, *Needs, Values, Truth*, Oxford: Blackwell, 1987.

Wilkins, John (ed.), *Understanding Veritatis Splendor*, London: SPCK, 1994, 41–5.

Williams, Bernard, *Ethics and the Limits of Philosophy*, London: Collins, 1985.

Willis, Robert, *The Ethics of Karl Barth*, Leiden: E. J. Brill, 1971.

Wright, Crispin, 'Truth Conditions and Criteria', *Aristotelian Society Supplementary Volume*, 50 (1976), 217–45.

Wuthnow, Robert, *Christianity in the 21st Century*, Oxford University Press, 1993.

Yeats, Charles (ed.), *Veritatis Splendor: A Response*, Norwich: Canterbury Press, 1994.

Yoder, John Howard, *The Politics of Jesus*, Grand Rapids: Eerdmans, 1972.

Young, Iris Marion, 'The Ideals of Community and the Politics of Difference', *Feminism and Postmodernism*, Linda J. Nicholson (ed.), London: Routledge, 1990, 300–23.

Index